German Rearmament and Atomic War

The Views of

German Military and Political Leaders

German Rearmament and Atomic War

The Views of
German Military and Political Leaders

Hans Speier

ROW, PETERSON AND COMPANY
Evanston, Illinois

White Plains, New York

Copyright © 1957
The RAND Corporation

5291

Library of Congress Catalogue Card Number 57-11348

MANUFACTURED IN THE UNITED STATES OF AMERICA

For Lisa

Preface

This research is a part of a larger investigation of Western European military and political trends undertaken by The RAND Corporation for the U.S. Air Force.

The study discusses the views of German military and political leaders on current international affairs, on the prospects and shape of war in the future, and on German rearmament. The study covers the period from 1952 to 1957. It is divided into two parts. The first part presents primarily opinions of former German generals, some of whom have resumed a military career or are active in German politics, and views of former military officers in the younger age groups who have maintained an active concern with military affairs. In the second part, the main arguments for and against Chancellor Adenauer's military policy advanced by deputies of the *Bundestag* (the Lower House in the Federal Republic) are reviewed and compared with the less publicized opinions of German military leaders.

The study was undertaken for three reasons. First, the military policy of West Germany will be influenced, in some measure, by members of the former military class. It is hoped that knowledge of the political and military views of German leaders in military thought will contribute to an appraisal of Germany's value as an ally in the Western defense system. Second, the foremost representatives of the former German military class are men of intellectual distinction. While they are subject to bias and prejudice like everybody else, they are serious observers of world events. Even when they are opinionated, their views should be a challenge to further inquiry rather than a reason for complacency. The views of former German officers contain much food for thought on the effects of U.S. foreign and military policies in the last six years. Third, the parliamentary debates on rearmament afford an opportunity to review American military policy toward Germany from the viewpoint of German politicians. It is hoped that this review will contribute to a better understanding of the problems which the atomic age has created, not merely with regard to American policy on Germany but to the Western coalition at large.

Most of the material for the first part of this study has been gathered from interviews. The discussion is therefore based to a large extent on data not available elsewhere. In addition, postwar German military writings have been closely scrutinized. Many of them deal with historical problems or are biographical and apologetic in nature, and so proved to have only limited value for the purposes of this study. In the last two years, however, a fair amount of German professional writing on current military problems has become available. Most of it has been published in professional military journals, of which *Wehrkunde* is the most important. Also, a growing number of newspapers and many periodicals which do not specialize on military affairs have extended their coverage of this subject in recent years. Several foreign books on nuclear problems have been translated into German. Volumes by P. M. S. Blackett, F. O. Miksche, G. C. Reinhardt and W. R. Kintner, Jules Moch, Charles Noël-Martin, and the AEC publication on weapons effects, to mention only a few, are now consulted by German authors who write for military journals. The writings of Liddell Hart and J. F. C. Fuller on warfare are popular among military men in Germany; in general, British military authors have succeeded in establishing closer contact with the leaders in German military thought than have their American counterparts. Important speeches or lectures by the military leaders of NATO are also often published in full in German periodicals.

Military books and articles in magazines or the daily press have been considered source material for this study only to the extent that they were written or cited by persons who were interviewed or to the extent that they contained opinions that illustrated or amplified the views obtained in interviews.

The record of the *Bundestag* sessions on military affairs served as the main source of information for chapters 8 to 11. This information was supplemented, however, by interviews with most of the deputies who are specialists on military policy, with a few other deputies, and with a number of officials in various ministries of the Federal Republic. Finally, some journalists, businessmen, lawyers, theologians, and members of other professions were interviewed, if they were known to be especially interested in military affairs or in one or another aspect of German rearmament.

In the course of gathering material for this study, it became evident that the interviews were bringing to light certain views and attitudes that had not been expressed in public. A number of studies of the German press, conducted in Germany at the time that the conversations with German leaders were held, showed this observation to be true beyond any doubt.[1] It is not possible to say that the difference between private and public opinion on political issues is greater in Germany than it is elsewhere, but students of the German political scene are well advised not to take publicly stated German views as being a necessarily reliable indication of the opinions that Germans hold in private.

The Appendix contains a summary of the public responses to questions about air war and nuclear weapons that were asked in mass-opinion surveys conducted in Germany. This summary can be used by the reader to compare the divergence of mass and elite opinion on some of the issues with which this study is concerned.

The interviews, more than 200 of them, were conducted in West Germany and in West Berlin for periods of about ten weeks each in the spring of 1952, the spring of 1954, and the winter of 1955. The sample included 120 former officers. The majority held a rank higher than colonel at the end of World War II. Some of them were retired or were filling civilian jobs at the time of the interview, but have since resumed military careers. In general, those interviewed included Prussians and South Germans, and Catholics and Protestants, in sufficient numbers to ensure that important variations in views due to regional or religious background would be represented.

---

[1] See the studies by E. W. Schnitzer: *Public Discussion in Western Germany of the Defense of Europe*, March to June, 1952, The RAND Corporation (Santa Monica, California), Research Memorandum RM-981, October 31, 1952; *German Geopolitics Revived: A Survey of Geopolitical Writing in Germany Today*, The RAND Corporation (Santa Monica, California), Research Memorandum RM-1210, March 19, 1954 (also published in *The Journal of Politics*, August, 1955, pp. 407–423); and *Some German Press Views on the Defense of Europe: A Survey of West German Press Opinion on Military Aspects of the Defense of Europe*, The RAND Corporation (Santa Monica, California), Research Memorandum RM-1372, November 26, 1954.

It was possible to maintain continuity of observation between the three interview periods by means of correspondence and occasional conversations with German visitors in the United States.

The selection of the persons who were interviewed was influenced by the objective of the study, which was to ascertain the opinions of thoughtful and articulate Germans on military affairs. This objective also influenced the character of the interviews. Most of the respondents were men of high intellectual caliber. They opened their homes or offered their time away from home and office for discussions on matters that were of interest to them as well as to the visitor. Any attempt, in such a situation, to adhere to a rigid schedule of questions would have resulted at best in amusement, at worst in annoyance; in either case it would have hampered the work. The author would have had fewer and shorter conversations, and consequently less opportunity to find out what he sought to learn.

The members of the former military class in Germany do not speak much in public. They differ in this regard from politicians and journalists. Many military leaders resent the press and suspect strangers who ask too many questions of being reporters or agents. Furthermore, former German officers of high rank live with uncherished memories of interrogations in Allied prison camps after the war. All of these facts called for establishment of more than the minimum rapport required in ordinary interviews. For these men do not care much for interviews, but do seem interested in conversations. Whoever wishes to ascertain their views and observe their attitudes must, therefore, be prepared either to converse with them or to resign himself to fruitless meetings.

Social and political scientists have to contend with the fact that the art of conversation has become atrophied as their techniques of scientific interviewing have been perfected. That is one of the reasons why today many technically excellent polls of popular opinion are available, but only a few competent studies of the private views of national leaders. People who enjoy conversation seem to dislike scientific interviews, perhaps because they render conversation impossible. Conversations are possible only between persons who like to exchange views on subjects of common interest. In conversation, pedantry and the appearance of inquisitiveness alike must be shunned, if only because they are ill-mannered. For the same reason, the course of the conversation cannot be rigorously determined in advance. In the interviews with military leaders, only the focus on the general subjects to be discussed remained unchanged; beyond that allowance was made for the particular interests and competence of each respondent. This apparent defect may have been compensated for, however, by the fact that the conversations offered many opportunities to go beneath the surface and to discover unforeseen attitudes. Common and apparent traits of the military class became less interesting as some hidden and little-suspected characteristics came into view.

Few of the conversations lasted less than one and a half hours; most of them were longer, and only a very few were limited to an hour. Many of those interviewed were seen more than once during the same year, or were visited a second time in later years; but the majority of respondents were different in each of the three years in which the interviews were conducted. Extensive notes of each conversation were made immediately after its conclusion. In addition, one round-table conference was held on each trip. Each dealt with a different aspect of the general subject of atomic war and German rearmament, and each was attended by fifteen former general officers and professional persons. These conferences lasted from one to two days each, and were recorded.[2]

Several of my friends and colleagues at The RAND Corporation took an interest in this study as it was being written. I am deeply grateful to Herbert Goldhamer for many valuable suggestions on the entire manuscript, and to W. P. Davison, Victor Hunt, and Nathan Leites for their critical comments on various chapters.

HANS SPEIER

Stanford
April, 1957

---

[2] All quotations in this study are statements made by German informants either in an interview or at a round-table conference, unless a source is cited.

Table of Contents

Introduction

ONE

U.S. Policy and German Rearmament

At the Quebec Conference of August, 1943, at a time when the United States was engaged in a serious effort to prevent the domination of the continent of Europe by Nazi Germany, Harry Hopkins had with him a document entitled "Russia's Position," which quoted as follows from "a very high-level United States military strategic estimate":

> Russia's postwar position in Europe will be a dominant one. With Germany crushed, there is no power in Europe to oppose her tremendous military forces. . . . Since without question she will dominate Europe on the defeat of the Axis, it is even more essential to develop and maintain the most friendly relations with Russia.[1]

This estimate was correct in its forecast. Since the end, and largely as a result, of the war, the Soviet Union has indeed become the dominant power in Europe. It has extended its hegemony toward the West beyond the borders of the realm over which Emperor Otto the Great ruled in the tenth century.

Yet, despite the growing Soviet threat, American early postwar policy toward Germany was based on the expectation that the wartime alliance with the Soviet Union would continue after the war, and that the preservation of peace depended on the elimination of *Germany* as a world power. It was not appreciated that the international struggle for power would go on after victory, and that the principal contender would be the Soviet Union rather than Germany.

At Yalta, President Roosevelt had told Stalin that American forces

---

[1] Robert E. Sherwood, *Roosevelt and Hopkins,* New York, 1948, p. 748.

would leave Europe soon after the war. In March, 1945, the conquest of Berlin was left to the Red forces, and General Eisenhower pushed ahead in the direction of Dresden.[2] The following May, prior to the Potsdam Conference, the troops that had liberated Czechoslovakia were withdrawn, despite requests by Churchill that they remain. A part of what is now the Soviet Zone of Germany was evacuated, and free access from the West to Berlin was not ensured.[3]

Germany was partitioned. In accordance with the Potsdam Agreement of August, 1945, West German industry was subjected to controls, restrictions of output, and considerable dismantling. West Germany was disarmed and demilitarized.

At a time when the Western European powers were weak, and when the United States was disarming with a speed that drove Mr. Forrestal to despair, the Soviet Union tightened its grip over Eastern Europe and the Balkans. It created a belt of satellite strength between Russia and the West, and attempted to foster and exploit for its own ends the popularity of communism in Italy and France.

Gradually, it became apparent to the West that the Soviet Union might weaken the political stability of Western Europe by means other than force. Western strength might be reduced further before the outbreak of a war—a peacetime loss that might be unacceptable to the West despite its superiority in the air and on the seas. Western Europe, it was believed, could not, like China, be permitted to fall under communist domination in a period of peace between the United States and the Soviet Union. Europe had to be held. With this decision came recognition that Germany was potentially in a position to tip the balance of power in Europe.

President Truman announced the policy of containing Soviet expansionism in 1947, and, in the same year, the United States began to provide economic aid to Western European countries by means of the Marshall Plan. In April, 1949, the United States joined NATO, a step for which the Vandenberg Resolution of the preceding summer had paved the way.

It had become apparent as early as the spring of 1946 that the Soviet government did not intend to co-operate with the Western

[2] For a critical discussion of these decisions, see Chester Wilmot, *The Struggle for Europe*, London, 1952, pp. 690ff.

[3] Sumner Welles considered the withdrawal from Czechoslovakia and the failure to ensure access to Berlin to be one of the gravest mistakes responsible for Soviet policy after Potsdam. (*Seven Decisions that Shaped History*, New York, 1951, p. 202.)

occupation powers in efforts to establish the economic unity of Germany that had been envisioned in the Potsdam Agreement. This realization hastened the end of the initial, punitive period of American occupation policy in Germany. On September 6, 1946, Secretary of State Byrnes addressed an audience of high American and German officials in Stuttgart. He announced American support of the French claim to the Saar, recognized the rights of Poland to the annexation of East German territory, and repeated the American determination to demilitarize and denazify Germany, to exact reparations, and to punish German war criminals.

German hopes were spurred, however, by other statements which Mr. Byrnes made in his address. He said that the army of the United States would be part of the occupation forces, "as long as an occupation force is required in Germany"; that the Oder-Neisse line, as a boundary between Germany and the East, was provisional; that a final decision would be made only at a peace conference; that the United States favored German retention of the Rhineland and the Ruhr, and that "the American people want to help the German people to win their way back to an honorable place among the free and peace-loving nations of the world." According to General Clay, Karl Geiler, Minister-President of Hesse, "had tears in his eyes as he expressed his appreciation" to Secretary Byrnes.[4]

The United States took the initiative in consolidating the three Western occupation zones of Germany, thereby factually, if not formally, basing its European policy on the idea that Germany could not be reunified unless the Soviet Union were ready to cede the Soviet Zone to a neutral or Western-oriented Germany. Early in 1948, the three zones of West Germany were included in the European Recovery Program, and their currency was stabilized. In the fall of 1949, the Occupation Statute was introduced. It was revised in March, 1951, to give the government of the new Federal Republic some degree of independence in the field of foreign affairs. West Germany then joined the Council of Europe and the Schuman Pool. During all this time, there was a gradual relaxation of controls over Germany, and a lifting of ceilings on industrial production which had originally been very low. West Germany began its economic recovery with a speed and vigor that astonished the world and worried France and Britain.

[4] Lucius D. Clay, *Decision in Germany,* New York, 1950, p. 80.

Important as American economic and political measures were for the well-being of the people of Western Europe, economic help did not create military strength. The defense of Europe was singularly weak at the time of the Berlin blockade, at the time of the *coup d'état* in Czechoslovakia, and for more than a year after the signing of the Atlantic Pact, when the Korean war broke out in June, 1950.

In the Moscow and London conferences of 1947, the foreign ministers of the three Western powers had vainly tried to win Soviet consent to settle the German question by forming an all-German government and concluding a peace treaty with it. They failed again at the Paris Conference in 1949. As early as 1947, the communists had begun to rearm East Germany by creating a militarized police force.

Given the increasing danger of Soviet aggression, American policy toward Europe had to be re-examined in the light of a strategic concept that included the possibility of a major war with the Soviet Union. It appeared at the time that eventual U.S. victory in such a war might require a reconquest of Europe, since, regardless of damage inflicted upon the Soviet homeland by strategic air attacks, the strong ground forces of the Soviet empire could overrun the Continent during the first phase of a war. Such an initial advantage, it was reasoned, would give the Soviet Union additional resources, especially in the Ruhr area, and would render ultimate victory costly. It would be better to try to hold Europe. Once this was seriously considered, the United States had to work toward mobilizing, equipping, and organizing ground forces that would be available in Europe at the outbreak of war.

In the summer of 1950, President Truman decided to seek Congressional approval of stationing more American troops in Europe. The decision was defended before Congress by Generals Marshall and Bradley early in 1951, and it was approved by the Senate, after seven weeks of bitter debate, on April 3, 1951. Four additional divisions were to be stationed in Europe, and a total of eight American tactical air groups for Europe were authorized. Following the limited mobilization of its economy on the basis of the Defense Production Act of 1950, the United States allocated a larger share of its armament output to its allies than it had since the end of the war.

The U.S. government could not have won the domestic political struggle for increased commitments to Europe without at the same time pursuing a policy of helping others only if they helped us, or as we preferred to put it, if they helped themselves. Accordingly, the United States urged its European allies in NATO to increase the mobilization of their manpower and economic resources.

The participation of West Germany in European defense appeared imperative when the balance of forces was reviewed from a military point of view. West Germany had a population of fifty million people, while France, for example, had forty-two and one-half million. German military manpower resources were untapped. Unlike France, Germany had no colonies and no territory to defend in Asia or Africa. Germany's geographical location would place German reserves where they might be needed in the event of a Soviet attack; they would not first have to be moved into the combat area. Former German officers of all ranks, and millions of German men, had had experience in fighting Soviet forces. Millions of Germans had had close contact with Soviet communism, and with the Red army as an occupation force; they were not, therefore, ready victims of communist propaganda, whereas the communist parties of France and Italy had been able to muster considerable popular support in those countries. Finally, the participation of Germany in Western defense could ease the burden of armament which the other European powers had to bear. It seemed unfair to let vanquished Germany develop her economy, while the victors assumed the entire responsibility for her defense. Sir Ivone Kirkpatrick, British High Commissioner in Germany, said in an interview with Alistair Horne on August 12, 1952:

> If we do not support a German arms contribution, we shall be encouraging competition in the field of foreign trade which may eventually ruin us.[5]

Thus, toward the end of 1950, the American policy of disarming Germany, which had prevailed since the end of World War II, was reversed for political, strategic, and economic reasons. As late as the spring of that year, both the U.S. Secretary of State and the U.S. High Commissioner for Germany had publicly declared that America did not intend to change its policy of keeping Germany demilitarized. But in August the Council of Europe approved a proposal by Churchill to create a European army, and the need for a

[5] Alistair Horne, *Return to Power*, New York, 1956, p. 28.

German contribution to Western defense was being strongly urged in the Pentagon. Strictly military considerations first led to the change of American policy. On August 23, 1950, the U.S. High Commissioner for Germany announced that the defense arrangements for Western Europe must provide for German participation,[6] and, a few days later in New York, Dean Acheson proposed to the foreign ministers of Britain and France that approximately ten German divisions be raised and incorporated into NATO.

This proposal was made without much diplomatic preparation, and without full anticipation of West European reaction to it. The United States did not realize that, while it had been possible for the Allies to enforce German disarmament in 1945, rearmament in 1950 required the consent of both Germans and Allies. The European Consultative Assembly had sought to link West German rearmament to arrangements and plans for the political and economic integration of Western Europe, such as the European Coal and Steel Community. But the American proposal was not in accord with that plan. From a military point of view, re-establishment of German armed forces on a national basis seemed the most efficient measure to suggest. The French, however, balked at the idea of remilitarizing West Germany, and presented the Pleven Plan as their initial counterproposal. Politically, that plan was based on the ideas suggested by the European Consultative Assembly; militarily, it sought to prevent a revival of German military power by proposing that small German combat teams be incorporated into international divisions. The Pleven Plan would have permitted some exploitation of German manpower for military ends without granting West Germany political equality and military independence. Furthermore, the plan envisioned the political integration of Europe as a prerequisite of control of Europe's military resources. Finally, it permitted France to exempt from integration in the projected European army those of her own military forces that were stationed outside Europe, and thus to retain her status as an independent military power. Clearly, the French were more concerned about German dominance in Europe, and about their own military prestige, than about the menace of Soviet aggression.

[6] John J. McCloy, "Western European Defense Includes German Participation," *Department of State Bulletin,* September 4, 1950. For a review of the early history of German rearmament, see Lewis J. Edinger, "West German Armament," Documentary Research Division, Research Studies Institute, Air University, October, 1955.

General Omar Bradley, for the Joint Chiefs of Staff, and General George C. Marshall, the Secretary of Defense, described the Pleven Plan as impractical, because it did not allow for full exploitation of West German manpower for military ends. The Germans strongly objected to it on the ground that it perpetuated the dependent status of the Federal Republic, while asking the vanquished foe to supply auxiliary soldiers to the West. The Germans were encouraged by American opposition to the plan. Even when Secretary Acheson finally endorsed the idea of a European army in February, 1951, West Germany held out for her own "Petersberg Plan," which had been evolved in secret conversations between American and German military experts. This plan was reported to be an endorsement of the original American idea, which called for a national German military establishment.

No international agreement had been reached by July, 1951. The United Kingdom, Denmark, Norway, and Portugal were not willing to join the proposed European defense organization. Germany was not interested in rearmament, but, if it had to be, she wanted political equality and a national army. The French favored continued discrimination against Germany, and a strictly controlled German contribution to European defense.

In June, 1951, General Eisenhower, the Supreme Commander of the NATO forces in Europe, intervened in the dispute. He realized that the political problems associated with German rearmament had to be solved in a way satisfactory to both France and Germany before German soldiers could be added to his command. Renewed negotiations led finally to an agreement in May, 1952, to form the European Defense Community (EDC). It was a compromise that failed just over two years later. EDC did not meet German wishes for full political equality, and yet it left France with wounded pride and unallayed fears. The German socialist opposition succeeded in delaying the ratification of EDC for many months, and in August, 1954, the French Assembly undid all planning and negotiating by its refusal to ratify the treaty.

The French vote could have created an acute political crisis if it had not been for British initiative, which quickly found a way to mend the European fences. The original American idea of a national German army, which the French had opposed so strongly, was resurrected in the Paris Treaties of October, 1954, four years after the first negotiations aimed at rearming Germany. The West European Union based on the treaties was formed with German and Italian participation; the Federal Republic was granted virtually full sovereignty and became a member of NATO. And, most important in allaying French apprehensions about German military power, the British agreed to participate in the new arrangement for the defense of Europe.

Apparently, arming a coalition in peacetime is even more difficult than conducting a coalition war, which is not easy. The first German soldiers—102 of them—donned their uniforms in January, 1956, five and one-half years after the issue of German rearmament had first been raised. By the end of 1956, Germany had about 96,000 men under arms, less than one-fifth of the strength which she was expected ultimately to contribute to NATO. In the summer of 1956, it was estimated that the maximum could be reached in 1959 or 1960, but toward the end of that year, the intermediate force goals for 1957 were reduced by more than one-half. Moreover, it is not certain that NATO will still exist in its present form in 1960, or that the then-existing German government will still deem it desirable to form a military establishment of half a million men.

During the long debate on German rearmament, almost all the political gains on the international scene have been made by West Germany and the Soviet Union. The Federal Republic was recognized as a sovereign power and became a member of NATO, without taking a single practical step toward rearmament. The Soviet Union had time to strengthen its position in nuclear weapons and to weaken the political cohesion of NATO, without the embarrassment of active German participation in the defense of the West. Moreover, the actions of the Soviet Union succeeded in proving both to Dr. Adenauer and his socialist opposition that no Western policy of unification had any chance of success as long as the Federal Republic stood firmly in the Western camp and wished to maintain the social and political institutions of a free country.

Dr. Adenauer has often been hailed in the West as a great German statesman. Upon sober reflection, it appears rather that he steadfastly promoted a policy that was forced upon West Germany by its geographic location, by the anticommunist feelings of its population, and by the cold war. Aided by the spectacular prosperity of the West German economy, the Chancellor was able—as any anticommunist German government would have been—to attain an important short-term objective: he rehabilitated the political standing of West Germany by rejecting neutralism in the East-West struggle and by favoring rearmament. Until 1957, his policy was supported by a large, though dwindling, majority in the *Bundestag*. Adenauer appreciated the fact that the Soviet Union, rather than the Western powers, held the key to the attainment of Germany's long-range objective, the peaceful reunification of the country, and he was probably aware of the danger of an East-West understanding about Germany at her expense, if a disunited West was hard-enough pressed by the communists in other areas of the world, or if the United States returned to an isolationist policy in Europe. Thus Adenauer's course did not bring his country closer to unification, but he was at least not subject to the illusions of the socialist opposition that a Western solution of the unification question could be found without paying a price unacceptable to government and opposition alike. His actions did not advance the prospects of unification, as he claimed until the end of 1955, but neither is it likely that they diminished them, as the socialists have never ceased to aver.

By the middle of 1955, Dr. Adenauer stood as the representative of a phase of German foreign relations that had come to an end.[7] In consequence of political and military developments that he could not control, Adenauer seemed to have become a man of the past.

From 1949 to 1955, Adenauer's commitment to the anticommunist rationale of the political course he had taken was so strong that he risked remaining behind the development of Western policy toward Russia. In order to continue his course and obtain legislation honoring Germany's international obligation to rearm, the Chancellor had to continue to appeal to the need for containing Soviet aggression in Europe. He had to do so at a time when some of his Western allies had lowered their contributions to NATO, either as a result of military engagements outside Europe or of budgetary considerations, and at a time when, by the testimony of leading political and military spokesmen in the West, there was no longer an imminent danger of Soviet aggression in Europe.

[7] F. R. Allemann ("Das Ende einer Epoche," *Der Monat*, February, 1956, pp. 1–13) reached the same conclusion by analyzing the results of the second Geneva Conference in 1955.

The policy of peacefulness and coexistence with which the Soviet leaders impressed the West and the neutral powers after Stalin's death seemed to lessen both the danger of communist aggression in Europe and the prospect of general war. The pressure exerted for the unity of NATO, which had been intense in 1950, was relaxed. At the same time, the efforts of the communists to change the balance of power in their favor had extended to the preindustrial areas of the world, where several NATO powers resisted further losses of their influence and power.

Strength was thus diverted from the alliance in Europe by the divisive pursuit of national interests elsewhere. France wished to maintain her possessions in Asia and Africa, and she could hope to do so only at a price in blood and treasure that virtually stripped her of military power on the continent of Europe. In 1956 Great Britain was spending proportionately almost twice as much on defense as were the other European NATO powers, and, given the precarious state of her trade balance, reduction of her forces in Germany looked extremely attractive, at least from the viewpoint of the Exchequer. Gone were the days of 1952, when the NATO powers had agreed in Lisbon to have ready, by the end of 1952, twenty-five divisions for D-day plus three, twenty-five reserve divisions for D day plus thirty, and four thousand combat aircraft. And they had set even higher goals for 1953.

By 1956, there were planners in all major Western countries who considered reducing the strength of NATO in Europe to a token force that could, in the event of attack, give the signal that would call the strategic forces of the United States and Great Britain into action. All the while, in view of the incalculable effects of general nuclear war, it was hoped that the Soviet Union would never make that attack. This became known as the strategy of the "trip-wire" or "plate-glass window." Such a policy would mean a return, under thermonuclear conditions, to the defense policy that prevailed prior to the formation of NATO, and would require a new Western approach to the German problem. Unofficial recommendations were made—by Winston Churchill, John J. McCloy, and George Kennan, to mention only a few—that were predicated on a change of Germany's projected military contribution to NATO.

On his visit to Washington in June, 1956, a month before the second and third parliamentary debates on the Conscription Law, Adenauer was reassured by high American officials that U.S. policy would not change, although he had some uneasy moments when reporters at a press conference asked for his reaction to the possibility of such a change; he warned that Soviet policy was as dangerous as ever. It is true that, despite the procrastinations of the French on EDC, and the reluctance of the Germans to rearm, the American government has never wavered in its insistence on German rearmament. And, by now, a reversal or drastic modification of its policy seems possible only at the risk of weakening NATO as a military organization even more than it has already been weakened—a step that the United States is as yet unwilling to take. For it is uncertain that a stronger emphasis on the political and economic tasks that NATO might perform could revitalize the alliance.

However, the political difficulties that Adenauer faces as a result of post-Stalinist Soviet policy and, particularly, of the weakening of NATO cannot be entirely removed by continued American support of his efforts to rearm. For ever since 1954 he has pursued his course against the background of an American defense policy that has placed increased reliance on atomic weapons for the defense of Europe. This American policy has, in the minds of many Germans, raised problems which they did not have to face when rearmament first became an issue.

In January, 1955, Admiral Arthur W. Radford and Defense Secretary Charles E. Wilson put forth the rationale of this policy in a briefing to the House Armed Services Committee on the reductions of the U.S. Army. Admiral Radford, in a prepared statement, referred to the free world as a "pool of collective strength," and spoke of achieving "balanced forces on a global scale":

This balance can best be achieved by each nation contributing to the pool those forces and facilities that it is most proficient in and best capable of developing.

In view of our industrial capacity, technological ability, and limited manpower, we believe that the most effective contribution which the United States is capable of making consists of complex technical weapons and equipment, modern air and naval power, and highly mobile offensive combat forces backed by ready reserves.

On the other hand, we feel that the other free nations can most efficiently provide in their own and adjacent countries the bulk of the defensive ground forces and local naval and air power.[8]

Secretary Wilson put the matter most succinctly by saying, at the same briefing, that many of our allies "can't build airplanes but have manpower." [9] The strategic concept underlying this view was that of massive retaliation, which was incorporated in the National Security Policy Plan No. 168 of 1953. This concept "was essentially an elaboration of General Eisenhower's campaign statement in 1952 that 'Asians should fight Asians.' " [10] Under the policy of the New Look, the total number of American men in uniform was reduced from 3,450,000 in December, 1953, to 2,815,000 in 1955. The army suffered the bulk of these reductions, and by the middle of 1956 it was expected that it would be further reduced by 80,000 or 100,000 men in 1957.

Shortly after the passage of the conscription bill by the German *Bundestag* in July, 1956, *The New York Times* reported that Admiral Radford, Chairman of the Joint Chiefs of Staff, had proposed a reduction of the U.S. Armed Forces by approximately 800,000 men, to be attained by 1960. The American service chiefs were said to be united in protest against this proposal on the grounds that, among other things, it would involve a very drastic reduction of the American contribution to the defense of Europe. Total U.S. Army strength as of June 30, 1955, was a little over one million men. The proposal for further reductions, attributed to Admiral Radford, would have involved lowering the strength of the U.S. Army to about 580,000 men in 1960.[11]

Admiral Radford immediately issued a statement to the effect that the story in *The New York Times* "was based on partial information," and that he had "not yet reached" the view attributed to him. He said, however, "it is possible that manpower requirements for the future security of the United States can ultimately be lowered because of the introduction of new weapons." Regarding American military commitments "in connection with the security of the free world," Admiral Radford merely declared that they would not be changed "unilaterally." [12]

[8] *The Washington Post,* January 26, 1955.
[9] *Ibid.*
[10] *The New York Times,* July 15, 1956.
[11] *Ibid.,* July 13, 1956.
[12] *Ibid.,* July 14, 1956.

The German press was much alarmed by the leak concerning the Radford Plan, and by Prime Minister Eden's almost simultaneous hint that the United Kingdom as well favored replacement of conventional forces by nuclear weapons. Following a comment published in *The New York Times,* German newspapers wrote about the possibility of an isolationist retreat of the United States to "Fortress America." General Adolf Heusinger, one of the two highest-ranking officers in the new German defense establishment, visited Washington to find out how matters stood. He was given assurances that the Radford Plan did not constitute U.S. policy. Also, Secretary Dulles and Foreign Secretary Selwin Lloyd told Heinrich von Brentano, the Foreign Minister of the Federal Republic, that no reduction of Anglo-American forces stationed in Europe would take place "for the time being." [13]

At the end of August, Dr. Adenauer was reported as feeling alarmed and betrayed at not having been given any indication of the Radford Plan on his visit to Washington in June. He decided to attack U.S. military policy in public, which he had never done before. Writing for the official *Bulletin,* published by the Bonn government, he said:

As to the debate which was started by Americans about the relationship between conventional and nuclear weapons, I would like to stress that I regard shifting the principal emphasis to atomic weapons at the present time as a mistake.[14]

Countering an East German invasion of West Germany with nuclear weapons, he said, would almost certainly

. . . trigger an intercontinental rocket war. . . . I am of the opinion that it is of special importance to localize small conflicts that may occur, and for this we need divisions with conventional weapons.[15]

Thus by August, 1956, Dr. Adenauer found himself pressed to fight not only for German rearmament, but, with a somewhat belated understanding of the New Look, also against a reduction of Anglo-American ground forces.

These developments involved two important changes in the Amer-

[13] *Bulletin* of the Press and Information Office of the German federal government (German ed.), August 21, 1956.
[14] *Ibid.*
[15] *Ibid.*

ican attitude toward the Western coalition. First, in 1950 the United States had urged the European allies to increase their ground forces, and had authorized the addition of several U.S. divisions to the military manpower then available in Europe. But in 1955 a *cutback* in American army strength was justified on the ground that the main manpower contributions to NATO should come from the European allies. Second, it was clear in 1950 that, in the event of war, Western Europe would have to be defended by conventional weapons. There still was hope, however illusory, that a strategic atomic war, should it occur, might bypass Europe. The decision to plan for an atomic defense was not reached by NATO until December, 1954.

By 1955, both the American and Soviet leaders seemed to have reached the conclusion that general thermonuclear war would destroy civilization, and therefore had to be avoided. By the same time, it became certain that if war came to Europe, NATO planned to use atomic weapons. It was only natural, therefore, for many Europeans to ask why such a war would not destroy European civilization.

The socialist opponents of Adenauer's rearmament policy made capital out of these developments, and used them in a blistering attack on the government. With faulty logic, but powerful appeal to popular feeling, they demanded that the defense effort of the Federal Republic be much smaller than then planned. They hoped, naïvely, that postponement of rearmament would induce the Russians to concede German reunification. That hope is now crushed. It was crushed many times: once after the Geneva Conference of July, 1955, when the Soviet leaders insisted that in a reunified Germany the so-called "social achievements" in the communist part of Germany would have to be preserved; again in September, 1956, when Adenauer reduced the term of service for German conscripts, yielding to domestic political pressure without the slightest compensatory international gain; and above all, toward the end of 1956, when the Soviet forces brutally suppressed the Hungarian revolution with the West looking on horrified but impotent to help the cause of liberty beyond the Iron Curtain.

All the while, however, socialist views of unconventional weapons were more realistic than those of Dr. Adenauer and his supporters. And it is largely for fear of strengthening the opposition to Adenauer that the implications of the atomic war plan for the defense of Europe still have not been explained sufficiently to the German people, either by Adenauer or by the American military and political leaders.

The German people have been enjoying the spectacular economic prosperity that West Germany has experienced under Adenauer's government, and they have paid inadequate attention to questions of European defense. Even the German political and military leaders who support rearmament have not thought very carefully about the military realities of the nuclear age. By August, 1956, they had done no more than reach the publicly professed conclusion that rearmament would help Germany avoid atomic war.

In September, 1956, however, the German government suddenly became interested in tactical atomic weapons. At the NATO meeting of December, 1956, Franz-Josef Strauss, the new Defense Minister, supported other European NATO powers in their requests for such weapons. Ever since that time, German political and military leaders have been increasingly inclined to adopt the American view that tactical atomic weapons are "conventional" means of ground warfare. When the British decided in April, 1957, to base their defense on strategic nuclear deterrence in the future and to reduce their conventional forces, including those stationed in Germany, Adenauer seized upon the occasion again to advocate the equipment of the *Bundeswehr* with tactical atomic weapons. Apparently, he no longer doubted that these weapons were conventional arms, since he pointed out that they were "a further development of modern artillery."[16] Thus under the impact of the Radford Plan and the British New Look, Adenauer quickly reversed his views on atomic weapons.

In general, public understanding of the impact of nuclear weapons on questions of war and peace has improved in the last few years, and it is likely that it will improve further. The American policy of rearming the Germans, however, has not yet been fully successful, and it may not be. Setbacks or successes of Soviet policy, the strength or weakness of NATO, American and British defense policies, and the courage to live and act under the fear of nuclear war—all these will influence the future of Germany's place in the Western coalition. So will the wisdom and candor of American policy.

[16] *The New York Times*, April 6, 1957.

TWO

The Military Class

Defeat in World War II turned German society into a temporary vacuum. There was no governing class, the political ideas of the Third Reich had been shattered, and cigarettes and coffee served as currency in the barter economy that prevailed for a time. Foreign administrators in the two parts of the divided country remade society after the conflicting images of the communist and capitalist orders of life existing in their respective home countries.

After 1948 the old class structure re-emerged in the wake of spectacular economic recovery, but without a functioning military elite. The earlier military class had been eliminated by demilitarization. Its leaders had been deprived not only of their functions, but also of prestige and respect among large parts of the population. However, short of physical extermination, a social group with distinctive beliefs and a characteristic code of conduct cannot be deprived entirely of its identity. Its spirit cannot be quickly eliminated by radical changes in the social roles of its members. Old functions may wither, old influence may be broken, rewards and recognition may be withheld; even expectations regarding the future may be completely altered. But the image of the self and the habitual outlook on life are too intimately connected with the past to be erased by political dictum. From 1945 to 1950, therefore, despite social dispersion, the old German military class survived in the habits and memories of its members.

This is not to say that a uniform spirit of militarism lingered on after the war like a suppressed religion. On the contrary, the old schisms of the military elite persisted, for the German military leaders never had a solidly common outlook on political, military, and moral issues. Their attitudes had been divided according to regional and religious backgrounds, by service rivalries, by differing traditions, and, from 1933 onward, by different views about Hitler and National Socialism. Despite patriotism and sworn loyalty, some officers had joined the resistance to Hitler that culminated in the assassination attempt of July 20, 1944. That event, along with Germany's defeat and the subsequent prosecution and denunciation of the military profession, exacerbated the conflicts among the professional soldiers and led them, after the war, to contemplate the past chiefly in order to justify their roles in it. When the issue of rearmament was raised in 1950, their past roles influenced the generals in their attitudes toward the new German military establishment.

The Allies had not realized during and immediately after the war that the relationship between Hitler and his generals had been a complex one, involving both strife and co-operation. In Fascist Italy the military had enjoyed the protection of the crown and had finally turned against Mussolini. In Russia Stalin liquidated many military leaders before the war broke out. In Germany the situation was different from both: Hitler subjugated, corrupted, and distrusted the generals whom he used.

After Hindenburg's death he no longer had to fear them, because they did not resist the degradation of their honor and the curtailment of their prerogatives. Hitler dominated the generals by enlarging the armed forces and creating opportunities for rapid promotion, by exploiting internal conflicts of interest, and, finally, by creating rival military and semi-military organizations. When Hitler became Supreme Commander of the German army in December, 1941, he told General Halder that he had "a National Socialist air force, an imperial navy, and a conservative army." [1]

More specifically, the German military officers fell into four groups according to their attitude toward the Nazi regime:

1. Devoted followers of Hitler.
2. Critical followers who served the dictator as experts, as they would have served any head of state, especially in wartime.
3. Conspirators who wanted to deprive Hitler of power either by arrest or assassination but without giving aid or assistance to Germany's enemies.
4. Radicals who were so outraged by Hitler's policies that they

[1] Peter Bor, *Gespräche mit Halder*, Wiesbaden, 1950, p. 112.

were willing to add co-operation with the enemy (*Landesverrat*) to revolt against the authorities (*Hochverrat*).

Most of the generals belonged to the second group. Some of the more senior ones, particularly on the General Staff, entertained conspiratorial ideas at one time or another, but few had a persistent will to act. Included in the first group were most air force and naval officers, many younger army officers, some old members at the top of the army hierarchy, such as Blomberg, Keitel, and Jodl, and Hitler's military protégés, such as Schoerner and Model. The fourth group was very small, and most of its members died along with the other conspirators after July 20, 1944, when Hitler avenged himself cruelly by finally "purging" the class.[2] Many of his active opponents were younger officers. Most prominent in this resistance were Colonel General Kurt Freiherr von Hammerstein-Equord, who died in 1943, Field Marshal Erwin J. von Witzleben, and Colonel General Ludwig Beck, who had resigned his office as Chief of Staff of the army in 1938.[3]

Ever since 1933, and especially during World War II, the conservative military leaders had been criticized both by devoted Nazis and by opponents of the regime. The Nazis distrusted conservatism, and the anti-Nazis despised political irresolution. This two-pronged critical attitude persists in the Federal Republic.

The Nazi critics—whose heroes are men such as Ernst Remer, who helped crush the rebellion of July 20, 1944, Field Marshal Albert Kesselring, and General Ramcke [4]—are now to be found chiefly, though not exclusively, among former SS officers. They condemn the

[2] Twenty generals and one admiral were executed, and five other generals attempted suicide after the unsuccessful attempt to assassinate Hitler. No *Luftwaffe* generals were murdered. Many more of the younger officers who participated in the conspiracy were killed thereafter. See Josef Folttmann and Hans Moller, *Opfergang der Generale*, Berlin, 1952. For an incomplete list of victims of July 20, 1944, see John W. Wheeler-Bennett, *The Nemesis of Power*, New York, 1954, Appendix D.

[3] About Beck, see Wolfgang Foerster, *Generaloberst Ludwig Beck. Sein Kampf gegen den Krieg*, Munich, 1953, and the Introduction by Hans Speidel to Ludwig Beck, *Studien*, Stuttgart, 1955. Much has been written about the German generals and the resistance. For general orientation, see Wheeler-Bennett, *op. cit.;* Gordon A. Craig, *The Politics of the German Army 1640–1945*, Oxford, 1955, chaps. VI–XII; Fabian von Schlabrendorff, *Offiziere gegen Hitler*, Zurich, 1946; Walter Görlitz, *Der Deutsche Generalstab*, Frankfurt, 1950; Gerhard Ritter, *Carl Goerdeler und die deutsche Widerstandsbewegung*, Stuttgart, 1954; Hans Rothfels, *The German Opposition*, Hinsdale, 1948; and Eberhard Zeller, *Geist der Freiheit*, Munich, 1954.

[4] See Ernst Remer, *20. Juli 1944*, Hamburg, 1951; Albert Kesselring, *Soldat bis zum letzten Tag*, Bonn, 1953; and H. B. Ramcke, *Fallschirmjäger. Damals und Danach*, Frankfurt, 1951.

men who attempted to remove Hitler from power, and suggest that Germany may have lost the war precisely because generals of high rank sabotaged Hitler's strategy. For example, General Franz Halder, Chief of Staff of the German army until the defeat at Stalingrad, has been attacked for belittling Hitler's generalship and for failing to serve him loyally at all times.[5]

The general political views of these critics have been stated aggressively by a German academician writing in 1952 under the pseudonym of Hugo C. Backhaus. According to him, National Socialism advanced a revolutionary principle in German history, while the generals clung to a conservative tradition. Unfortunately, Backhaus said, the two leading groups, the party functionaries and the military leaders, did not co-operate harmoniously, but developed a fatal rivalry which led to Germany's defeat and domination by foreign powers. He deplored the fact that the military had remained aloof from the regime even after Hitler had demonstrated in 1934 (by a blood purge of stormtroop leaders, including Hitler's friend Röhm) that he was determined to suppress the radical elements of his party in order to gain the support of the *Wehrmacht*. Harmony between the army and party leaders, Backhaus concluded, existed only during the period of German successes in the lightning campaigns of 1939 and 1940.[6]

It is indeed true that, among the military, discontent with Hitler's rule increased as the days of the so-called "flower wars" against Austria and Czechoslovakia passed and the early victories in Poland, Norway, and France were followed by mounting sacrifices and defeats. But the majority of the discontented confined themselves to griping, to occasionally failing to comply with a particular order, to offering their resignations (as long as they were not forbidden to do so), and to private forecasts of Germany's doom: they did not act. They were caught in a web of fear of the Nazis—for themselves or their wives and children—a sense of professional or patriotic duty, moral indifference, and political apathy.

---

[5] Halder attacked Hitler's strategy after the end of the war in *Hitler als Feldherr*, Munich, 1949. For attacks on Halder from the political right, see, for example, Erich Kern, *Der grosse Rausch*, Wels, 1950, pp. 168 and 269.

[6] Hugo C. Backhaus, *Wehrkraft im Zwiespalt*, Göttingen, 1952, p. 67. The communist-sponsored monthly, *Nation Europa* (September, 1952), said about Backhaus' pamphlet: "Since 1945, hardly another book of such impact and lucidity has appeared in the German language. . . ." See also Ernst Remer, *op. cit.*

Precisely for this reason, the former generals have been attacked also by survivors of the resistance movement and by those who now sympathize with it. This censure, too, dates back to the days of Hitler, and it is as much a part of the Nazi heritage in present-day Germany as is the nostalgia of men such as Backhaus for a Fourth Reich. For example, the diary of Ulrich von Hassell, secretly written during the war years before his execution in 1944, contains many outcries of despair about the political myopia and irresolution of the military leaders:

The longer the war lasts, the less I respect the generals. They are technically competent and physically brave, but have little courage when facing authority (*Zivilkourage*); they lack broad judgment of world affairs, intellectual self-reliance and strength of character—the fruits of true culture. Hence they are completely inferior to, and at the mercy of, a man like Hitler. Moreover, to most of them careers in the lowest sense of the term, donations and field marshal's batons, are more important than larger considerations and moral values. All those upon whom hope has been based are failing and this in a peculiarly abject manner, as they engage in the most dangerous talk but lack the courage to act.[7]

Hassell's moralism was born of the bitter disappointment of an intelligent man whose diplomatic career had come to an end in 1938 after five years of service under Hitler, and who, like all moralists, ascribed the obligation of free moral choice to the men who remained in office. He overlooked the fact that only exceptional persons are sincere enough to act in defiance of their associates, to give up their careers, and possibly to risk their lives for an unpopular cause. The moral failures of a class or a nation always are first of all a verdict against the traditions of that class or nation. No social class, except a leisure class, can maintain values that conflict with the

[7] Ulrich von Hassell, *Vom andern Deutschland,* 2d ed., Zurich, 1946, pp. 308–309. The cited entry was made under the date of April 20, 1943. In a recent discussion of the military efforts to resist Hitler, the bitterness of the anti-Nazis about the generals during World War II is summarized as follows: "*Canaris to Hassell:* he had given up all hope as far as the generals were concerned. *Stackelberg to Hassell* on a trip to Norway: Falkenhorst is the usual general without political will and courage. *Gisevius to Hassell:* he no longer expected anything from the top-level generals; they were being fed with titles, Knight's Crosses and donations. *Hassell himself:* 'Whoever has gained some clarity about the development is being seized by flaming rage about our high military leaders, whose servility excells that of the lowest bureaucrat.' *Popitz:* 'The military think of nothing but their Knight's Crosses.' In this way they thought and spoke among themselves in the Foreign Office, in the Ministry of Economics, in the editorial offices of the *Frankfurter Zeitung* and in many other places in Germany" (Margret Boveri, *Der Verrat im XX. Jahrhundert,* Hamburg, 1956, Vol. II, p. 35).

structure of the society in which it functions. If society changes and class traditions are modified, adherence to old values survives in some individuals, but only in a pragmatically useless, atypical form which isolates them from the new dominant type.

When Hitler came to power, the German military class still bore faint traces of aristocratic and humanistic traditions which many critics of German militarism overlook, but the class as a whole had long since spent its moral energy. Its leaders had been instrumental in the downfall of the Republic, and they believed they could dominate Hitler. Instead, Hitler dominated them.

The humanism that had distinguished the German military reformers after the Napoleonic wars had long since faded, in the military class as well as in German society at large. The last influential military representatives of that tradition in Germany had been Helmuth von Moltke and, already to a considerably lesser extent, men like Schlieffen and Falkenhayn. Thereafter, nothing distinguished the class but *expertise* and political ambition; a broader outlook and adherence to the old standards were confined to a few exceptional persons.

Under Emperor Wilhelm II, the industrialization of German society changed the balance within the German officers' corps in favor of the industrial spearhead of the middle class, lowering the number of the aristocracy and the influence of the corps' traditions. These traditions themselves were weakened by the growing industrialization of German society. The new dominant class valued success, wealth, efficiency, and expansion. While army leaders were more reserved toward the feverish spirit and ostentatious manners of the times than were the newer navy officers, they proudly associated their profession with the political success of the Reich, and expressed their loyalty to the Kaiser through aloofness, among other ways, from the lower reaches of civilian life.

The generals became bureaucratic specialists in the management of military affairs. After 1918 they developed the conceit that the political ends of power were not their concern and they claimed to serve "the state" rather than the Republic; but in fact they exerted considerable political influence on the composition of the Weimar governments and their foreign policies. Their dominant attitude toward democracy was one of indifference and contempt.

Seeckt, the acknowledged leader of the military class in republican Germany, had stated that he differed from Hitler not in his aims but merely in his methods.[8] The generals accepted the regime which introduced the methods of gangsterism as a glorified form of statecraft in both domestic and foreign affairs. They were outraged only by the political ambitions of the stormtroopers and their leader Ernst Röhm, who threatened the political and military privileges of the army.

For that reason, the highest-ranking generals condoned Hitler's Blood Purge of 1934, which rid the *Reichswehr* of its plebeian rivals.[9] A few weeks later, the generals again accepted murder as an instrument of national policy when the Austrian Chancellor Engelbert Dollfuss was shot down by Nazis and left to bleed to death. In August of that year the military leaders paid their price for Hitler's betrayal of the stormtroopers: they swore before God unconditional obedience to Hitler as Führer of the Reich and Supreme Commander of the *Wehrmacht*. Four years later, in 1938, some of the leading generals were appalled by the risks Hitler was taking in his foreign policy and plotted against him. Ever since, they have conveniently excused their failure to act at that or any later time by pointing to Chamberlain's futile attempt to appease Hitler at Munich.

Hitler's early successes in World War II almost overcame military opposition to his policy. Only a few officers in the armed forces remained firm in their resistance; most of these were young men, inspired not by the code of their class but partly by religion, partly by ethical socialism, and partly by esoteric conservative values.[10] However, as defeats began to mount in 1943, opposition to Hitler increased among high-ranking officers, although some of the most senior officers in the *Wehrmacht* hastened to congratulate Hitler on his

---

[8] Friedrich von Rabenau, *Seeckt. Aus seinem Leben,* Leipzig, 1940, Vol. II, pp. 347–348, quoted by Wheeler-Bennett, *op. cit.,* p. 118.

[9] It should be mentioned, however, that Hammerstein and the aged Mackensen were tirelessly active to prove the innocence of Schleicher and Bredow, who had been murdered in the Blood Purge. Indignation about the murder of many other militarily less prominent victims was less intense.

[10] For example, the brothers Stauffenberg were followers of the poet Stefan George. The military participants in the conspiracy were mainly young professional officers, and many of the older officers who joined them were either in retirement or holding high positions in the home army and in occupied areas rather than at the front. The younger officers were often urged to action by those of the older conspirators who had been retired. The list of the victims of July 20, 1944, given by Wheeler-Bennett, *op. cit.,* consists of 160 names. Seventy-five of these were professional officers, 55 holding up to the rank of colonel. Of the civilians, a relatively high proportion were foreign-service officers or members of the civil service. If the 160 victims are divided according to family background, the ratio of aristocrats to commoners is very high: no less than 60 of the victims were noblemen.

miraculous survival of the abortive *putsch* of July 20, 1944. Then a military Court of Honor expelled the conspirators from the army, and handed them over to the Nazi authorities for sham trial and cruel execution.[11]

Since the war, only a few German officers have dared to ascribe the political and moral failure of the German military class under Hitler to the earlier fading of aristocratic and humanistic traditions and to the political ambitions of the generals. Such occasional self-criticism has come primarily from anti-Prussian South Germans such as Geyr von Schweppenburg, Faber du Faur, and Robert Knauss.[12]

Violating many of the taboos on class criticism which the conservative German generals observe, Geyr has spoken of the "sergeant's mentality" of the General Staff. The officers' class, he says, had for a long time lacked the spiritual resources to resist the anti-Christian forces of the age, when they found a new champion in Hitler. The class had been hostile toward the socialists under the Kaiser and in the Weimar Republic, and it has yet to realize that the workers, whom it despised, and the Social Democratic Party, which it considered a party of treason, have done no harm to them, whereas National Socialism, with which the generals did not find it impossible to compromise, ruined them as well as Germany. Geyr's scathing remarks hit not only Nazi generals like Reichenau and Jodl, but also persons like Halder[13] and Rundstedt. In fact, Geyr did not even spare such older German military leaders as Seeckt and Schlieffen, who still are regarded by most of the German generals as paragons of military virtue and beacons of a glorious past.

Similarly, Faber du Faur has considered the decay of the German military class in the wider context of what he regards as the general cultural deterioration in Germany that has occurred in the last seventy years. In a highly evocative manner, and with considerable

[11] The members of this Court of Honor included not only Keitel and Guderian, but also Field Marshal von Rundstedt, who today is still held in high esteem by many conservative military leaders.

[12] See Leo Freiherr Geyr von Schweppenburg, *Gebrochenes Schwert*, Berlin, 1952; Moriz von Faber du Faur, *Macht und Ohnmacht*, Stuttgart, 1955; and Robert Knauss, "Vom Geist eines deutschen Kontingents," *Europäische Sicherheit*, March, 1951, and "Der innere Aufbau eines deutschen Verteidigungsbeitrags," *Deutsche Rundschau*, March, 1952.

[13] "Halder did not have the strength to do as Beck had done, and say 'no' to the demands of the 'unconditionally obedient'" (General Geyr von Schweppenburg, *The Critical Years*, London, 1952, p. 197). See also Geyr's castigation of Halder for having tolerated, and collaborated in, the violation of Belgian, Dutch, and Danish neutrality in 1940, in *Gebrochenes Schwert*, p. 64. For other criticism of Halder by members of the resistance, see Rudolf Pechel, *Deutscher Widerstand*, Zurich, 1947, p. 151.

literary skill, he has contrasted the lost charm of patriarchal, aristocratic life in nineteenth-century Württemberg, its modesty and devotion to crown and country, with the rootless interest in success, the worship of power, the vulgarity and shiftlessness of the later generations. Few of his peers escaped his derision for having served Hitler. Faber du Faur scandalized most of his military readers. The president of the aristocratic *Johanniter Orden* expelled the author when his book first appeared in the *Stuttgarter Zeitung*. Similarly, Geyr's book has been removed from the shelves of some military libraries. And whoever else has dared to criticize the German military tradition has been regarded by the conservative elements of the class as a biased outsider, if not as a traitor. This attitude was, of course, strengthened by the wholesale condemnation of the German military profession by the victorious Allies during and after World War II.

Most of the former military leaders have shunned a review of their past political conduct. Very few of them would admit, as Robert Knauss has done, that the *Reichswehr* contributed to Hitler's rise to power.[14] In almost all of the numerous military memoirs that have been published in recent years, the German military tradition has been accepted as good and sound. Responsibility for Germany's downfall has been placed on the Nazi leaders. In the conservative military view, Germany was defeated by Hitler. His political and military errors have been scorned with pedantry, with no mercy, and sometimes with bureaucratic blindness.[15]

[14] "When we ask the question, 'Why did not the *Reichswehr* prevent Hitler's seizure of power?' it must be answered that already a year before that, in the spring of 1932, we opened the door to National Socialism by overthrowing Groener." (Robert Knauss, "Vom Geist eines deutschen Kontingents," *loc. cit.,* pp. 5–6.) For an account of Groener's place in the Republic and the role of the *Reichswehr* in overthrowing him as Secretary of Defense, see Gordon Craig, "*Reichswehr* and National Socialism: The Policy of Wilhelm Groener, 1928–1932," *Political Science Quarterly,* Vol. LXIII, No. 2 (June, 1948), pp. 194–229.

[15] High-ranking staff officers, like Halder, Heusinger, Zeitzler (Halder's successor), and even Guderian (who became Chief of Staff of the army after July 20, 1944) have made every effort to exculpate themselves after the war by showing that their professional judgment was superior to that of Hitler, the amateur, and of his military minions such as Keitel, Jodl, and Schmundt. See Halder, *op. cit.;* Adolf Heusinger, *Befehl im Widerstreit,* Tübingen and Stuttgart, 1950, pp. 209 and 247; Kurt Zeitzler, "Das Ringen um die militärischen Entscheidungen im zweiten Weltkrieg," *Wehrwissenschaftliche Rundschau,* 1951, Nos. 6/7 and 8/9; and Heinz Guderian, *Erinnerungen eines Soldaten,* Heidelberg, 1951. Many anti-Nazi, frontline commanders, however, have held these staff officers co-responsible for some of the militarily disastrous orders issued by the Supreme Command of the army, and have blamed them for not having resisted Hitler and his yes-men strenuously enough.

Some feeling of shame may be now hidden by silence or repressed in defiance of the moralistic postwar propaganda of the victors. From a large spate of German military memoirs, however, it transpires that it was neither Hitler's cruelty and vulgarity nor the imperialist aims of his policy that aroused the conservative generals, but rather his usurpation of supreme military power and the *risks* he took in directing Germany's foreign policy. In particular, the generals could not forgive the dictator for disregarding the work of the General Staff and for curtailing the privileges and responsibilities of the army in favor of the Joint Command of the *Wehrmacht* and of civilian Nazi authorities. From this vantage point, Hitler's immorality has come into view only in characteristic distortion: as unfairness to competent commanders, as supercilious disregard of military *expertise,* or simply as "demonic" power—a nonbureaucratic and hence seemingly supranatural force which no ordinary mortal could be expected to curb.

Thus it appears that the conservative generals have learned little from the past about their own tradition. They now feel abused in three ways: by Hitler, by those foreigners and Germans who had the temerity to denounce them after the war for their co-operation with him, and again by those Germans who charged them with sabotaging the war effort. A few military writers of conservative persuasion have searched more deeply for the reasons underlying the subjugation of the generals by Hitler and the political failure of the class. Even in these accounts, however, the responsibility which the military leaders bore because of their exalted position is befogged by references to Hitler's popularity in *other* groups, to "fate," and to "tragic circumstances." [16] Having taken a stand with regard to their political past that amounts to a conspiracy of evasion, and believing that their professional competence and patriotism are beyond reproach, the conservative group of German generals sees no reason why the future of their class should deviate from its past. As experts they served those who held political power; they stand ready to do so again, hoping that their *expertise* will be respected.

Since the war, the political orientations of former German military leaders have been most sharply divided by conflicting attitudes

---

[16] The more searching books include Adolf Heusinger, *op. cit.,* and Siegfried Westphal, *Heer in Fesseln,* Bonn, 1950. For contrast, compare Albert Kesselring, *op. cit.,* and Lothar Rendulic, *Gekämpft, Gesiegt, Geschlagen,* Heidelberg, 1952.

toward the events of July 20, 1944. While the unreconstructed Nazis criticize those who rebelled against Hitler and regard them as traitors, the conservative leaders have adopted an attitude of neutrality toward the military conspirators. Unwilling to join the fanatics who condemn the attempt at assassination, but also unwilling to exalt those who broke their oaths and tried to overthrow the government while Germany was at war, they evade the moral issue and perpetuate the irresolution which plagued them while Hitler was still alive. Taking a stand now would imply either a belated admission of their own failure to resist Hitler or a condemnation of their comrades-in-arms who were murdered by him. The conservative leaders try to bypass this moral dilemma by means of various rationalizations. Some of them hold that the twentieth of July is "unique" in history: nothing like it happened before and nothing resembling it will ever recur; the events of that day cannot be judged in the light of general moral principles, nor is there a need to do so. Others regard the plot against Hitler as a morally indifferent process resembling an organic upset. Still others simply say that one ought to keep silent. "The less said about July 20, the better." "Let's forget about that. Why stir up old ashes?" "It is something we must *digest.*"

Reserve is broken only when the question of co-operation with the enemy comes to mind. Stauffenberg can perhaps be forgiven for having placed a bomb in Hitler's headquarters, but General Hans Oster, who gave military information to the enemy, cannot. It is held that in extreme circumstances a German officer may commit tyrannicide, but he must never betray his country. Characteristically, even those who have dared to defend Oster have usually done so by adducing *patriotic* reasons for his action. Oster is said to have been so consumed with hatred because of Hitler's defilement of Germany's good name that he felt justified in committing *Landesverrat* for the sake of his country.[17]

---

[17] Only Schlabrendorff has freed himself of the nationalist prejudice that is inherent even in this apology and spoken of Oster's faith as being of a higher order than loyalty to the fatherland: he has said that "Oster was a man as God meant men to be"—*ein Mann nach dem Herzen Gottes.* See Schlabrendorff, *op. cit.,* p. 21. See also his evidence at the trial of Ernst Remer on March 10, 1952 (cf. Margret Boveri, *op. cit.,* Vol. II, p. 27). Geyr von Schweppenburg, too, has publicly stood up for Oster after the war, in the English edition of his autobiography, *The Critical Years.*

Sometimes conservative military leaders try to belittle the differ-ence between the conspirators and the men who continued to serve Hitler by stressing that the former had hailed or supported him ear-lier in their career "like everybody else." The point is not that these observations are factually incorrect—even men like Ludwig Beck and Claus von Stauffenberg had indeed sided with Hitler; the point is that these observations are not made in praise of the men who corrected their political errors, but in justification of those who clung to them. The opinion that Stauffenberg would have had "a right" to take Hitler's life only if he had been willing to perish in the attempt is fairly widespread among former German officers. They seem to believe that revolutionaries must kill themselves in order to atone for the guilt of rebellion. Thus a former air force general remarked in 1955,

Stauffenberg had as much right on his side as the others who con-tinued fighting the enemy. But consider that instead of shooting Hitler down, Stauffenberg tried to save himself by depositing a concealed bomb in Hitler's quarters. He left before it exploded.[18]

In contrast to both the unreconstructed National Socialists, who condemn the resistance to Hitler, and the conservative military ex-perts, who try in one way or another to deny the moral significance of July 20, the critics of the German military tradition believe that the anti-Nazi resistance in Germany saved the claim of their nation to freedom despite Hitler's shameful rule. These men consider July 20 as the day on which a number of upright and intrepid men preserved the political self-respect of the nation.

A true reconciliation between the proponents of these conflicting views is extremely difficult to effect. In modern society, political sin can hardly ever be forgiven, since agreement on the nature of sin is wanting. For the same reason, there is no way for great civic virtue to command universal respect; for many people who lack civic virtue would have to be forgiven their failing first, or at least be willing to recognize it themselves. Since modern society cannot forgive political sin, it can live on only by forgetting the past. It is difficult, however, to forget that Hitler ever existed or that many of the best Germans,

---

[18] Stauffenberg had been severely wounded in North Africa and lost one of his eyes, his right hand, and two fingers of his left hand.

who were *not* persecuted by him, died because they tried to rid their country of him. In Germany a truly unresolved past thus intrudes upon the present.

The past has reasserted itself in Adenauer's present military policy in more ways than one. When the Federal Republic began its preparations for rearmament, it could not obtain the assent of the German people merely by pointing to the new moral and expediential issue of the defense of freedom against the communist threat. It had to reassure the war-weary Germans that in the new military institutions the past would not be revived. Adenauer appointed Theodor Blank, a Catholic trade-union leader, to head the office that developed later into the Ministry of Defense, and the new agency was staffed with former officers who had not been devoted Nazis. The government felt it necessary to seek the co-operation of radical anti-Nazis in the defunct military class as well as of recognized experts with conservative leanings. But officers who were radically compromised as uncritical Nazis had to be kept away in order not to strengthen national and international resistance to the American policy which Adenauer followed. From its inception, however, the conflict between the reformers who found fault with the German military tradition, and the conservatives who saw no reason for deviating from it, was firmly lodged in the new Defense Ministry itself, with the reformers supposedly seeing to it that the new German army would be nonmilitaristic, and the conservatives ensuring that the nonmilitaristic forces would be efficient.

Reformers and experts have clashed on various occasions, and both of them have been subjected to public attacks, because civilian as well as military observers in the Federal Republic judge the government plans from the vantage point of an oppressive, vividly remembered past.

The intellectual leader of the reformers in the Defense Ministry has been Wolf Graf von Baudissin. While the influence of his faction in the Ministry has receded with the failure of the European Defense Community in 1954 [19] and with the growth of the Ministry, he has survived all attacks by colleagues and outsiders, partly because he enjoys the support of German youth organizations and of the Social Democrats.

In an effort to preserve for the future the best in Germany's recent

[19] In May, 1954, a number of young reformers quit the Ministry.

military past, Baudissin has openly and with some show of defiance endorsed the revolt against Hitler:

Consciously and unequivocally, we take a stand for a definite tradition, the direction of which—in any event for myself—is indicated by the name of Colonel General Ludwig Beck.[20]

Very few of the older conservative military leaders, however, have taken Baudissin seriously. They deride his idealism and view his efforts to instill a democratic spirit in the new German armed forces as a result of insufficient military experience.[21]

But the traditionalists in the Defense Ministry have been assailed no less than the reformers. Social Democrats and the military critics of Germany's military tradition distrust them on political grounds. Many conservative officers outside the Ministry regard many of them either as "paper-pushers" of dubious professional qualification or as faint-hearted men who lack the energy to restrain the reformers.

What may be called "the official view" of July 20, 1944, and of the role of the military in it is a compromise of conflicting opinions, and the whole German rearmament effort has been based on this compromise. It is now held that it was possible to serve Germany in the last war by opposing Hitler as well as by fighting the enemy, the implication being that both resistance to Hitler and lack of resistance were justified. In March, 1954, a conference of delegates of the *Deutscher Soldatenbund,* the largest German veterans' organization, adopted a resolution which expressed this view. Similarly, the principles for selecting officers up to the rank of lieutenant colonel, which the new Personnel Selection Board published in October, 1955, contain the following statement:

The soldier's conscience is bound by eternal moral laws. Aware of his transtemporal responsibility, he respects the rights and the religious and political convictions of his neighbor. From this orientation it follows that the future soldier must accept the conscientious decisions of the men of July 20, 1944. He will combine this acceptance with respect for them and

[20] Wolf Graf von Baudissin, "Soldatische Tradition und ihre Bedeutung für die Gegenwart," *Wehrkunde,* September, 1956, p. 437. See also *idem,* "The New German Army," *Foreign Affairs,* October, 1955.

[21] Baudissin was taken prisoner as a young officer early in World War II. For conservative criticism of his postwar views, see especially Werner Picht, *Wiederbewaffnung,* Pfullingen, 1954; see also *Deutsche Soldaten-Zeitung,* April, 1957.

for the many other soldiers who out of a feeling of duty risked their lives until the end.[22]

In order to ensure that the new military establishment became democratic, the Blank Office enlisted the help of many civilian and military advisers. Particularly in the early fifties, some conservative officers who privately spoke scathingly about various members of the government and about some of their former comrades in the Blank Office participated at the same time in endless deliberations on training, education, and the desirable relations between officers and men in the future German contingents.[23] Much energy of former military leaders was thus channeled into discussions of the so-called "inner structure" of the military establishment that the government wanted to create. In the absence of progress in rearmament, this discussion assumed inordinate public importance, giving to the early armament debates an almost quixotic air.

In contrast, the strategic issues of the defense of the West received considerably less attention. The government did not want to alarm the public by discussions related to war, and the generals, smarting from the criticism to which they had been subjected and cut off from up-to-date information on the development of modern weapons, hesitated to speak in public on strategic issues.

In conversation the conservative members of the group often justified their public reticence on other grounds. They pointed to a need for secrecy and to the fact that their standards of security were higher than those observed in the United States. Such beliefs served, of course, also to soothe their injured self-respect, since they implied a claim of correct conduct in an area in which Americans were allegedly careless. Devotion to secrecy was reinforced by the tradition of military aloofness from the civilian sector of society,

---

[22] "Richtlinien für die Offiziersauswahl," as published in *Wehrkunde*, November, 1955, pp. 514ff. For the "official" view of July 20, 1944, see also Theodor Heuss, *20. Juli 1944*, Berlin, 1954.

[23] Concerning the objectives of these deliberations, see Adelbert Weinstein, *Armee ohne Pathos, Die Deutsche Wiederbewaffnung im Urteil ehemaliger Soldaten* (hereinafter cited as *Armee ohne Pathos*), Bonn, 1951. The response of the conservative elements in the older German military elite is illustrated by the critical discussion of that book in Georg von Sodenstern's *"Bürgersoldaten," Wehrwissenschaftliche Rundschau*, June, 1952. See also *Der deutsche Soldat in der Armee von morgen*, Veröffentlichungen des Instituts für Staatslehre und Politik, e.V. Mainz, Vol. IV, Munich, 1954; Erich Dethleffsen and K. H. Helfer, *Soldatische Existenz morgen*, Bonn, 1953; and the official brochure, *Vom künftigen deutschen Soldaten: Gedanken und Planungen der Dienststelle Blank*, Offenbach, 1955.

and especially from professional talkers or writers; [24] in German the very word "journalist" has a pejorative meaning. Conservative German officers regard the press as a basically opportunistic institution. For example, they readily predict that, in the event of political adversity, Adenauer would quickly lose the support of those journalists who have applauded his actions in the past. "These men are hyenas waiting to tear corpses to shreds." Only the reformers among German military leaders have felt it necessary or desirable to enlighten civilians on military affairs, while the conservatives have regarded such matters as a strictly professional concern. Among the reformers, interest in secrecy is not shared but criticized. The dissenters from the tradition consider unnecessary military secretiveness a feature of German militarism and additional proof of the undemocratic character of the former military class. [25] They deplore also the corresponding confidence of the public in secretive military *expertise*.

In the last few years, public discussion of strategic issues has increased somewhat in Germany. It has become evident that the views of army and navy officers on war and strategy are more clearly articulated than are those of air force generals. There is no German strategic doctrine which reflects a distinctive view of the former *Luftwaffe*. Traditionally, German strategic thinking has been landbound and has tended to underrate the importance of naval power in global conflicts and of joint operations in general. Similarly, the strategic importance of air power has been characteristically underestimated. Douhet's doctrine of the war-decisive importance of air power used to be held in high esteem only in the leading circles of the *Luftwaffe*, while it was rejected by the General Staff of the army. [26] Service rivalry between the German army and the *Luftwaffe* was intense, partly because the German air force was directed by Göring and was more nazified than the army, and partly because it became less and less effective after the Battle of Britain and the first campaign in Soviet Russia. Since the war, it has been most difficult

[24] In the days of the Weimar Republic, General von Schleicher once remarked, "The people must have a vague and respectful opinion of the General Staff, but it must not know anything whatever about it." Cited in H. R. Berndorff, *General zwischen Ost und West*, Hamburg, 1952, p. 15.

[25] On German military attitudes toward secrecy, see Hans Speier, "German Rearmament and the Old Military Elite," *World Politics*, Vol. VI, No. 2 (January, 1954), pp. 147–168.

[26] See Adolf Galland, "Defeat of the Luftwaffe: Fundamental Causes," *Air University Quarterly Review*, Vol. VI, No. 1 (Spring, 1953), p. 23; and Siegfried Westphal, *op. cit.*, p. 46.

for the older, conservative German generals to develop an appreciation of strategic air power and its capabilities in the atomic age. When, in the early fifties, the subject of the bombing of German cities was mentioned by German generals, they cited unfailingly British professional criticism of its wastefulness and cruelty, hiding their own condemnation of strategic air war behind the opinions of such writers as J. F. C. Fuller and Liddell Hart.[27]

Nuclear power and its role in future war are subjects which many former German generals still view with a bias born of ignorance and prejudice. It has been chiefly the civilian opponents to rearmament and former officers in the younger age groups who have concerned themselves seriously with the future.[28]

It is difficult to obtain accurate and comprehensive information on the present economic status of the thirteen-hundred former German generals.[29] By and large, their age and the location of their prewar property determine their present standard of living. Those who owned property or immobile capital in the communist part of Germany, but now reside in the West, have suffered a sharp economic decline in comparison with those who have property in West Germany. Similarly, unemployed older generals who have not reached the age of 62, when they are entitled to receive a government pension, are worse off than the younger officers, most of whom have found a new gainful occupation. Government benefits are small, and many high-ranking older officers who lost their property because of the war have had to lower their standards of comfort, some of them drastically. Many have tried to supplement their income in one way or another. In the early years after the war, before German military publications reappeared, British and Swiss military magazines, rather than American journals, provided a minor source of additional income to German military experts. Many generals wrote memoirs or historical accounts of World War II. The historical divisions of the U.S. Army, Navy, and Air Force provided former German officers with work and pay. Similarly, a

[27] Similarly, critical British writings by Paget and others on the issues of war crimes and unconditional surrender were popular in postwar Germany.

[28] One of the important exceptions is the discussion of U.S. strategic problems contained in the widely read article by former General Frido von Senger und Etterlin, "Strategie in Amerika," *Deutsche Zeitung,* December 17, 1955.

[29] There are about 300,000 former officers of lower rank in West Germany today.

large number of German officers who had been active in military intelligence work, including experts with a doubtful political past, were enabled to continue in their jobs without loss of income in the "Organization Gehlen," so called after General R. Gehlen, who had headed G-2 in the German army.

Most former German officers, however, left their profession entirely in the years of demilitarization and sought civilian employment. Since the social and political connections between German heavy industry and the officers' corps had been close ever since the reign of the Kaiser, many former generals found a place in German industry, especially after the stabilization of the currency in 1948. The demands for executive ability in modern military organization are similar to those of modern business, so that changing from one to the other is easy in all industrial societies. As in the United States, where generals after retirement are frequently offered lucrative positions in business, such change from military to civilian seems on the whole to have been financially advantageous to the persons concerned. The generals who have profited in this way are inclined to deny that economic improvement has been frequent in their ranks. One of them said in 1955 that there had been no more than ten cases of this kind. But this estimate was evidently much too low.[30] It is refuted, among other things, by the concern voiced by officials in the Blank Office in the early fifties that it would be difficult to find officers to fill vacancies in the Defense Ministry and in the high echelons of the new German contingents, because so many suitable persons had found more rewarding jobs in business and were unwilling to accept a loss in income by returning to a military position.[31]

Not only heavy industry, but also other business enterprises, have absorbed a large number of high-ranking military personnel. Some of them have become salesmen of various goods, ranging from champagne to Geiger counters. Younger former officers seem to have been quite successful in their new civilian careers. One general said as early as 1950 that he would wager that none of the younger General Staff officers were unemployed or had turned out to be failures in

[30] The sample on which this study is based itself comprises more than ten such cases.
[31] This unwillingness was often attributed to the wives of these former officers. It should be added that in the early fifties employment in the Blank Office was made only on a limited-time basis.

civilian jobs. He attributed their success proudly to the high standards of selection and training of the former General Staff.

In general, the economic boom after 1948 which provided the propertied class in West Germany with the highest profit rates of any European country in the postwar era has aided in the absorption of the former professional officers into civilian life. No doubt not only the severity of Germany's defeat in World War II, but also this economic boom has been a powerful influence in preventing the rise of political extremism among former German officers. Different from the adventurism that was rampant after World War I when, under the influence of socially displaced officers, nihilistic contempt for work and peace made inroads in German middle-class youth, the German political scene after World War II has been tranquil, if not complacent, despite the partitioning of the country, the elimination of Prussia as a state, the occupation, and the influx of millions of refugees. The quick re-emergence of the class structure under conditions of prosperity has channeled energy away from political activism throughout West Germany. It is the maimed, the old people in the lower-income groups, war widows, and economically useless elements of the population that constitute the equivalent of a lower class in modern Germany; but if there is ferment in German postwar society, it does not consist in radicalism but, paradoxically, in the absence of deep political commitments among German youth to the defense of freedom against foreign threats. A recession could provide an arena to irresponsible activists, but probably only for men with a neutralist bent.

Democracy in Germany has no political tradition that unites people despite barriers of class, party, and denomination. Nor have the citizens of the Federal Republic much patriotic self-assurance. They eat well, but not the fruit of common national achievement. Several older generals alluded to this fact by remarking that the Federal Republic was "no state," that no "values" are firmly upheld in the community, that there is "distrust" of words denoting "ideals." Having passed within thirty years from the Kaiser Reich through the Weimar Republic and the National Socialist era to foreign occupation and finally to a government that owes its existence to foreign sufferance and encouragement, many Germans distrust political ideals of any kind. Owing to their recent history, they exemplify in a particularly radical form the crumbling of political ideologies from which all Western civilization suffers. Even in the *Bundestag* today, where orators might be expected to assume a modicum of common beliefs, tolerance for any words that denote such beliefs is extremely low. On June 28, 1955, Richard Jaeger, Vice-President of the *Bundestag,* spoke of "the acceptance of freedom as the basis of private and public life" and "the common love of our homeland." He was immediately heckled, and added hastily, "We do not want to lose ourselves in false pathos," at which point some Social Democratic deputies shouted, "Very true." Jaeger continued, "We do not want to use words here which may be interpreted in a National Socialist way." [32]

The quick succession of five different political regimes in the last forty years in Germany has also increased the importance of age differences in the political climate of the Federal Republic. The past experienced by Adenauer and the older military leaders extends to the Kaiser Reich and the early years of the Republic, when these men were active adults, whereas the youngest German voters today were small children when Germany was plunged into war by their elders. Given this rapid rate of political and social change, the influence on political ideologies of the present political structure and of class position in it is refracted by various age-differentiated images of the past. Thus the structure of present society is less "real" than it would be in a society with more durable political institutions.

The political and military views of German professional officers appear to vary with age, service affiliation, and regional and perhaps religious background, rather than with economic position. Above all else, however, the roles played in the Nazi era subtly affect their outlook.

The direct political influence in the Federal Republic of the former military class is not great. The *Bundestag* and the parliaments of the *Länder* in the Federal Republic have a few members who were officers of higher rank. Until 1953 their number was even smaller than it has been in the second *Bundestag,* when the rearmament discussions made it possible and, in view of the legislative tasks ahead, desirable to elect some deputies with military knowledge and experience. Without exception, however, these "military deputies" have turned civilian in outlook. Never has there been a session in the

[32] *Verhandlungen des Deutschen Bundestags* (hereinafter cited as *Bundestag Record*), June 28, 1955, p. 5227.

Bundestag in which any of them has made a speech that could be called militaristic in any sense of the term. Instead, deputies of all parties have protested on numerous occasions that German militarism is dead, that German youth is anything but enthusiastic about military service, and that another war would be disastrous for Germany and the world at large.

There have been occasions in the *Bundestag* when the antimilitary feeling was expressed with unusual candor. In many debates on rearmament it has been necessary for the speakers of the government parties to protest that Switzerland and the United States prove the compatibility of freedom and democracy with military service. The Defense Minister himself said in the *Bundestag* that it was understandable that German youth looked at military service "with reservations." [33] And he had to plead, "The soldier must not be regarded by the citizen as a necessary evil," [34] because he is being regarded precisely in this way even by many supporters of German rearmament. According to international agreement, the function of Germany's navy will be confined in the main to coastal protection, minesweeping, and, together with the Danish navy, to keeping control of the sea lanes in the western part of the Baltic Sea. In December, 1954, a deputy of the Christian Democratic Union (CDU) said in the *Bundestag* that it would, of course, be nonsense to have German battleships "which would cost billions and on which an admiral would then take his constitutional." [35] The absence of certain modern weapons such as bombing planes in the projected German armed forces, or the prohibition of heavy-weapons production has not been deplored or criticized in parliament. General von Manteuffel, deputy of the Free Democratic Party (FDP), explained in December, 1954, that he and his party welcomed the renunciation of a higher defense effort, since the prevailing restrictions would in time offer opportunities for security arrangements between East and West. [36]

With regard to the rejection of "militarism," there is little difference between the members of the opposition and the coalition parties in the *Bundestag*. In fact, there have been occasions when both of them joined in voting down proposals submitted to the

---

[33] *Ibid.*, June 27, 1955, p. 5214.
[34] *Ibid.*
[35] Will Rasner, in *ibid.*, December 16, 1954, p. 3190.
[36] *Ibid.*, p. 3199.

Bundestag by the Blank Office. This happened, for example, in the summer of 1955, when Theodor Blank presented a bill on the so-called "Volunteer Law" with the approval of the Chancellor. Deputies of Adenauer's own political party rebelled, and the *Bundestag* as a whole opposed the first real step toward rearmament, because it was felt to be hastily and inadequately prepared.

Similarly, in September, 1956, the restriction of military service to a period of twelve months was forced upon the government by the fact that many influential members of Adenauer's party opposed the plan for longer service on which the Defense Ministry had insisted.

With respect to military representation, the only difference between the Social Democrats in the *Bundestag* and the deputies of the other parties consists in the fact that the opposition has no high-ranking former officers. The leading Social Democratic expert on issues related to rearmament is Fritz Erler, a civilian who spent time in Nazi prisons. The principal military adviser on the staff of the Social Democratic Party is a former professional officer with the rank of lieutenant colonel. Like Erler, he is respected outside his own party and in the Defense Ministry for his judgment and moderation. Fritz Erler is Vice-Chairman of the Parliamentary Defense Committee. It is largely due to him that the Social Democratic Party has not opposed rearmament to the point of surrendering all influence upon the structure and organization of the new German forces to the government and to the parties supporting its rearmament measures. Such radicalism might have alienated the military establishment from the people and fostered the development in the military forces of such independent political power within the state as contributed to the downfall of the Weimar Republic.

Among the deputies of the CDU, Adenauer's party, the leading members of the former military class are Fritz Berendsen, a former army colonel on the General Staff, and Vice-Admiral Hellmuth G. A. Heye. Berendsen's influence in the party is greater than his distinction as a debater, because of his close connection with heavy industry. In the second *Bundestag,* Berendsen has made many of the main speeches for the Christian Democrats in defense of rearmament, although his colleague Richard Jaeger, a lawyer in the Bavarian Christian Social Union (CSU, which is allied with the CDU), is the Chairman of the Parliamentary Defense Committee.

Among the *Bundestag* deputies, Fritz Berendsen and former General Hasso von Manteuffel are probably the two men who are closest to the Prussian tradition of the German army. Admiral Heye, another CDU member of the Defense Committee, entered the German navy in 1914 and was an officer throughout the Weimar and Hitler periods. He ended his professional career as commander of the midget submarines (*Kleinkampfverbände*). Before becoming a *Bundestag* deputy he worked for the historical division of the U.S. Navy. Admiral Heye is a politically moderate man with an understanding of world affairs wider than that of the average German Deputy. He and Admiral Friedrich Ruge, who became chief of the new German naval forces, have been the two most distinguished German professional authors approaching the defense problems of the West from a distinctly naval point of view.[37]

In the CSU, the outstanding military expert is Franz-Josef Strauss, who is not a professional officer but a historian. A man of great political ability, Strauss defended Adenauer's policy with considerable skill and fervor in the early *Bundestag* debates on rearmament. He again came to the government's aid in 1955 when the NATO atomic exercise CARTE BLANCHE was used by the opposition as an occasion for a withering attack on Adenauer and the Blank Office. In 1955 Strauss was appointed Minister for Atomic Affairs, and in October, 1956, finally succeeded Theodor Blank, his old rival, as Defense Minister. It is significant that the new Defense Minister, rather than any of the military representatives in the *Bundestag,* has been associated with the recent interest of the West German government in receiving tactical atomic weapons.[38]

The FDP has at least one outstanding military representative in the *Bundestag,* namely, former General Hasso von Manteuffel, scion of an old military family and commander of an armored army that participated in the German advance in the Battle of the Bulge. Soon after the war, Manteuffel found a position in an industrial firm in the Rhineland and was elected to the *Bundestag* in 1953. He represents his party on the Defense Committee. He remained loyal to the government when a large part of the FDP faction in the *Bundestag,* headed by its party chairman, broke with the Chancellor and went into opposition early in 1956.

[37] See especially Friedrich Ruge, *Seemacht und Sicherheit,* Tübingen, 1955.
[38] See Chap. 12.

There is no former air force officer of high rank in the German *Bundestag*.

Direct influence of former German officers by pressure groups upon postwar politics in Germany has been small. In the first years of demilitarization no veterans' organizations were permitted. They began to form after 1950, and have confined themselves primarily to representation of the economic interests of their members and to the advocacy of release of war criminals. The biggest organization—the *Deutscher Soldatenbund*—has consistently supported Adenauer's policy of rearmament and has followed an anti-Soviet line. Its organ, *Die Deutsche Soldaten-Zeitung,* has participated in the discussion of controversial issues only by condemning attacks on militarism such as those contained in the best-selling series of novels by Hans Hellmuth Kirst that were published under the title *0815.*

The organization *Stahlhelm,* under the leadership of former Field Marshal Albert Kesselring, is more nationalistic than the *Deutscher Soldatenbund*. After his release as a war criminal, Kesselring occasionally made international news by public statements which intensified antimilitaristic feelings among German youth and anti-German feelings abroad.

There are innumerable smaller veterans' organizations, called *Traditionsverbände,* primarily devoted to maintaining contact among their members and the *esprit de corps* of the units to which they belonged, and there are a few relatively unimportant political veterans' organizations with openly antidemocratic leanings.

The most important organization promoting professional interests in military science is the *Gesellschaft für Wehrkunde*, with headquarters in Munich, which has local chapters throughout West Germany. From the accounts of their activities appearing in its journal, the government-sponsored military monthly *Wehrkunde,* it appears that the discussions held in these groups are devoted primarily to military history and current international affairs. An *Arbeitskreis für Wehrforschung* (Working Group for Military Research) publishes a number of military journals, which, different from *Wehrkunde,* contain primarily historical studies, although current military problems are not entirely neglected.[39]

---

[39] The publications of the *Arbeitskreis* are *Wehrwissenschaftliche Rundschau, Marine Rundschau, Wehrtechnische Monatshefte,* and, beginning in 1956, a series of monographs, *Studien und Dokumente zur Geschichte des Zweiten Weltkrieges.*

Former German generals have exerted political influence neither through pressure groups nor through their writings on current affairs, but rather through personal contact with politicians, businessmen, and government officials. Informal contacts between the Blank Office and former military leaders on the outside have been intense and widespread. Many former German generals have served in an advisory capacity to the Blank Office and to the Defense Committee of the *Bundestag*.

Most prominent, of course, have been those military leaders who were reappointed to serve the Federal Republic in a military capacity, and the former generals who became members of the *Personalgutachterausschuss* (Personnel Selection Board), created by the *Bundestag* in 1955 to screen the highest officers in the new German *Bundeswehr* for their political reliability and professional competence.

The Board contains a few members who were closely associated with the resistance to Hitler, and a number of former German generals with anti-Nazi tendencies, a high sense of civic responsibility, and forward-looking democratic ideas about military organization.[40] By contrast, the highest military functionaries in the Defense Ministry are as a group more nondescript in their political outlook. This is particularly true of Adolf Heusinger, one of Germany's two three-star generals. Until July, 1944, Heusinger was Chief of the Operations Division in the High Command of the army. He is credited with unusual strategic talent, sobriety, and caution. Under Hitler, he was disturbed by Nazi interference with military efficiency, smooth coordination, and time-honored, proper procedures. He confined himself to giving expert advice and considered Hitler's disregard for it as one of the major faults of the regime. In his postwar memoirs Heusinger has described the many conflicts of competence between the *Wehrmacht* and the army as though they had been fights between hostile forces, and has reported with satisfaction the ambiguous phrasing of orders so as to comply with Hitler's commands and yet to permit their violation by field commanders.

Hans Speidel, Germany's other three-star general, is a military scholar and a military diplomat with more than a common under-

---

[40] These military members include former General Frido von Senger und Etterlin, one of the German military publicists who, beginning in 1955, has concerned himself with the strategic issues of nuclear war.

standing of foreign affairs, particularly French-German relations. In the latter part of the war, Speidel was Erwin Rommel's chief of staff. Due to his considerable adroitness he survived his own and Rommel's late association with the resistance.[41] In the last few years Speidel has worked for German rearmament to the satisfaction of his Minister and the Allies. In January, 1957, he became the first German commander of NATO troops.

By September, 1956, the Personnel Selection Board had passed judgment on 322 former officers with the rank of general or colonel and rejected 30 candidates. Twenty-four other submissions had been withdrawn by the Defense Ministry upon advice of the Board. Seventy-five further cases remained to be examined.

The Board has extraordinary powers. It is authorized to determine its own procedures. Its decisions are made in secret and require a two-thirds majority. The Board does not publish the grounds on which it reaches its decisions, and in case of rejection no appeal is possible. The Board has passed judgment not only on candidates for the highest military positions to be filled, but has also claimed authority to examine the suitability of the top incumbents in the Defense Ministry. Since it decided unfavorably on the political suitability or military competence of some prominent and trusted men in the Ministry, it challenged by implication the political competence of the Defense Minister and created a series of political sensations. For example, in one of its earliest decisions the Board decided against the suitability of one of Blank's officers who enjoyed the confidence of Allied military personnel at SHAPE. Similarly, the Board declared Adolf Heusinger to be "unsuitable to be Supreme Commander of the Armed Forces or Supreme Commander of the Army." Thereupon Blank saved his face by appointing Heusinger Chairman of the *Militärischer Führungsrat* (Military Council), an agency corresponding to the U.S. Joint Chiefs of Staff. In this position, Heusinger has no command function.

Early in 1957, it became known that not only Speidel but also Heusinger might be given a position that would take him away from Bonn. He was slated for transfer to Washington if a German representative were to be added to the NATO Standing Group. In the process of reorganizing his ministry, Strauss was expected to ask for legislative approval to appoint a four-star general as Inspector

[41] See Hans Speidel, *Invasion 1944,* Stuttgart, 1949.

General of the *Bundeswehr*. The names of Walther Wenck, a former general of armored troops and now managing director of a steel plant, and of General Josef Kammhuber were mentioned as candidates for this position. Kammhuber was appointed in 1956 to fill the highest position in the German air force. He had been a very competent commander of night fighters under Hitler, who fired him twice during the war. It would be an extraordinary departure from tradition if the highest soldier in Germany should be an air force officer rather than an army general.

The Department of the Army is headed in the Defense Ministry by General Hans Röttiger, a former general who entered the army as a volunteer in 1914 and received General Staff training in the Weimar Republic. At the end of World War II he served as Chief of Staff of Army Group C (Southwest) and played an important role in the surrender of the German forces in Italy to Field Marshal Alexander. In order to effect that surrender, Röttiger bypassed his new chief, who had been appointed just after an agreement with the Allies had been reached. He prevailed upon the subordinate army commanders of Army Group C to cease fire according to the agreed-upon terms, thereby avoiding further useless bloodshed.[42]

Kammhuber is one of the relatively large number of Bavarians who have become influential in German military policy. After the cabinet shake-up in October, 1956, Bavarian representation in German defense policy became even more prominent. In addition to Franz-Josef Strauss, the new Defense Minister, Fritz Schäffer, the Minister of Finance, is a member of the CSU; so are Siegfried Balke, the new Minister for Atomic Affairs, who took Strauss's old place in the cabinet, and Richard Jaeger, Chairman of the Defense Committee in the *Bundestag*. Minister-President Hoegner, the Chairman of the Defense Committee in the *Bundesrat,* is a Bavarian too, though a Social Democrat.

In short, toward the end of 1956 it appeared that the direct political influence of the Prussian tradition upon German military institutions was being definitely superseded by that of Bavarian politicians, some of whom, such as Strauss and Jaeger, are among the ablest new

[42] The moral problem of surrender has occupied German generals after the war almost as much as has July 20, 1944. For a discussion of surrender see, for example, Albert Kesselring, *op. cit.,* pp. 411–412, 418–420, and 423–427; and Hans Speidel, *op. cit.,* pp. 69–70. Kesselring's conduct in the surrender negotiations in Italy was criticized by Allen W. Dulles, *Germany's Underground*, New York, 1947, p. 39.

younger men in the *Bundestag*. If the elections in 1957 should lead to the formation of a coalition cabinet, the Bavarian wing of the Christian Democrats and some of its prominent leaders might be more acceptable to the Social Democrats as partners than Adenauer or his fiercely antisocialist backers.

Part I

The Views of the Military

THREE

The Cold War: 1952–1954

When former German military officers talk about foreign affairs, they rarely repeat the opinions voiced in parliament or in the press. Nor do they show much interest in the niceties of diplomacy and the details of international negotiation, or in the manipulative aspects of foreign relations. Instead, they call attention to basic conflicts of national interest, and to secular trends of power politics. They tend to review the relations between states in the light of historical precedents, and to describe them in terms of military power, geography, population pressures, economic resources, and massive ideological forces. This tendency is characteristic especially of the older generation of German military leaders. It gives their views on international affairs both a broad sweep and a doubtlessly cherished appearance of disregarding the ephemeral and temporary in favor of the essential.

Minor and passing events figure in such assessments of the cold war only if they can be endowed with what is believed to be brilliant meaning that casts light on a broad-stroked picture of the world scene. Generally, careful examination of political detail is lacking, and is, one feels, disdained. Talk with a German newspaperman about American foreign policy and, more often than not, he will mention a recent press conference given by a high American official, a German grievance, or (in order to show his sophistication) an issue on which Executive and Congress in the United States are deadlocked. In contrast, members of the former military class will, in similar situations, compare American policies in Asia and Europe, discuss the trends and prospects of U.S. policy toward the Soviet bloc, or point to the difficulties which any democracy faces in shaping foreign policy. Whereas the newspaperman may take pleasure in parading bits of inside information, the former general likes to take a view which he believes exhibits originality and breadth of thought. The military man gives the impression that he has looked at globes of the world and read books on history. Although his thinking on military affairs may be bounded by tradition and personal experience, his mental horizon on foreign policy extends beyond the borders of Germany and Europe, and encompasses more than a life span of history.

German military leaders believe that the current period of the cold war is but a phase of a continuing total and global war. One general recalled in 1952 that it had taken the United States some time after 1945 to realize this fact. He had startled his American interrogators immediately after the war by remarking that "Germany can now wash her hands of it: it will be up to the Western Allies to cope with the Soviet Union." Similar views were voiced vociferously by General Guderian and in many German popular writings on the postwar role of the United States.[1] But by 1952, malicious lack of interest in the cold war was no longer a common attitude among former military officers. The more detached among them now regarded Guderian's opposition to German rearmament within EDC as the opinion of a firebrand: they had turned their attention from the past American policy of collaboration with the Soviet Union to current prospects in the struggle between East and West. As one former general put it,

people resent the fact that while the United States followed a policy of German disarmament and of friendship with Russia after the war, it now advocates rearmament. They could just as easily argue that it was admirable of the United States to realize its mistake in hoping for cooperation with the Soviet Union and to change its policy.

German military leaders changed their views on the nature of the cold war less than might have been expected as a result of changes in the world, and particularly in the Soviet Union, between 1952 and 1955. They did so precisely because they are swayed by minor political news less easily than are politicians. In particular, they attributed much less importance to the changes in Soviet political

[1] Heinz Guderian, *Kann Westeuropa verteidigt werden?* Göttingen, 1950; and *idem, So geht es nicht*, Heidelberg, 1951.

tactics after Stalin's death than to the military balance of power. They pointed to the increase of Soviet military pressure on the West, and they never assumed that the basic aims of Soviet policy had changed.

German military observers point out that, in order to appreciate the true nature of the cold war, one must remember that the struggle between East and West has a long history. During the twentieth century, the struggle has developed in favor of the East: first, by the disintegration of the Austro-Hungarian Empire in World War I; second, by the dismemberment of Germany and the defeat of Japan; third, by the victory of communism in China; fourth, by communist inroads in many other parts of the world during the so-called "cold-war period"; and, finally, by the breaking of the American monopoly in nuclear weapons.

In March, 1952, the late General von Sodenstern published an article on the strategic situation in the East-West conflict, which was read with much approval, and often quoted, in German military circles. Sodenstern said that Bolshevik strategy represented a reversal of the teachings of Clausewitz; according to the Soviet version, peace was a continuation of war, with other means thrown in. The use of armed force on a large scale, in the Bolshevik view, is merely the final stage of a long-term war that has already been won politically, economically, and ideologically. The current war between the East and the West, then, goes on in Korea, Indonesia, Malaya, Greece, Indochina, and other countries; the battles in this war include liquidations in the European satellite countries, labor strikes in the harbors of Australia and the Pacific ports of the United States, and nationalist activities in Persia and Egypt:

World War III, the outbreak of which is continuously feared in Europe, has long since started. It began when Roosevelt's 'Old Joe,' certain of German defeat, turned to the final bolshevization of China, while Americans and Englishmen were busy achieving freedom of action for him by the invasion of France (instead of the Balkans) and the destruction of Japan's position as a great power. Stalin needed this freedom of action in order to attack his former allies in the East as well as in the West.

With the destruction of Germany and Japan, a radical change of the world picture took place, which at the time was recognized only by . . . General MacArthur: the predominant power of world revolution was mobilized for the decisive battle against the noncommunist world. Ever since, not a cold war, but a total war has been in full swing. The Kremlin determines its fronts, and decides about the methods to be used.[2]

According to German military opinion, the Soviet Union was not ready to resume military hostilities on a large scale in the first years after the termination of World War II.

It had pushed westward in Europe and consolidated its positions there. Until 1956 it had suffered only one major defeat in the cold war, the defection of Tito, and that was not the result of Western initiative. Then the Soviet leaders concentrated their attention on the non-Western areas of the world, using, to attain their ends, all means at their disposal short of overt military action by their own forces. They sought to weaken the West by forcing it to deplete its military strength in Europe and violate the principle of the concentration of forces in defense of British and French overseas interests. Similarly, the commitment of U.S. forces in Korea, much as it helped to brace morale in Germany, and though it proved to the West that America was willing to sacrifice more than dollars in order to contain communism, played into the hands of the Soviet Union by diverting Western power to a strategically unimportant area. Interestingly enough, German military observers did not view communist aggression in Korea as a Soviet mistake prompting the United States to assume a stronger defense posture. Nor did they suggest that the conflict in Korea provided the United States with an opportunity to improve its position in what German generals considered the ongoing third world war. It seems that they regarded the Korean war rather as a military mistake of the United States, committed in violation of the principle of the concentration of force and leading to a dissipation of effort. Nonetheless, it is likely also that they would have criticized American policy strongly if the communist attack in Korea had not been resisted at all. It cannot be said that the German military views on this issue were well considered, and this lack of objectivity may be interpreted as an indication of hidden hostility toward the United States.

While they see no essential change in the nature of the cold war, German military leaders have, in the past three or four years, grown increasingly pessimistic about the West's prospects of winning it.

[2] Georg von Sodenstern, "Die strategische Lage der Welt," *Wehrwissenschaftliche Rundschau,* March, 1952.

They are discouraged by Soviet successes, by the lack of American initiative, and by increasing Soviet capabilities in unconventional weapons. This pessimism was expressed most sharply in the spring of 1954, at the time of the Geneva Conference on Indochina.

Asia

American policy toward Asia after China fell to the communists baffles many German military leaders. Few of them consider this policy sound. Lacking an understanding of its background, and failing to appreciate the strategic issues of the Pacific as readily as they do those of Europe, they criticize United States policy toward China as serving to cement the Chinese-Russian coalition instead of seeking to drive a wedge between the two biggest communist powers.

Even those German generals who do appreciate the strategic issues involved stress the possibility of a conflict of interests between the Soviet Union and China. One of Germany's former leading strategists said in 1954 that it was clearly against the interests of the United States to have any single foreign power dominate either the eastern Atlantic coastline or the Asiatic coastline of the Pacific and the Indian Oceans. China was already in communist hands, and control of the rest of the Pacific coastline in Asia might also fall to the communists. It was therefore understandable, he continued, that there were people in the United States who wanted to contest Chinese power.

But one must think further, the general continued. If the United States were to engage in a war against China, the Soviet Union would sit back, pleased that both the United States and China were locked in war. Its own day would come at the end of such a war, which would be a long and exhausting struggle, for "one knows from history that China cannot be defeated militarily."

Similar views were expressed, especially in April, 1954, by some other military observers, when they considered it possible that American intervention in Indochina might lead to war between the United States and Communist China.

Very few of the German military experts who were interviewed for the purposes of this study addressed themselves to the domestic causes of the new nationalism in the underdeveloped countries of Asia, Africa, and the Middle East; nor did they respond to introduc-

tion of this topic in the course of discussion. All anti-Western sentiment and action in those areas were attributed to communist in-
stigation and to Western failure to take appropriate defensive action.
German generals fail to distinguish between simple Soviet support
and more insidious manipulation of native independence move-
ments in non-Western countries. Economic misery and social in-
justice seem to be matters beyond the ken of these military observers.
The non-Western world does not appear to them to have a life of
its own. They tend to view it, rather, as a chessboard on which the
Soviet player is moving his black pieces more skillfully than his
Western counterpart is playing the white. And white, quite clearly,
in their opinion, is losing the game.

The Middle East

The Middle East has long appeared to many German military
leaders to be an especially important area in the cold war. They
believe that this area is vulnerable both to direct communist infiltra-
tion, and to the communist-inspired, anti-Western activities of the
Arabs. As early as 1952, several former generals singled out the
Middle East as an area in which they expected to see major cold-war
developments that would embarrass the West. This forethought
probably resulted in part from strategic preconceptions about the importance of the deep southern flank in any Soviet attack on Central
Europe.[3] Thus some informants said that solid Arab opposition to
American policy might weaken Turkey decisively, and reduce its
value to the Western defense system. But they also pointed to the
offensive value of the Middle East. One of them illustrated this
value by remarking that the Soviet Union could be strategically
defeated from a strong base system in the Black Sea area.

The importance of areas adjoining the Middle East is also mentioned, especially by former *Luftwaffe* officers. The latter are especially likely to insist that, in view of the exposed position of Western

[3] Similarly, the importance of Scandinavia as the northern flank of any such attack has
often been commented upon. For example, Leo Freiherr Geyr von Schweppenburg wrote in
1951 that, next to the destruction of the American war potential from without, and the sap-
ping of the morale of the American working class from within, the main danger to Western
defense would be the establishment of Soviet submarine and air bases on the Atlantic coast
and in Scandinavia. ("Will They Attack?" in *The Western Defenses,* ed. Brig. J. A. Smyth,
London [n.d.; probably 1951].)

Europe, Spain and North Africa must be regarded as part of the Western defense area, and one unusually well-informed officer explicitly mentioned in the spring of 1954 that not only the Middle East but also Kenya and the Union of South Africa are regions in which a step-up of Soviet cold-war activities could be expected.

France and EDC

When German military leaders look at the various theaters of the cold war, they often concentrate on regions rather than on countries. Even in their comments on cold-war developments in Europe, they take a continental view and rarely lose themselves in narrow issues. This is illustrated by the fact that, despite their undoubted patriotism, most German military leaders were intensely interested in European integration during the early fifties. A desire to regain sovereignty for Germany coupled with concern about the balance of military forces in Europe led most of them to favor some measure of European solidarity. What probably made it even easier for the military to hold this attitude was their belief that in due time Germany would recapture a position of strength, if not indeed of dominance, on the European continent.

After initial blasts against EDC by General Guderian, German military opposition to EDC was not vocal, although many former officers outside the government thought very little of the military efficacy of the proposed arrangement. All of the military criticized and deplored the slow progress toward an increase in European strength, though most of them showed restraint toward the French when commenting on the length of time that it was taking Paris to ratify EDC. One former general had this to say about the various delays: "America is strong enough to prevent a war, but not so strong as to render the quarrels among pygmies [i.e., in Europe] tolerable." [4] Another remarked in 1952 that, if the French insisted on a French commander for the land forces in EDC, he would favor their proposal, because building up defensive strength for Western Europe as a whole was more important than matters of national prestige.

In 1952 the French proposed a protocol to the EDC treaties accord-

[4] Leo Freiherr Geyr von Schweppenburg, *Die grosse Frage,* Berlin [n.d.; probably 1950], p. 22.

ing to which the Supreme Commander of the NATO forces would be obligated *in advance* to approve withdrawals of the French EDC contingent for colonial tasks. German generals took a dim view of this proposal. General Hasso von Manteuffel, now a *Bundestag* deputy supporting Dr. Adenauer, wrote at the time that the defense of Europe would "work better in a good coalition than in a less good integration." He thus threatened German abandonment of EDC if the French proposals were adopted, and suggested that, under such conditions, a German national army would be preferable. The strength, composition, and armament of the German contingents, he wrote, should, in any event, be determined by military rather than by political considerations.[5]

German generals have not regarded the issue of the Saar as a serious obstacle to French-German military collaboration. In general, territorial questions following World War II have aroused much less emotion in Germany than did the issues created by the Treaty of Versailles after World War I. The military in particular have been more concerned about the strength of the communists in France, whom they regard as a very serious liability in case of war, than about the policies of the various French governments regarding the Saar.

This "tolerant" attitude toward France, which is indicated by the various concessions that the German military class would be prepared to agree to in the interests of European defense, probably has two main components: political unwillingness to pressure the French and appreciation of a certain defensiveness on the part of the French when faced with the greater military potential of Germany. In addition, the German military leaders undoubtedly preferred any impatience with French procrastination to be shown first by the United States, so that they could then "share" in such impatience with a powerful ally without being responsible for originating it.

Regarding the French attitude toward EDC, the Bonn government in general, and the German military leaders in particular, felt that it would be impolitic for West Germany to urge the French to make haste. If anyone was to put pressure upon the French, it should be the United States government, and, in private conversations, many German generals indicated that they thought that just this

[5] Hasso von Manteuffel, "Mitentscheidung bei der Verteidigung des Westens," *Deutsche Soldaten Zeitung,* May 2, 1953.

should be done in the interests of improving Western strength in the cold war.

As late as the spring of 1954, it was still the official American and German position that the French Assembly might yet ratify the EDC treaties, although many observers outside government had long considered that the idea of EDC had failed.[6] But by that time, strong disappointment with French delays was expressed in German military circles. Most of the military showed their scorn of France more freely than they had before; some of them pointed out that EDC, once designed as a "motor" to power the process of European integration, now functioned in fact as a "brake" on progress toward that end. Finally, all persons in any way connected with the Bonn government who were interviewed during spring, 1954, managed to suggest with suspicious uniformity that Adenauer, and the United States government along with him, would be in trouble if EDC were not soon ratified by the French.

A high official in the Blank Office remarked that if, in the event that the French failed to ratify, the United States had no alternative to EDC, the situation in West Germany would become "very difficult indeed." He said that continued French indecisiveness and the lack of an alternative American policy for improving the Western defense system might have grave repercussions on German domestic politics. The Chancellor was "already fighting with his back to the wall." Failure of EDC would be interpreted by many West Germans as a failure of Adenauer's foreign policy. Nothing drastic need happen immediately as a result, but nobody could predict how things would develop in West Germany later. He added ominously that, in such a contingency, "forces" might emerge in Germany that would be ready to turn a more friendly eye toward the East, "perhaps not immediately but, say, in two to three years." He was, of course, entirely correct.

A second reason for the restrained attitude toward France was that members of the German military class saw French procrastination on EDC as a result of French weakness and apprehension or "envy" of Germany's potential strength. They appreciated those feelings, because they were fully aware of Germany's superiority in manpower, economic productivity, and industriousness. One general

[6] For example, as early as August 2, 1953, Hanson W. Baldwin said in *The New York Times* that EDC was "obviously deader than a dodo."

bared his conceit as early as 1952 by remarking that he did not hesitate to say in private what could not be stated publicly: "If the French want the Saar, for heaven's sake, let's give it to them to get going." Then, as an afterthought: "In thirty years we'll have it back anyhow." A few of those interviewed showed openly how little they thought of the French as prospective comrades-in-arms, while others were careful not to give the impression that they considered the French poor soldiers.

In 1954, two former officers, who were employed in the Bonn government, took pains to point out that the difficulties that France was facing overseas were not always sufficiently appreciated in West Germany. French setbacks in Indochina could easily have repercussions in Morocco, they said, and a major defeat in Indochina might create a crisis for the French in all of French North Africa. They added that this interdependence of her "colonial difficulties" on her policy in Europe affected French-German relations, but that this was not always as readily appreciated in Germany as it was in France. It would be going too far to speak of a French feeling of "inferiority," they suggested; the correct word, rather, was "weakness."

One of these officers related an incident which he thought might be symptomatic. His son, who was seventeen years old, had asked him to talk to his classmates about the political situation. During the talk, the father pointed out, among other things, that the French had been among the victors during the last war. The young listeners reacted forcefully to this statement, he said, and expressed the opinion that the French had never been victorious since 1815. The youngsters averred that the French had been beaten by the Germans in four wars (thus implying that the Germans had defeated the French also in World War I). The man who told this story said that he did not wish to suggest by it that all German youth shared the feelings expressed by these boys; but he did manage nicely to suggest that there were feelings involved in German opinions about current French policy that Americans might not always understand or take into account.

Finally, the German generals may temper their condemnation of France because the United States does not condemn her; they respect strength and like to be in favor with the strong. It was felt that French resistance to EDC and German rearmament served to enhance the importance of Germany in American eyes. This attitude was never shown openly, but it could be inferred, during many conversations, from a sense of comfort displayed by several of the generals when they discussed the French problem and deplored the inability of the French to see that the Soviet Union was a greater menace to France than was Germany. In speaking thus, these military people were able to suggest a picture of Germany as *sharing* the American concern about the tardiness of the French. Any such attitude must be an ambivalent one, however, for the German military believe that power must be used effectively in order to be power. A truly powerful United States would overcome the obstacles to the attainment of its objectives in Europe. Conversely, since the United States did not overcome French resistance, the reality of its power was open to secret doubt.

German Reunification

Prior to 1955, German reunification was hardly ever mentioned by German military leaders when they talked about the cold war and German rearmament. This may have been due, in part, to political caution, for it would be strange indeed if these men were indifferent to the dismemberment and division of their country. Another reason for their reticence was probably their unwillingness to have it said of them by foreigners that their interest in German rearmament was prompted by nationalistic sentiments. The German military are above all realists in anything that concerns military power. In this instance, their relative disinterest in the issue of reunification followed from their conviction, which they voiced readily, that the Soviet Union would not voluntarily withdraw its forces from East Germany. Nor did they expect such a withdrawal as a result of negotiations, since they believed that the West was not strong enough to negotiate with that much success. Thus, to the German generals, talk about achieving reunification by "negotiating from positions of strength" was mere political rhetoric long before that slogan faded out of political discourse.

The military were aware that their Western neighbors, and particularly the French, feared that German rearmament might lead to revival of a German military adventure eastward, thus possibly setting off a major war. Their understanding of these fears was all the easier, since they never doubted the superiority of the German military potential to that of the French. In addition many of them pointed out that Germany was the only nation with experience in fighting Red forces. But the notion that the Germans, rearmed as members of EDC, or of the Western European Union (WEU) and NATO, might attempt to reconquer the eastern parts of Germany appeared to them too absurd to merit refutation. The prevailing balance of power deprived such considerations of meaning. None of them commented on the possibility that a rearmed Germany, by an attack on the East, might present the West with a *fait accompli,* thus requiring it either to abandon Germany to the Soviet Union or to take arms to come to her rescue.

Whenever, before 1955, military people raised the issue of unification at all, they always did so in the context of conversations on the general question of the defense of Europe. In 1954, one former general officer said that he regarded the whole question of German reunification as a false one. Then he added that the American "general staff" might yet come to realize that Western Europe might be better defended farther east than either the Rhine or the present eastern border of the Federal Republic. But this general was discussing the defense of Europe from a global rather than a European point of view, and he regarded the German preoccupation with the security of the Federal Republic as a distinctly parochial bias. He even considered it possible that Central Europe might be a secondary theater in a third world war, and he spoke of the possibility that strategy might require the temporary sacrifice of West Germany and other parts of Western Europe. In such an event, he continued, German contingents would have to fight elsewhere. Such ideas, however, though willingly discussed by the military in private, could not be then and are not now aired in public, not because their aggressiveness might alarm the French and the West, but because such apparently callous boldness in subordinating German interests to those of the Western coalition would scandalize the German public.

We have discussed the opinions of German military leaders on some of the important political issues of recent years, and we have seen, in these opinions, the bases on which these men, in 1954, judged the prospects of the West in the cold war. For various reasons, American political prestige in Germany sank low in 1954. The Berlin

Conference at the beginning of that year had brought no progress on German reunification, and the French were defeated in Indochina. For a while, the German press was intensely concerned that U.S. intervention in Indochina might lead to war. That fear had been nurtured by official American statements about meeting communist aggression with massive retaliation, and apprehension tempered with an element of malicious satisfaction resulted from the common knowledge that there was less than complete agreement in the highest councils of the U.S. government about what to do with Indochina.[7] Some influential commentators lost their sense of proportion completely. One widely read weekly wrote, "William II was a timid schoolboy by comparison with the Republican leaders in Washington. There is a difference between rattling one's saber and brandishing an H-bomb."[8] The press in general attributed the passing of the crisis to the success of British statesmanship in checking American rashness. By the end of the first week of the Geneva Conference, it appeared that American diplomacy had suffered a serious setback. Germany's leading monthly on foreign affairs later published evidence of this in the form of an article by an American journalist, which minced no words about the American diplomatic setback. "For the moment," it read, "the Western alliance had practically lost all effectiveness. . . . The initiative had passed from Washington to London and Paris."[9]

The German military looked at the developments in Geneva from a viewpoint that differed radically from that of the opinions expressed in public. In assessing the state of the cold war, they attributed the greatest importance to the growth of Soviet capabilities in the field of nuclear weapons, that is, to authoritative American statements, early in 1954, that the Soviet Union might attain effective parity in thermonuclear weapons and delivery capabilities within a few years. In addition, many of them held the British responsible for the crisis at Geneva.

These military observers were convinced that, under conditions of

[7] In its issue of May 13–14, 1954, for example, *Süddeutsche Zeitung* featured a summary without comment of the contradictory statements about the crisis in Indochina made by President Eisenhower, Vice-President Nixon, Secretary Dulles, and Senator Knowland from March 30 to May 13, 1954.

[8] *Der Spiegel*, April 28, 1954.

[9] Joseph C. Harsch, "Präventivkrieg und militärisches Gleichgewicht," *Aussenpolitik*, November, 1954.

nuclear parity, the Soviet Union's prospects of advancing its interests by cold-war methods would be better than before, while those of the United States and the West would continue to decline. This belief was based on certain assumptions that were rarely stated explicitly.

For example, irrespective of the state of thermonuclear armaments, German military officers believed that the Soviet Union used cold-war methods more effectively than the West did; they found the West outstripped in both variety of political techniques and ruthlessness of their employment. Also, the German military regard peacetime policies as the direct derivatives of military capability: the greater the military strength of a nation, the larger and bolder can be its peacetime political designs. That is why these military observers were disappointed by American "lack of initiative" in the cold war during a period when the United States enjoyed military superiority. Conversely, they expected that an increase in Russian military power would be reflected in more aggressive measures that could only work to the disadvantage of the West.

Unlike the German press, the older generation of officers did not believe that American policy in Indochina was reckless. Rather, they directed most of their criticism at Churchill. It seems that Churchill is the only foreign statesman who can throw the conservative members of the German military class into a rage. Perhaps the intensity of their venomous reaction to Churchill's every conciliatory statement on the international situation stems from old hatreds, and from memories of the time when Germany was deprived of her triumph.[10] The memory of the combination of British staunchness and the Western-Soviet coalition is apparently still very much alive.[11] Ostensibly, however, the former generals reacted fiercely to Churchill's warnings that the West should compose its differences with the Soviet leaders, because they considered the cold war a blessing in disguise; so long as it lasted, the Soviet menace was generally recognized. But when "coexistence" became the image of international relations between East and West, the basic conflict, they believed, was

[10] It is interesting to note that many German generals who now criticize Hitler for his decision to go to war in 1939, when Germany was not strong enough to win, also criticize him for not having crushed the British at Dunkirk.

[11] Adenauer himself has often justified his pro-American foreign policy by evoking in parliament the specter of a *rapprochement* of the Big Four at Germany's expense. Neither he nor anybody else in the *Bundestag,* of course, has ever publicly denounced Churchill.

not abolished; it was merely ignored, to the detriment of the West.

On May 1, 1954, Churchill said in a speech at the conservative Primrose Club that the West longed to see the Russian people *and the Soviet government* assume a proud and splendid role in the leadership of mankind. One German general, asked why Churchill might have made this statement, replied contemptuously: "Perhaps it looks to him like better business"; this contemptuous reference to business was an allusion to a distinction made in a book by Werner Sombart that appeared in Germany during World War I: *Händler und Helden,* that is, (British) *merchants* and (German) *heroes.* Another commented that the British no longer have a commonwealth, "although they pretend to have one." He bristled with indignation at Churchill, and asked his American interviewer why Churchill was supposed to be a great statesman. "He has led his country twice into misfortune. Only recently he made this incredible pro-Soviet speech stabbing your country in the back."

Still another of the generals interviewed charged Churchill with preventing an aggressive Western policy in Indochina, and with bringing about the Western diplomatic defeat at Geneva. He made sarcastic reference to the French, Italian, Swiss, and German newspapers, which had all praised the British at the beginning of the Geneva Conference for having saved the peace. He said the popular notion that Churchill makes his own decisions is "of course" quite false. Churchill relied on "committees" and on individual advisers; Lord Cherwell had great influence over Churchill, while Eden was only waiting for his demise. Churchill, a very old man, wished to become the mediator between East and West before joining his forebears. He wanted also to make Europe—a Europe that would include the Soviet satellites and European Russia—into a "third power" between the two giants.[12] This general concluded by saying that the power of the old generation in world politics was very great indeed, and that much of "the mess" in which the world found itself had to be attributed to just that fact. This was true not only of Great Britain, he added, but of France and Germany as well.

A fourth informant pointed out in explanation of the Primrose speech that Churchill's reasoning power was at times impaired by old age: "He forgets that Stalin is dead, wants to telephone him,

[12] On May 10, 1956, Churchill said in Aachen that the spirit of NATO "should not exclude Russia and the East European states."

and so forth." In an entirely different vein, this general said that Churchill might be seriously disturbed by the prospect of large-scale atomic war and its incalculable destructiveness. Then, shifting his attitude once more, he spoke of the British insistence that consideration of the Southeast Asia Security Pact be postponed until it was certain that the 1954 Geneva Conference had failed. He suggested that one of the long-range aims of British policy might be to recapture British prestige in Asia, and to resume leadership of a combination of powers that might be able to hold its own against the United States in world politics.

In short, it transpired that, in the spring of 1954, German generals were far more critical of British political intentions than they were of French weakness and tardiness. Their criticism was focused on what was held to be British unwillingness to abide by the stern terms of the cold war. This, combined with French procrastination and with what they regarded as the dwindling of American strategic superiority over the Soviet Union, as well as the general disunity of the West as shown at Geneva, led to the over-all pessimism of the German military class in 1954.

One former general, a man of caution and circumspection, remarked in May of that year that, by comparison with the Soviet Union, the United States was a sea power rather than a sea-and-air power. He explained that the Soviet Union had been making great strides toward becoming an air power, and might soon match the United States in that regard. "I am no longer sure what the outcome of an all-out war between the Soviet Union and the United States would be." Another officer, limiting himself to the subject of the cold war itself, regarded the breaking of the U.S. atomic monopoly as one of the decisive developments in the postwar period. He said that, in the American presidential campaign of 1952, Republican leaders had spoken of "rollback" of communism and "liberation" of satellite areas. Then he reviewed the developments in Asia, Africa, and Europe since that time and concluded: "The facts present a picture of 'rollback in reverse.' One is reminded of Stalin's prediction that the West will disintegrate automatically." Still another former general said that the three most important developments of the postwar era were the rise of communism to power in China, the "near-achievement" of atomic parity by the Soviet Union, and the continued political successes of the Soviet Union. He then gave a succinct picture of the European situation as it might be evaluated by the Soviet Union:

1. In the last three years the United States has proved unable to attain a position of intellectual and political leadership in the West.
2. In the same period Europe has proved to be incapable of unification.
3. The German miracle of economic recovery, based upon German industriousness, is the best guarantee against the unification of Europe.
4. The United Nations organization has proved incapable of united military action.
5. As though stung by the tsetse fly, Europe is periodically afflicted with attacks of sleeping sickness in the cold war, and it is not to be expected that this disease will be cured in the next three years.
6. There is a certain chance that the absence of any prospects of German unification may slowly transform German immunity to communism into readiness to negotiate with the Soviet Union and into a state of low resistance to communism.

The last point concerns German neutralism.

FOUR

Neutralism

For West Germany, neutralism does not mean continuation of a state of independence and noncommitment in the conflict between East and West. It means, rather, disengagement from the United States in order to *attain* independence and freedom of choice.

Since such freedom would involve a serious risk of Soviet domination, the advocates of a neutralist policy for West Germany have felt it necessary to be strongly anti-American and extremely generous in attributing selflessness to the Soviet Union. They have not favored retention of West Germany's territorial *status quo*. Instead, they have encouraged hopes that—if the Federal Republic left NATO and rid itself of American political influence—the Russians would desire the formation of a truly independent, noncommunist West Germany, larger in size, population, and other resources than at present. The tenuous character of such political speculation has been obscured by emotions, chiefly by German anxieties about war, and, to a lesser extent, by nationalist sentiments.

Prominent among those who do not allow their attitude toward neutralism to be colored by emotionalism are the German military leaders. That is probably because a rational view on the question requires substantially those elements of judgment in which the old military leaders are strong. Therefore it is particularly important to know what they think about neutralism, since any government (in contrast to an opposition which may indulge in judgments based on emotionalism) is unlikely to make foreign-policy decisions without being influenced by military advice. In this chapter we shall present the opinions of the military leaders, and contrast them with the most prominent opinions of other groups in Germany.

To the extent that German neutralism derives emotional strength from anxiety about war, it has been rejected out of hand by the older military leaders, partly from professional notions about courage, and partly because of confidence in Western strength. Adherence to the professional code may also account for the fact that German generals have not criticized, on moral grounds, the *military* spokesmen for neutralism. In their eyes, military neutralists are wrong, but neither cowardly nor dishonest, whereas civilian neutralists are quite readily suspected on both grounds. Similarly, Germany's former military leaders have, since the beginning of the rearmament debate, shown leniency toward the patriotic argument, often used by neutralists, that West German soldiers could not be expected to shoot at East Germans in the event of war. But the generals have not agreed with this view. They have sought to temper the argument by expressing doubts that very many people were troubled by such scruples, by denying that a war was imminent, by voicing hatred of communism, or in some other way.

Another source of neutralist sentiment in Germany is the desire to escape in some miraculous way from the conflict between East and West in order to enjoy peace and prosperity. Many Germans have felt as a result that West Germany might be "punished" by the Soviet Union, or by "fate," for its close ties with the Western powers. The military leaders have not entertained such notions, partly at least because they believe that "fate" resides in military strength, and that economic prosperity is not the highest national value.

West Germany's dependence on the United States has no doubt been resented by many Germans, and there may also have been feelings of guilt about collaborating with the conquerors in World War II. Such feelings were repressed, immediately after the war, as a result of economic misery and, later, the success of Adenauer's policies. Only Nazi diehards and a few political moralists [1] voiced them, but they made little headway against the fact that collaboration was economically rewarding and publicly justifiable on grounds of anti-Nazism. As Germany's economic and political self-reliance grows, however, the anti-American component of neutralism may prove more important than it has seemed to be in the past. [2]

[1] See, for example, Margret Boveri, *Der Verrat im XX. Jahrhundert,* 2 vols., Hamburg, 1956.
[2] The popularity of the German press campaign in 1956 against the allegedly immoral conduct of the American soldiers in Germany affords an illustration of anti-American resentment.

Among former professional officers, anticollaborationist feelings were strong only at the beginning of the rearmament debate, when neutralist sentiment centered about the issue of the military war criminals. Since then, virtually all former war criminals have been released from prison, and statements about the "defamation" of the German military class have died down. Anticollaborationist sentiment is still strong, however, among those former SS officers who are barred from military re-employment, and thus from "collaboration."

Potentially the strongest basis for neutralist sentiment among the military is fear of Western weakness. If the Western coalition were to break down, German military leaders would probably not find it difficult to adjust themselves to the changed situation. They might then fall back on the political and military traditions of Germany which, under the banner of *Realpolitik,* point to the advantages of orienting German policy toward the East. Such a development would probably give prominence to new names: a military counter-elite could emerge, made up of people who are now without political influence. By the same token, some of the military leaders who have identified themselves strongly with the cause of the West might, in such an event, lose political responsibility and public influence. The opportunists, who are numerically predominant in the military as in all other social classes, would simply follow the trend toward political reorientation. Since many generals value military *expertise* more highly than firmness of political conviction, the reorientation could be accomplished without political difficulty and without moral qualms.

On the following pages we shall discuss in detail attitudes of the military (1) toward German neutrality and *Realpolitik,* and (2) toward neutralist arguments that have been advanced by (*a*) German politicians, (*b*) a few former officers, and (*c*) German journalists. The chapter will end with a discussion of (3) the reasons which antineutralist military observers give for the growth of German neutralism.

Neutrality and Realpolitik

In the early fifties, German military leaders scorned the idea of German neutrality and tended to equate it with the contention that

Germany could or ought to stay neutral in the event of war.[3] Some former generals, in conversation, rejected that contention with a sharpness so startling as to suggest that neutrality appeared to them not only absurd but also shameful. Perhaps they felt that only the small powers in Europe had managed to stay neutral in the last two world wars, and that for Germany to aim at neutrality implied too radical a reduction of national aspirations.

This sense of national identity also led them to favor some form of military establishment of their own. While they preferred borrowed military power in the form of American troops in Germany to naked exposure to the Soviet menace, they also preferred even a token of German preparedness to complete dependence on other powers. The latter preference was usually expressed obliquely. In 1952, for example, when there was talk of twelve German divisions in EDC, one general, disregarding the cost of modern armaments, said that according to a rule of thumb "a country can put up a number of divisions equal to about half the number of millions of population; since West Germany has a population of about fifty million, twenty-five divisions would not strain the economy too much." Several others pointed out, rather vaguely, that the United States could not be expected to meet German security needs forever. Germany had to assume a defense posture of her own, they said, which would guarantee peace even when, sometime in the future, Allied troops were withdrawn. While such desire for military autonomy was never expressed by the military supporters of Adenauer's policy, and while the possibility of American withdrawal was felt to be utopian in view of the prevailing balance of power in Europe, it is likely that speculation about the prospect evoked at once dismay and gratifying associations of national independence.

The attitudes of the former German military class toward proposals that the Federal Republic disengage itself from American leadership, or at least develop a livelier initiative in its relations with both the Soviet Union and the Western powers, are considerably more complex than are its views of neutrality. From 1950 to 1955, most professional officers in West Germany opposed all tendencies toward loosening the ties with the West in order to gain some freedom of bargaining with the East. But this opposition, unlike the re-

---

[3] For example, Erich Dethleffsen, *Das Wagnis der Freiheit,* Stuttgart, 1952; Günther Blumentritt, *Deutsches Soldatentum im europäischen Rahmen,* Giessen, 1952; and H. Müller-Brandenburg, *Neutralität?* Berlin, 1952.

jection of neutrality, was not based on principle. Nor was the generals' support of Adenauer's policy rooted either in loyalty to the Chancellor or in adherence to the political values dearest to him. It followed rather from estimates of the prevailing political situation in both Germany and the world, and in part from personal aspirations to military re-employment. It would therefore be hazardous to predict that many former German officers would continue to oppose a more flexible, independent German foreign policy if disengagement of the Federal Republic from American policy appeared politically feasible to them.

This should not be surprising in view of the fact that the German military class has always held the German proponents of *Realpolitik* in high esteem, whether they were called Bismarck or Seeckt, who was the commander of the German army under the Weimar Republic. The old conflict between the Eastern and Western orientations of German policy had not even been absent in the military circles that conspired during the last world war to overthrow Hitler. Seeckt's prestige continues high among many former German military leaders. In the conversations held from 1952 to 1955, however, no German officer advocated collaboration with Russia, a policy which Seeckt had secretly condoned during the Weimar period. Some younger former generals did mention, in 1955, that Seeckt's views on the advantages of an elite force might again become timely if, under the conditions of modern technology, a small professional army were found to be superior to the mass armies raised in the past by conscription. But these opinions were not advanced in order to recommend a return to Seeckt's policy of collaboration with the Soviet Union.

Approval of Adenauer's antineutralist foreign policy by the former German generals did not mean that they shared all its basic motivations. Adenauer himself was guided in his foreign policy by ideas that originated between the two world wars, which centered on the importance of peace between France and Germany. To these ideas Adenauer added, in the postwar period, a keen appreciation of the conditions favoring Germany's political comeback and a deep distrust of the Soviet Union. The German military are not anti-French, but they did not share Adenauer's eagerness in pursuing conciliation with France. In particular, the Protestant and Prussian generals, who partake more intimately than the officers of Catholic and South

German origin of the German military tradition, attributed to conciliation with France nothing but *instrumental* value. To them it was not an emotionally central concern as was the Soviet menace, which alarmed them as much as it did the Chancellor.

Conversely, rearmament itself had greater sentimental value to the professional military elite than to Adenauer, who was a civilian with no competence in military affairs. The Chancellor felt more strongly than the military that, if it was to succeed, German rearmament would have to appear not to jeopardize German democracy. The generals, like Adenauer, were products of their early experiences; they were impatient with any criticism of "militarism" and unwilling to face their own compromised past. They felt critical of Adenauer's effort to organize the new German forces in a democratic spirit. Their sharp criticism, however, which was deflected onto the Defense Minister, Theodor Blank, reached the public only on a few occasions; and any objection to Adenauer himself has been kept altogether private.

But it has not been wanting. Many German officers readily ascribe to Kurt Schumacher, the late leader of the Social Democratic Party, an understanding of military matters superior to that of the Chancellor. In a conversation in 1954, two distinguished former officers even maliciously compared the Chancellor's lack of military sense with that of Adolf Hitler. In 1955 another former general deplored the fact that air defense had received only inadequate attention in German plans, and attributed this fault to Adenauer's preoccupation with the political bargaining value of rearmament at the expense of German security.

Many military leaders refrained from criticizing Adenauer in public, however, because they feared they might suffer in consequence of such criticisms. A particularly striking example of such restraint was offered in conversation with a prominent and well-informed general in 1952. He was much concerned about the future of democracy in West Germany, because he held the Americans to be ignorant of the reactionary forces at work, charged the Blank Office with incompetence, and attributed to the "Gehlen organization" [4] a politically sinister influence on the selection of former

[4] This organization, headed by General Gehlen, the former chief of intelligence in the German army, has collected information on communism in satellite countries since 1945. At the time of Otto John's "defection" to East Germany, it was reported in the German press that the Gehlen organization was supported by American funds.

military personnel for government positions. When asked why he did not take his case to the public, since he felt so strongly about it, the general replied that such responsibility lay with the *Bundestag*. Any private citizen who dared to tell the truth would risk "defamation," and, if he was a former officer, he would forfeit any chance of getting back into the armed forces. "If I were asked to join a group of citizens who made it their business to expose the politically reactionary forces in the Federal Republic," he said, "I would have to refuse the invitation, because I wish to get a command position in the army when it is being established." Similar views were expressed by others.

The Arguments for Neutralism

Military attitudes toward neutralist policies vary with the social and political positions of those who advance them. This bias has taken the form of imputing intentions to the proponents of neutralist policies and then judging the proposals in the light of those intentions. By and large, the military class readily attributes ulterior motives to the socialist opposition to Adenauer's policy, is more tolerant than the Chancellor of efforts by other politicians to explore the possibilities for German initiative in foreign affairs, and does not question the moral integrity of those neutralists who have high military standing.

From politicians. Except for military officers who had become professional politicians and for a few others, such as Field Marshal Kesselring and Generals Ramcke and Remer, the military class as a whole avoided participation in the public discussion of German foreign policy. In particular, it left public advocacy of foreign policies that deviated from that of the Chancellor to politicians and journalists, and to a few of its more impetuous comrades. Some of the latter were disqualified from military re-employment by reason either of age or political record.

German military leaders did not associate themselves with the criticism of Adenauer's policies which Hermann Rauschning advanced in 1953 and 1954. Rauschning, originally a prominent lieutenant of Hitler's and afterwards his critic in exile, spread the neutralist theses of his book *Is Peace Still Possible?* [5] in many well-attended

[5] Hermann Rauschning, *Ist Friede noch möglich?* Heidelberg, 1953, p. 58.

public lectures in 1954. Without restraint, he cast doubt and aspersion on the political intentions of the United States, charging that
the Germans did not really know what those intentions were.
American policy, he suggested, might well be governed by secret
calculations which conflicted with its professed aims:

> Many Germans are of the opinion that the real intention of the [U.S.]
> policy on Germany which President Roosevelt approved is not yet def-
> initely abandoned, and that merely the means for realizing it have been
> changed. In addition to the destruction of communism, a future war
> could have the not altogether undesired consequence of completely
> de-industrializing Germany and reducing the German nation definitely
> to forty million people.[6]

Rauschning's attack on American policy, and on Adenauer, constituted an adaptation of early postwar German anti-Americanism
to the struggle against EDC. His appeals fed on German fear and
resentment caused by Secretary Morgenthau's policy and by the early
occupation policy of holding German industrial production to a low
level.

German military observers attributed the public interest Rauschning's lectures aroused in 1954 to lack of political understanding on
the part of his listeners, and, occasionally, to alleged desires of certain
business circles not to be caught napping if Adenauer's policy failed.
These comments suggested, more or less directly, that, in the opinion
of the generals, commercial interests provided no vantage point from
which to view the cold war intelligently, but offered eloquent neutralists such as Rauschning an opening for spreading their own
political confusion.

Heinrich Brüning's attack on Adenauer was taken somewhat
more seriously by the generals. Unlike Rauschning, Brüning (the
former Chancellor of the Weimar Republic) was not an intellectual.
Addressing the Rhein-Ruhr Club on foreign policy on June 2, 1954,
Brüning called Adenauer's policy "dogmatic," and advocated a re-
turn to the course of mediation between the East and West which the
Weimar Republic had followed in the period of Locarno and Rapallo.
Brüning warned that the dependence of the Bonn government on the
United States might cost Germany dear in the case of an economic
slump in America. Brüning's speech was applauded widely in the

[6] *Ibid.*, p. 65.

press; even newspapers that had staunchly supported the government endorsed his arguments. But Brüning's prestige was no match for Adenauer's. When the government turned sharply against Brüning, the CDU press quickly resumed its support of Adenauer, and the incident was forgotten. Military observers sided with the Chancellor without maligning Brüning; they were uninterested in the economic warnings that Brüning had sounded, and they attributed the loud but quickly passing acclaim he had received to the fickleness of the press.

Almost all parliamentary advocates of specific foreign-policy plans and actions that deviated from Adenauer's policy have come from the Free Democratic Party. The deputies Karl Georg Pfleiderer and Thomas Dehler—and in 1956 Erich Mende as well—repeatedly tried to find opportunities for German initiative in foreign affairs to correct the inflexible dependence of Adenauer's policy on the United States. Indeed, until late in 1956, the only concrete proposals for new ways to break the deadlock between East and West over Germany came from the FDP rather than from the *Sozialdemokratische Partei Deutschlands* (SPD). For example, the so-called "Pfleiderer Plan" for the establishment of a third, central zone in Germany from which both Eastern and Western occupation troops would be withdrawn was publicly discussed in Germany as early as the spring of 1952, three years before Eden made a similar proposal at the Geneva Conference of July, 1955.[7]

After the failure of EDC in 1954, when the substitute plan of WEU was agreed upon in London, Thomas Dehler proposed that West Germany should prevail upon the Western powers to negotiate with the Soviet Union before the signatures were affixed to the treaties. Like some other deputies of the FDP, Dehler believed that the mere prospect of German rearmament might provide an opportunity for the Bonn government to capitalize on the Soviet interest in loosening Germany's ties with the West without compelling the Federal Republic to sever them more than the French Assembly had done by its refusal to ratify EDC. These were tenuous speculations in view of Germany's military weakness, but they expressed dissatisfac-

[7] In June, 1952, a Social Democratic leader remarked privately that he had been informally approached by American officials, who, he said, were critical of American support of EDC, to launch a plan closely resembling the Pfleiderer Plan on his own initiative. He had refused to do so, "because all opposition to the Pentagon is futile."

tion with Germany's dependence on the national interests of the Western powers, and they reflected German desires for further national advancement.

Most of the older military leaders realized that Germany lacked sufficient strength for any independent diplomacy. They also realized that, under the cold-war conditions of the early fifties, any middle-sized power would find it extremely difficult to execute diplomatic maneuvers.[8] Thomas Dehler was frequently called "erratic" by military observers, while Pfleiderer appeared to be held in higher respect. It was known that some FDP leaders, unlike the socialists, considered the Chancellor not so much a captive of "the Pentagon" as a man who lacked the traditional skills of a diplomat. In particular, Pfleiderer, who had made the German diplomatic service his early career, was reported to regard Adenauer as a man with the limited experience and the autocratic habits of a mayor running municipal rather than national affairs. Such sarcasm was not entirely lost on the older military leaders, but Adenauer's relentless intolerance of the slightest opposition to his policy, even if it came from a coalition party, and his dogged adherence to the objective of rearmament strengthened the conviction of the military that it was the Chancellor rather than his FDP critics who pursued a realistic policy.

From the military. The most powerful attack on Adenauer's military policy did not come from politicians, however, but from former Colonel Bogislav von Bonin, an insubordinate officer in the Defense Ministry, who early in 1955 shattered public confidence in the federal government's ability to safeguard German security interests. The incidental merit of Bonin's inexcusable insubordination consisted in confronting the German public with the defense issue in terms more specific than those in which the government had chosen to present it. The opinions of former German officers concerning the various aspects of the affair reveal their attitudes toward neutralism on the part of the military with extraordinary clarity.

In June, 1952, Colonel von Bonin was appointed Chief of Planning in the Blank Office. Bonin had distinguished himself in World War

[8] At that time, neither military nor civilian observers in Germany were prepared to examine the proposition that the Soviet government might be more strongly opposed to European unification than to German rearmament, and that the chances of exacting concessions from the Soviet Union at the price of stopping German preparations to rearm might have *lessened* after the failure of EDC.

II in various staff and command posts and had ended his wartime career as Chief of Operations on the General Staff of the army, a position in which he succeeded General Heusinger, who had been wounded in the attempted assassination of Hitler on July 20, 1944. Bonin's reputation among his former comrades was high. Many officers believed that his presence in the Blank Office would counterbalance the influence of the "theorists" and "reformers" who wanted to prevent the resurrection of militaristic practices in the training of the new German forces.

No sooner had Bonin entered the Blank Office than he found himself in conflict with these reformers, his principal antagonist being Baudissin. Blank supported Bonin, but the conflict kept smoldering in the Blank Office until March, 1955, when Bonin was dismissed as a result of another more important incident, which involved the issue of neutralism.

As Chief of the Planning Section, Bonin questioned the soundness of the plans for the organization of the German contingents which the Temporary Committee of the Conference for the Organization of EDC had developed in Paris. He believed it would be impossible to set up twelve German divisions in two years, which was the plan in 1952–1953. Subsequent events proved him to be entirely right on that point. He feared, furthermore, that during the period in which the German forces were to be built up Germany would be defenseless. He quoted Allied military leaders to the effect that "forward defense" east of the Rhine would become possible only after the addition of the German divisions to the NATO forces. For this reason he proposed that, contrary to Allied plans, the German units be stationed near the Iron Curtain, so as to provide West Germany with an emergency defense force from the beginning. Furthermore, only the deployment of the German military forces for the defense of German soil, Bonin argued, would have a chance of overcoming the resistance of German youth to military service.

Bonin's plans were predicated on the assumption that Allied forces would come to the defense of West Germany even if Germany failed to collaborate in Western defense in accordance with Allied plans. Disregarding the possibility that Germany would be at the mercy of the enemy if his assumption was wrong, Bonin was willing to risk losing Allied support by defying NATO and by insisting on a German national strategy. At first, General Heusinger authorized

Bonin to concern himself with "emergency planning" for the build-up period of German rearmament. This decision was based on the fiction that a distinction could be made between "planning" and "emergency planning," and on failure to realize that German rearmament as a whole was an emergency measure.

By 1953, Allied concern that Bonin's work evaded or thwarted German preparations for rearmament on the basis of NATO and EDC plans had become so acute as to force Bonin's superiors to deprive him of his planning function. Bonin was replaced by Colonel Fett, who was later found politically unsuitable for his job by the German Personnel Selection Board. Bonin was sent abroad, to Paris, England, and the United States. He returned in the summer of 1954, convinced that American illusions about the speed of German rearmament had been nurtured by German political authorities, that NATO strategic plans did not meet vital German interests, and that American planners placed too much stock in the experiences gained in Korea while neglecting those that Germany had had at the eastern front in World War II.

On July 14, 1954, Bonin submitted to his superiors his views on German defense. Still without raising the political issues involved in German rearmament, he advocated a German force of about 120,-000 to 150,000 volunteers, organized and equipped as defensive blocking units (*Sperrverbände*), and deployed along the zonal border to a depth of fifty kilometers. Bonin's plan was based on the expectation that any war would begin with a Russian tank assault. His proposed defensive force, equipped with 8,000 antitank guns, would function as an *armée de couverture* which would hold the aggressor near the frontier until mobile Allied forces could mount their counterattack.

This plan was rejected in the Blank Office by Generals Heusinger, Speidel, and Laegeler because it conflicted with NATO plans and because it was judged militarily inadequate. His critics considered the thin antitank screen which Bonin recommended extremely vulnerable to penetration by enemy infantry and paratroopers. Moreover, Bonin's plan was held to be politically dangerous, because it was feared that the deployment of German forces along the frontier might be misread as West German recognition of Germany's partition, might strengthen popular illusions about German security, and might thus increase German apathy toward rearmament.

Bonin received orders from Minister Blank to discontinue his work on emergency planning. He disobeyed those orders and decided to take his case to the public. He probably believed that the collapse of EDC in August, 1954, provided a favorable climate for re-examination of German defense plans in the light of Germany's national security needs. Indeed, German hopes that European loyalties might develop through EDC and slowly replace nationalist interests and sentiments in Western Europe had been shattered by France. German nationalism and neutralism received powerful support through the French vote against EDC.[9]

In the summer of 1954, Bonin began to justify his plans on *political* grounds. He argued—perhaps upon the suggestion of neutralist politicians—that a small German army, organized exclusively for defense, could menace neither the Soviet Union nor France, and would thus facilitate reunification. A West German army equal in strength to the East German police force would create military conditions conducive to the withdrawal of Western and Soviet forces from German soil. Bonin also modified his original military plan by recommending a small armored reserve which would seal off any possible breaks in the defensive screen.

Bonin's efforts to mobilize support for his plan in the ministerial bureaucracy outside the Defense Ministry and among parliamentarians and former military leaders were not too successful, although W. W. Schütz and L. von Hammerstein promoted his ideas in the Ministry of All-German Affairs, which also provided Bonin with travel funds. He also received powerful support from Adelbert Weinstein, the military commentator of the *Frankfurter Allgemeine Zeitung,* and Major von Stülpnagel, an officer of the Border Police and editor of the *Grenzjäger.* Weinstein summarized his own views in a much-read pamphlet, *Nobody Can Win the War,*[10] in which he combined advocacy of Bonin's military plans with slashing attacks against Theodor Blank and SHAPE. For example, Weinstein wrote:

[9] Eight months later, at the meeting of the German-English Society held in Königswinter in April, 1955, some German participants shocked their British associates by suggesting that German officers who would have served for a while in the Western contingents might be unacceptable for service in the new all-German post-unification army, because their familiarity with NATO plans might render them incapable of a really neutral attitude. (*Deutsch-Englisches Gespräch 1955,* Königswinter, April 14–17.)

[10] Adelbert Weinstein, *Keiner kann den Krieg gewinnen,* Bonn, 1955.

If the Commissioner for Security [i.e., Theodor Blank] could still say, as he did in a speech early this year [i.e., 1955], that his ultimate aim remained the realization of EDC, then he has either still not comprehended the Carolingian character of European politics, or he must accept the charge that he intentionally neglects the idea of reunification. . . .

Our coming partnership in the Atlantic Pact must not consist in our being only on the giving side; in accordance with the meaning of partnership we must also receive something in return. Otherwise, this alliance is disingenuous in character from the beginning. There is more to it than the task of complying with Pentagon strategy by delivering twelve divisions, which will be employed only according to Atlantic principles: for the Federal Republic divisions make sense only if they increase defensive morale in West Germany without becoming an obstacle to the political future of a reunified Germany.[11]

Perhaps the most sharply neutralist aspect of Weinstein's views was revealed in his comments on the relationship between the *Bundeswehr* and the communist "People's Police" in East Germany. Weinstein contended that in the event of reunification the communist forces would not simply disappear, but might be merged with the West German NATO contingents. The Federal Republic as well as the East German government should therefore avoid "putting more than half of a later all-German *Wehrmacht* under arms."[12]

Toward the end of February, 1955, Bonin's plan was sent to Adenauer and to German party leaders, apparently by Stülpnagel. A few press notices disclosed the gist of the plan and intimated that a group of German officers supported it. At that time Bonin was discussing his ideas with a number of well-known former German military leaders, including Field Marshal von Manstein and Generals von Lüttwitz, von Wietersheim, Crüwell, Westphal, Kuntzen, Hossbach, Reinhardt, Busse, and Eberbach. The copy of Bonin's memorandum that had been sent to Erich Ollenhauer was forwarded by the recipient to Theodor Blank with the sarcastic notation "to the official in charge!" It was now public knowledge that an official in the Defense Ministry, possibly backed by a clique of former German generals, was defying the government on an issue of great political import. Blank had no choice. Bonin was dismissed on March 22, 1955, with Adenauer's knowledge and approval, as a government spokesman confirmed later.

[11] *Ibid.*, pp. 22–23, 65.
[12] *Ibid.*, pp. 55–56.

The Defense Committee of the *Bundestag* investigated the circumstances of the dismissal and came to the conclusion that the Minister could not possibly tolerate the insubordination of a government official's appealing over the heads of his superiors to the public for support of views which his superiors had disapproved. Four days after his dismissal, Bonin gave an interview to *Der Spiegel,* which in its next issue supported him against Theodor Blank and published a nearly complete text of Bonin's memorandum.[13] Thus it became widely known that there was dissension inside the government on German rearmament and reunification, and every German newspaper reader had an opportunity to side either with NATO and the German government or with the rebellious Colonel von Bonin. In addition, opinion was strongly divided about the disciplinary action taken against Bonin.

As in all other cases involving the issue of neutralism, the press did not respond wholly along party lines. Some newspapers that had usually backed the government found merit in Bonin's ideas or fault in Blank's action. In particular, many FDP papers showed sympathy for Bonin because he had scored NATO defense plans and the work of the Defense Ministry.

The FDP Deputy Erich Mende sided with Bonin. Only the CDU press defended Blank's action, although very few papers went so far as the *Kölnische Rundschau,* which rejected Bonin's proposals summarily as a plan for socialists, national bolshevists, and neutralists. The Social Democratic press reaction reflected disunity among SPD leaders on the issue. The party disavowed an article in its own Parliamentary-Political Press Service which had denounced Bonin as a reactionary. The party leaders, pleased with Bonin's attack on the Blank Office, and unwilling to forego using his arguments, apparently could not agree on associating themselves too closely with a man reputed to be militaristic in outlook. Although the SPD finally decided not to take Bonin's side, it has freely used many of his arguments in subsequent debates on German rearmament.

Bonin was not silenced. For several months, until he finally withdrew to a position in German industry, he continued his campaign as a journalist and as a speaker at public meetings. In doing so, the neutralist character of his political views became clear for all to see. The newspaper *Rheinisch-Westphälische Nachrichten,* for which he

[13] *Der Spiegel*, March 30, 1955.

served as editorial writer, was supported by communist funds. While Bonin's critical memoranda prepared in the Blank Office had been concerned primarily with what he held to be shortcomings of German defense plans, his journalistic activities broadened into attacks on Adenauer's whole foreign policy. The brand of neutralism he advocated was indistinguishable from communist policy objectives. For example, he wrote:

> He who sees and knows how to evaluate the American encirclement of the Russian colossus cannot doubt the rightful need of the Soviets for security.[14]
>
> I am convinced that the Supreme Command of NATO shares my idea that the defense of Europe in a new world war would be hopeless.[15]

Bonin advocated a neutralized, reunified Germany "on whose territory there would remain" no foreign troops, no foreign air bases, and, above all, no atomic weapons.[16]

On July 29, 1955, Rudolf Steidl, a former colleague of Hermann Schaefer's, the editor-in-chief of the *Rheinisch-Westphälische Nachrichten,* declared at a press conference that the paper, of which both Bonin and Rauschning had become editors, was being edited on behalf of Albert Norden, State Secretary of the communist East German government Office of Press and Information. He also charged that both Schaefer and the newspaper were being financed by the Communist Party of East Germany. Schaefer did not answer and Rauschning, who tried to do so, did not invalidate the charge. Bonin also became military adviser to the *Hanns von Seeckt Gesellschaft,* a communist-front organization founded by Hermann Schaefer, and to *Deutscher Club 1954;* both organizations promoted neutralism. Finally, he published articles in *Militärpolitisches Forum* and in *Das Gespräch,* communist-sponsored neutralist publications that tried to appeal especially to former officers in West Germany.

Most of the German generals whom Bonin had contacted failed to share his strategic views. Convinced of the merits of mobile warfare, they rejected the notion that the German army ought to

---

[14] Bogislav von Bonin, "Angst vor Neutralität," *Rheinisch-Westphälische Nachrichten,* October 8, 1955.

[15] Bogislav von Bonin, "Militärische Realitäten gegen Bonner Phantastereien," *Militärpolitisches Forum,* July, 1955, p. 20.

[16] Bogislav von Bonin, *Atomkrieg—unser Ende,* Düsseldorf, 1955, p. 22.

consist mainly of blocking units equipped and trained to fight in immobilized defense positions along the border. They showed more sympathy for Bonin's proposal that the first German units be stationed near the zonal border, and they fully subscribed to his criticism of plans for a quick build-up. In rejecting the strategy of immobile defense they agreed not only with Bonin's military superiors in the Defense Ministry, but also with those former professional officers who had become members of the parliamentary Defense Committee.

Bonin's strategic ideas were severely criticized in public by some members of the military profession, partly in the form of reviews of Weinstein's book.[17] None of the generals approached by Bonin in February, 1955, seem to have endorsed his ideas fully, press intimations to the contrary notwithstanding. When they learned that Bonin's plan conflicted with the policies of the office in which he was employed, some of them advised him to discontinue his private campaign. Most of the older officers also endorsed Blank's subsequent action against Bonin, although Blank was frequently criticized in conversation for not ever having given Bonin an opportunity to present his views personally to his Minister. The Defense Ministry must have felt uneasy about the dismissal; otherwise General Heusinger would not have deemed it necessary to call a meeting of leading former German generals, some of whom had been visited by Bonin, in order to explain and justify to them the action the Ministry had taken against the rebel.[18]

Many of the younger officers, however, were convinced that Blank had been wrong. They regarded Bonin as a victim of a bureaucracy that valued obedience more highly than truth and the courage to speak it. These younger officers failed to appreciate the requirements of public service. Even the members of the parliamentary Defense Committee were relieved when they visited Washington in the spring of 1955 and heard General Ridgway explain that in the United States a military official could uphold his opinions against his civilian su-

[17] See especially Joachim Rogge, "Strategie des Wunschtraums," *Wehrkunde,* May, 1955; Georg von Sodenstern, "Strategie oder Sicherheit," *Wehrkunde,* September, 1955; Frido von Senger und Etterlin, review in *Die Gegenwart,* July 30, 1955; and Friedrich Ruge, *Seemacht und Sicherheit,* Tübingen, 1955, pp. 66ff.

[18] At this meeting Field Marshal von Manstein and Generals Westphal, Kuntzen, Crüwell, and Blumentritt, among others, were present. The need to call such a meeting illustrates the fact that the German Defense Ministry cannot conduct its business without the good will of the former German military leaders.

perior, even before Congress, with his superior's foreknowledge, but that he would abide by a decision against him or else resign and continue his fight as a citizen. The German parliamentarians were reassured to learn that their support of Minister Blank against Bonin was consistent with democratic practice.

Bonin's neutralist *political* views did not arouse the public censure of his former comrades-in-arms. None of the generals seemed to attribute much weight to the fact that after his dismissal Bonin freely chose to serve the communist cause. His action was taken as proof either of his naïveté or of his need to earn a living. His patriotism and his honesty were not questioned. His military standing seemed to exempt him from the political suspicion with which many German generals view the politicians of the left. A former officer who was politically close to the SPD remarked in conversation that as long as Germany was divided the West might just as well accept the fact that cases such as the defection of Otto John to the East Zone [19] and Bonin's rebellion would recur. In order to stress Bonin's political purity, this officer called the colonel "a *Parzival*," just as other officers frequently spoke of Bonin's "naïveté." When those who seemed upset by the case were asked why they had not publicly exposed Bonin's ideas as communist propaganda, they replied that such action was up to the Defense Ministry.

A similar tolerance of military neutralism can be detected in the attitudes of West German generals toward Field Marshal Friedrich Paulus.[20] Paulus had been in command at Stalingrad. After his capture by the Red forces in 1943, he had served the Soviet Union as a star member of the Free Germany Committee, which carried on Soviet propaganda against Hitler at a time when the Soviet Union was allied with the West against Germany. Paulus lived in East Germany and was the most prestige-laden military participant in the communist effort to undermine support of Adenauer's policy among former German generals. In June, 1955, Paulus gave the main address at the "All-German Soldiers' Meeting," organized by the communists in Berlin. His speech summarized the communist arguments that have been used incessantly in the effort to spread neutralist senti-

[19] At the time of that conversation, in October, 1955, Otto John, the former head of the West German Internal Security Agency, had not yet returned to the West.
[20] Paulus died in East Germany in February, 1957.

ment and increase resistance among the military in West Germany to Adenauer's rearmament policy.

Paulus pointed out that, beginning in January, 1955, after an exchange of ideas by correspondence, former officers from East and West Germany had begun to hold "all-German soldiers' talks" in Berlin, "our German capital," in order to discuss the burning question of unification. Any war that might be precipitated by the division of Germany would inevitably develop into a world war, he said. For Germany, "the battleground of the first days," that would be tantamount to fratricide. According to Paulus, the Paris Treaties had increased the danger of war, and their allegedly defensive character was belied by the fact that the Soviet Union was not admitted to membership in NATO. In NATO, all German troops would have to be delivered to the command of "the American general Gruenther," which meant that they were to give their lives "somewhere in the world" in the service of foreign interests.

To ensure peace, Paulus continued, the two parts of Germany should set an example to the world. Their representatives should gather around the same table and talk about ways and means to unify peacefully the torn fatherland.

Paulus did not fail to mix threats with appeals to patriotic feelings. He said that the nations allied through the Warsaw Pact comprised 900 million people. "Nor should we forget that the Soviet Union has not merely reached parity but outstripped America both in the quantity and quality of nuclear weapons—a fact openly acknowledged today by western military experts." In truly communist propaganda style he ended his address with a series of demands:

We demand the withdrawal of all occupation troops.

We demand the elimination of all foreign military bases from German soil.

We demand membership of a Germany that is free of all alliances in a system of collective security.

We demand the establishment of a German national army which serves exclusively the protection of our homeland.[21]

No German general in the West publicly denounced the service that General Paulus rendered to the communist cause. In part,

[21] The address by Field Marshal Friedrich Paulus was published under the title "Bündnisfreies Deutschland—deutsche Nationalarmee" in *Militärpolitisches Forum*, Munich, July, 1955.

this was a consequence of class solidarity. To some extent, also, this failure can perhaps be explained by a desire not to increase his prestige by publicity, however adverse in spirit. Moreover, former German officers in the West denied that General Paulus exerted any political influence in West German military circles. Only one of them expressed concern about the possible political influence in West Germany of the memoirs Paulus was reported to have been writing. In the context of an analysis of military attitudes toward military neutralism, however, it is noteworthy that, even in private conversation, none of the generals who strongly support Western policies cast any aspersion on Paulus' political motives. The image they held of him was that of a highly competent and intelligent comrade, whose health had never been of the best. His political role was deplored, but regarded as the result of "tragic" circumstances. Just as they had called Bonin a *Parzival,* some of the German generals in the West said that Paulus himself was a "tragic" character.[22]

From the press. Although many German military leaders are apt to exculpate those of their former comrades-in-arms who have moved close to the communist position, they have little respect for journalists who reveal neutralist inclinations. Only conservative writers whose criticism of Adenauer's policy stems from a search for opportunities to resume some form of German *Realpolitik* are exempt from the prejudices with which most German professional officers regard "the press."

One of the most gifted critics of Adenauer's policy has been Dr. Karl Silex, a naval officer in World War I and a nationalist of the old school. After editing a small weekly paper, *Deutsche Kommentare,* in Stuttgart, Silex became editor of the Berlin daily *Der Tagesspiegel* in 1955, where he continued to expound his anti-American, neutralist views.

Silex at first supported EDC because he hoped that German rearmament would provide the West with an instrument for bargaining in negotiations with the Soviet Union on the future of Germany. Then, like many other German observers,[23] even outside the SPD, he attributed the failure of the Berlin Conference of Foreign Minis-

---

[22] It should be noted, however, that according to the "Principles for the Selection of Officers," prepared by the Personnel Selection Board, former members of the communist National Committee for a Free Germany, in which Paulus played a prominent role, cannot become officers in the new *Bundeswehr.* (*Wehrkunde,* November, 1956, p. 515.)

[23] Including the editors of *Aussenpolitik,* the leading German monthly on foreign policy.

ters early in 1954 to lack of serious interest on the part of the Western powers in German unification. The French debacle in Indochina in the spring of that year convinced him that the American "policy of strength" had failed, and that EDC was doomed. Only a policy of neutrality for West Germany now seemed to make sense to him, although he preferred to call neutrality "armed independence" in order to avoid the defamatory connotations which the term "neutralism" had acquired in German political discourse.[24]

As early as May, 1954, controversy arose over one of Pfleiderer's proposals that deputies of the *Bundestag* should establish personal contacts in the Soviet Union. Silex put this controversy in a larger context, demonstrating his ability to detect a new phase in East-West relations more than a year before the majority of his colleagues appreciated the turn that events were taking. Pointing out that ever since May, 1953, when Churchill had proposed a meeting of the heads of state, Western relations with the Soviet Union had been in a process of revision, he predicted that the United States, too, would revise its cold-war policy "because of the H-bomb tests." "A reexamination of the relations between East and West, which already occupies the whole world, is overdue as far as we [the Germans] are concerned." There was need, he said, for "an orientation toward the Moscow thesis of coexistence."[25]

In the spring of 1954, at the time these observations were made, most German military observers were unwilling to subscribe to Silex' views. They regarded "the Moscow thesis of coexistence" as a communist stratagem. They rejected the policy Silex advocated, although his was a kind of *Realpolitik,* which in general was congenial to them. They approved of Silex' reasoning in terms of the balance of power and world political trends, even though they believed that his conclusions were erroneous.

In contrast, military reaction was wholly negative to the German journalists who, in the summer of 1955, went to the Soviet Union and came back claiming that the Western cold-war image of Soviet communism had distorted "the reality" of Russian life and policy.[26] Despite the fact that millions of Germans had had a chance to ob-

---

[24] Similarly, Rauschning liked to speak of "equally favored status" (*Gleichbegünstigung*) instead of neutralism.

[25] *Deutsche Kommentare,* May 22, 1954.

[26] More than one hundred German journalists visited Russia at that time.

serve life in the Soviet Union during the war, and many of them for a long time afterwards as prisoners of war, these journalists acted as though they were the first discoverers of a world otherwise known only from Western propaganda. With no effort at modesty, the journalists referred to their visit as "a turning point in history," or spoke of "the world-historical hour" at which they were permitted to enter Russia. Many of them reported that, if one only shed one's prejudices, "the other Russia" emerged from the shambles of propaganda to which the West had been treated. One of them wrote:

The time of the revolutionaries [in the Soviet Union] has passed. This is probably one of the most essential findings for every visitor from the West. The new generation is free from the revolutionary spirit of their fathers. I dare say that this generation merely pays lip service to communist slogans and slowly even the interest in private property and the security of an absolutely middle-class existence will triumph.

Another journalist wrote:

The fairy tale of "the unhappy slaves" [in the Soviet Union] is an irresponsible propagandistic trick.[27]

Since, in the opinion of these journalists, a middle class and a middle-class mentality had developed in the Soviet Union, they concluded that its new rulers were reasonable men with whom coexistence was possible.

A similarly startling change in press attitudes toward the Soviet Union occurred in September and October, 1955, after the return of the Federal Chancellor and his party from Moscow. Moscow was pictured in German illustrated weeklies as being "like any Western capital." Adenauer shook hands with Bulganin, Khrushchev embraced Carlo Schmid, the socialist member of the German delegation, and called him "Mr. Great Germany"; Carlo Schmid visited the embalmed corpses of Lenin and Stalin; Adenauer prayed in a Moscow church; German and Russian leaders watched Shakespeare's *Romeo and Juliet,* which promptly assumed symbolical significance, since the Soviet authorities had changed the announced performance of *Boris Goudonov* to give Capulet and Montague a chance to make peace over the corpses of their children. Khrushchev admired the potency of German *Kirschwasser,* calling it "a drink for oxen";

[27] The quotations are taken from Clemens Ansbach, "Das Jahr in dem Moskau entdeckt wurde," *Der Monat,* January, 1956, pp. 80–85.

Carlo Schmid drank vodka out of waterglasses, Adenauer *liked* the Soviet leaders, except for morose Molotov, or so it was claimed in the German press. In his toast he mentioned not only "normal relations" between the Soviet Union and West Germany, but "friendly relations," and this nuance was found significant by German commentators as well as by Khrushchev.

All this and more was reported in the German press, with the result that the conference appeared as a mighty first step toward the *fraternization* of Germans and Russians. The term "fraternization" was used, perhaps ironically, in a caption of one of the conference photos appearing in a German weekly. Silex, who had been in Moscow at the time of Adenauer's visit, wrote that "no serious politician could now aver that it is heresy to think about possibilities of a solution [of the reunification issue] outside the Atlantic Pact." [28]

Although this pro-Russian sentiment did not persist in the German press for long, since it was quickly rendered incongruous by Soviet intransigence at the second Geneva Conference in December, 1955, it would be erroneous to dismiss it as an instance of journalistic sensationalism, which was the attitude adopted by many military leaders at the time. In the fall of 1955, several American observers noticed that German journalists talked about Adenauer's policy more critically among themselves than their writings would have suggested. It is possible that the change in the German press treatment of Russia expressed, in a politically permissible form, dissatisfaction with Adenauer's firm commitments to the West, and that it was rejection of rearmament which led to the discovery of the "real Russia." In any event, the growth of German neutralism in the fall of 1955 was acknowledged in conversation by people in various walks of life, not only by members of the opposition, but also by journalists, bankers, academicians, former officers, and even government officials.

Reasons for German Neutralism

In the last analysis, nothing but shifts in the world balance of power in favor of the East can shake the conviction of the former

[28] *Deutsche Kommentare,* September 24, 1955; similarly *Süddeutsche Zeitung,* September 28, 1955.

military leaders that West Germany is an antineutralist country. Many of them viewed the development of the cold war from 1952 to 1954 with apprehension, and they were not encouraged by subsequent events. In their opinion, three developments in particular pointed to a weakening of the West: the Soviet advances in nuclear armament, the fissures in the structure of NATO, and Western efforts toward coexistence with the Soviet Union.

The military leaders appreciated that the Soviet Union was moving toward nuclear parity with the West. Few of them believed the claims of nuclear superiority made by Soviet leaders and by such men as Bonin and Paulus in Germany, but the remaining superiority of the United States in this field was widely held to be insufficient to prevent further gains by the Soviet Union, by cold-war means and possibly by local wars.

Straight neutralist conclusions, however, were hardly ever drawn from this development by military observers, although some of them did suggest that nuclear parity would enable the Russians to put an ever higher price on their assent to reunification, that the American approach to this problem was in the nature of a pious wish, and that "nuclear stalemate" might give more leeway for political maneuver to the middle-sized powers, including Germany.

In the opinion of many German military observers, the capabilities of NATO decreased in 1955. They deplored the weakening of NATO which followed the commitment of French armed forces to North Africa and the policy, adopted by other powers, of curtailing their share in the coalition. The favored excuse of Western statesmen, that quality was to replace quantity in military contributions to common defense, did not convince the German military observers. While few of them were so rash as Adelbert Weinstein, who equated the NATO situation in October, 1955, with that prevailing in 1950, thus claiming that the organization was virtually impotent,[29] none of them credited NATO in 1955 with progress toward a military posture of strength. Former officers in the younger age groups were especially pessimistic.[30]

Because of their predisposition to underestimate the importance of

[29] Adelbert Weinstein in *Frankfurter Allgemeine Zeitung*, October 13, 1955.
[30] At his final news conference, before his retirement as Supreme Allied Commander in Europe, General Gruenther said, "The alliance had four to five times the armed strength it had in 1951" (*The New York Times*, November 14, 1956).

nuclear weapons, few of the older military leaders subscribed to Weinstein's thesis, according to which "the far-reaching loss of the mission of the Atlantic Pact" was attributable to the possession of H-bombs by both the West and the East and the "military equilibrium" established thereby. Instead, they pointed to the drain on conventional NATO forces by the military engagements of France in Africa, and they stressed the political fissures in the alliance developing over this issue and over other issues in Cyprus, Iceland, and the Suez Canal area. Since, in German eyes, NATO was militarily weak and politically divided, doubts were sometimes expressed about its ability to offer effective protection to Germany in the event of a crisis. The German general A. L. Ratcliffe, surveying the developments of 1955, stated his conclusions about NATO in a manner which summarized the comments made in conversations by many other military observers toward the end of that year:

As the immediate danger of general war abated, the readiness to defend itself waned very quickly in Western Europe and the moral foundation of the Atlantic Pact began to show deep fissures. . . .

While some countries [in NATO] want to preserve the *status quo,* i.e. continue the policy of strength, others expect large-scale disarmament and neutralization. In addition, the relations between some member nations have become tense so that the structure of the Atlantic Pact, especially in the South East, appears seriously shaken.[31]

Finally, German military leaders observed that responsibility for the rising opposition to Adenauer's antineutralist policy lay not only with tactical changes in Soviet policy, nuclear developments, and a decline of NATO, but also with American policy itself. It appeared to them that American foreign policy had adopted a more conciliatory attitude toward the Soviet Union ever since the Summit Conference in Geneva in July, 1955. After that conference, Adenauer was in danger of getting out of phase with the Western policy of "relaxing tensions." This fact was clearly reflected in the German parliamentary debate after his visit to Moscow. The leader of the opposition who approved of the results of the conference said, on September 18, 1955, that only a large and courageous initiative of the Federal Republic could save the Germans from becoming "the

[31] A. L. Ratcliffe, "Die militärpolitische Lage am Jahresende," *Wehrwissenschaftliche Rundschau,* December, 1955, p. 545.

last Mohicans of the cold war." And Thomas Dehler, the leader of the Free Democratic Party, which at that time still supported the government, exclaimed that the global relaxation of tensions among the big powers must not take place at Germany's expense.

Adenauer and his supporters in the *Bundestag* denied that the world political climate was changing, but the change was generally perceived nevertheless, even in political and military circles close to the Chancellor. A member of Adenauer's cabinet said privately in October, 1955, that he had suggested in June that the then forthcoming Summit Conference be used to probe the alleged change of Soviet foreign policy. He had proposed that the Western representatives ask the Soviet leaders at the conference in effect, "Have you departed from the Marxist-Leninist-Stalinist philosophy and policy? If so, will you publicly declare that you disavow them?" If they had been ready to make such a declaration, this official explained, its truthfulness should have been examined at the conference. If the Soviet leaders had not been ready to make such a declaration, the conference should have been called off and everybody might as well have gone home.

The same official linked Adenauer's visit to Moscow with the conference of the preceding July. He said one could not be surprised that, after the handshake of Eisenhower and Khrushchev, Adenauer and Bulganin "looked deeply into each other's statesmanly eyes." One could not be astonished that Adenauer put his hands on Bulganin's shoulders in the Bolshoi Theater in Moscow, he said, since Eisenhower had presented a gift to Zhukov in Geneva.

Both the Geneva and Moscow conferences, this official continued, had had certain undesirable consequences in the West. They had fostered unwarranted beliefs among people everywhere about the degree to which tensions had been relaxed. He believed that it had disheartened the opposition to communist rule in the Soviet satellite countries, and had led West Germans to ask why it was still necessary for them to arm. "Some years ago many people had said about German rearmament: 'Without me'; now they said: 'Against whom, for heaven's sake?' "

Such views were shared by several older German military leaders. Believing that the Soviet menace had not abated, they were apprehensive that Germany's most powerful ally might move toward a position in which the desire for peaceful coexistence with the Soviet

Union might isolate the Federal Republic in its strong anti-Soviet stand.

In 1956, it appeared that these apprehensions were not without some foundation. For example, on May 3, 1956, George Kennan, whose prestige in German political circles is high, said in an address before the World Affairs Forum of the Pittsburgh Foreign Policy Association that he had "always doubted the wisdom of the decision to rearm Western Germany and to bring her into the Atlantic Pact." It seemed to him "that American policy should be aimed at the reunification of Germany and the earliest possible establishment of that country as a neutral zone that can blunt the sharp edge of military bipolarity in Europe and help, eventually, to mitigate the intensity of the conflict between East and West." [32]

On May 10, 1956, Churchill addressed a German audience in Aachen, and pointed out that "we all must realize how deep and sincere are Russia's anxieties about the safety of her homeland from foreign invasion"; he suggested that the new anti-Stalinist Soviet Union might become a member of NATO.[33] Not long thereafter the German press reported that John J. McCloy, former U.S. High Commissioner for Germany, in an effort to find a new approach to the thorny problem of German reunification, had proposed that West Germany might be released from some of her present military obligations to NATO.

Finally, at his news conference on June 6, 1956, President Eisenhower spoke of the advantages of neutrality and the risks involved in military alliances with great powers. He said that "If a nation is truly a neutral" and becomes the victim of aggression, then "public opinion of the world is outraged." Conversely, if a nation militarily associated with a great power got into trouble at its border, people would say, "Good enough for it. They asked for it." [34] This statement, which pleased the uncommitted nations in Asia and Africa, sounded ominous to those, including West Germany, that had made collective-security arrangements with the United States.

[32] The address was widely discussed in both the American and German press and was subsequently published in *U.S. News and World Report,* June 29, 1956, from which the quotation is taken. The magazine published in the same issue a fierce attack on Kennan's views by William C. Bullitt.

[33] *The New York Times,* May 11, 1956.

[34] *Ibid.,* June 7, 1956. The President made these observations by way of argument for his foreign aid bill, which provided for support also of countries that were not members of any Western defense pact.

Mr. Eisenhower's statement seemed to be contradicted three days later by Secretary Dulles, in a major address on foreign policy at Iowa State College. While the President had pointed out that he could not see that freedom from military alliance "is always to the disadvantage of such a country as ours," [35] the Secretary of State said that neutrality "has increasingly become an obsolete conception and except under very exceptional circumstances, it is an immoral and short-sighted conception." [36] While Mr. Dulles could not fail to shock the governments of those countries that had been pleased by Mr. Eisenhower's remarks, and reassure those that had been baffled by the President, it became evident in subsequent efforts by the Administration to clarify its policy that the U.S. government was moving away from the blanket condemnation of neutralism that had characterized it in previous years.

In September, 1956, it was reported that Adenauer was trying to change the politically feeble Western European Union into a more viable political organization. Transformed into a European confederation, and free of the supranational features of EDC which France had found intolerable, this organization might determine international and defense policies for its member states, and could function as a "third force" independent both of the United States and the Soviet Union. Adenauer disclosed this idea on the occasion of a visit to Belgium on September 26. A few days later, he said at a press conference that Western Europe must cease to appear as the tail on the American kite.[37] He added that Belgium and France favored the plan; and it had been known since July, 1956, that Britain might be interested in joining a European arrangement that would provide for a free-trade zone in addition to a European customs union.

The press reported that Adenauer's renewed interest in some integration of Europe, and in European independence from the United States, had begun to take shape after the Geneva Conference of the Big Four heads of state in July, 1955. It was also reported that these interests had taken on new urgency in his mind as a result of two developments, the sharpening of the Suez crisis and the alleged intentions of the United States to reduce its conventional forces. Adenauer was said to fear that, if the Radford Plan were carried out,

[35] *Ibid.*
[36] *Ibid.*, June 10, 1956.
[37] *Ibid.*, October 2, 1956.

a reduction of American forces in Europe might be inevitable and German security therefore gravely endangered. At his press conference, Adenauer contended that the United States had always wanted an independent Europe. The next day Mr. Dulles backed him, explaining that such a move toward European independence should not be regarded as "a slap" at the United States.[38]

Perhaps this development did not come entirely as a surprise to former military leaders in Germany. In November, 1955, a few of them, distinguished by political acumen and imagination, had observed in conversation that in order to judge the prospects of neutralism in Germany one had to distinguish between its popular manifestations and the political and military developments in the East-West struggle which affected Germany's interests. German neutralist tendencies had risen in 1955, they admitted, but this fact might be discounted, since such tendencies were subject to the flow of news and the ups and downs of popular sentiment. In contrast, it was important to consider that Adenauer himself, pressed by world political developments beyond his control, might work for a consolidation of European interests in order to form an independent European "third force." At the time, these comments were not more than dispassionate speculations, made without indications of approval or censure.

[38] *Ibid.*, October 3, 1956.

FIVE

Atomic Blackmail

The uncertainty as to whether atomic weapons will be used in future war, either local or general, lends itself to political exploitation in the cold war. The efficiency of nuclear weapons in wartime and their resulting threat-value in either war- or peacetime constitute their political-military worth. In peacetime, the threat-value of weapons can be exploited in many ways: by an ultimatum, by authoritative or inspired statements on capabilities or intentions, by studied disclosures of new weapons on ceremonial occasions, by means of maneuvers, redeployments of forces, or by so-called "demonstrations."

In the pre-atomic age, naval demonstrations and partial mobilizations of ground forces were standard measures for bringing military pressure to bear on foreign governments in peacetime. In the present era, such pressure can be exerted also by using the threat-potential of modern air power and of the weapons of mass destruction. Evidence of this is seen in official statements on deterrence, in threats of instant retaliation in propaganda to foreign populations about the vulnerability to air or missile attack of their bases, industries, and cities, and in discussions of the vastly increased importance of surprise in war.

The political worth of modern military power does not reside merely in threats that certain weapons may be used or in promises that they will not be used. Political worth attaches also to technical and scientific accomplishments, for the power that is unlocked by such advances can, like all power, be used for military as well as for peaceful ends. Witness the political value of airlifts, of rescue missions and expeditions, of international exhibitions of advances in modern technology, of international congresses and "years" devoted to progress in the basic or applied sciences.

Yet it cannot be said that all of the many possibilities of peacetime exploitation of the political value of military power are being realized. This is particularly true with respect to certain military activities, such as weapons tests or training missions. Here military purposes usually overshadow consideration of the political advantages that might be gained or disadvantages that might be avoided by changes in the timing of military activities, and in the public information practices accompanying them. For example, the atomic exercise CARTE BLANCHE, which was held in June, 1955, largely in West Germany, took place just prior to a debate in the *Bundestag* on German rearmament, and it caused the federal government no little trouble. Better timing or a more carefully considered policy of informing the public could have saved some political embarrassment in this instance.

There exists no doctrine of the peacetime exploitation of military power comparable to military doctrines on the employment of military forces in war. That gap remains to be filled. The present chapter discusses only "atomic blackmail," one of the many ways in which the political worth of military power can be exploited. In view of the fact that Germany may become one of the victims of such blackmail maneuvers, the subject was taken up with former German officers in the spring of 1954. Their opinions will be presented at the end of this chapter, after a general analysis of atomic blackmail.

A government that is exposed to atomic threats in peacetime readily regards them as "blackmail," whereas the threatening power is likely to call them "deterrence." In order not to fall a prey to this confusion of terms, it is useful to distinguish threats according to (1) their nature, (2) their conditions, and (3) their terms of compliance. First, what actions are threatened; that is, what is the precise nature of the threat? Second, what actions does the threat seek to forestall; that is, what are the conditions under which it will be carried out? Finally, what alternative actions is the threat meant to induce; that is, what terms of compliance does it attempt to impose?

In the early years of the postwar period, Western statesmen used to speak of the deterrent power of the U.S. monopoly in atomic weapons. In Zurich, on September 19, 1946, Churchill put it this way:

> In these present days we dwell strangely under the precarious shield, and I might even say, protection of the atomic bomb. The atomic bomb is still only in the hands of a state and nation which we know will never use it except in the cause of right and freedom. . . .

The deterrent value of all such statements lay in their implied warning to the Soviet Union. Leaving aside the degree of verbal explicitness or directness of such warnings, what gave them force was the threat that the United States would employ atomic weapons against the Soviet Union. The condition of the threat—what it sought to forestall—was an attack by the Soviet Union upon the United States or Western Europe. Compliance with the threat required only that the Soviet Union abstain from such an attack.

In Secretary Dulles' doctrine of instant and massive retaliation, the nature, conditions, and terms of compliance of this threat were changed.[1] The new threat implied the possibility that thermonuclear weapons would be used, not only against the Soviet Union, but against any communist aggressor. It sought to forestall any communist attack (by Soviet forces or by proxy) anywhere (in Europe or elsewhere). Correspondingly, the compliance which the new threat hoped to enforce consisted in communist abstention from local aggression anywhere in the world.

This new threat was given its most radical expression by Vice-President Nixon:

> We found that economically their [the Soviet] plan, apparently, was to force the United States to stay armed to the teeth, to be prepared to fight anywhere—anywhere in the world—that they, the men in the Kremlin, chose. Why? Because they knew that this would force us into bankruptcy; that we would destroy our freedom in attempting to defend it. Well, we decided we would not fall into these traps. And so we adopted a new principle. And the new principle summed up is this: Rather than let the communists nibble us to death all over the world in

---

[1] John Foster Dulles, "Policy for Security and Peace," *Foreign Affairs*, April, 1954. See also Vice-President Nixon's radio and television address on March 13, 1954, published in *The New York Times*, March 14, 1954. For a useful discussion of the various forms and possible motives of Mr. Dulles' statements on the New Look, see E. Raymond Platig, "The 'New Look' Raises Old Problems," *The Review of Politics*, Vol. XVII (January, 1955), pp. 111–135.

little wars we would rely in the future primarily on our massive mobile retaliatory power which we would use in our discretion against the major source of aggression at times and places we chose.[2]

Mr. Dulles was more cautious when he clarified the newly announced policy in his *Foreign Affairs* article. He said:

obviously, the possession of that capacity to retaliate on a massive basis comprehends within it the capacity to retaliate on a less than global or massive basis.

He continued, explicitly:

. . . I believe that it is disastrous for us to believe that the danger can be met by our concentrating merely upon one form of defense or one type of deterrent.[3]

This last statement came very close to subscribing to the doctrine of graduated deterrence, in which the British have shown much interest.[4] Graduated deterrence is an attempt to scale down the nature of the atomic threat so that it will match less exacting terms of compliance. While there is still a threat that all-out nuclear war would follow any thermonuclear attack on the United States (and/or Western Europe) by Soviet forces, restricted or local communist aggression could be met by less than total retaliation. In the words of Admiral Buzzard,

The suggestion is that we work out and declare, without waiting for communist agreement, distinctions of the following order. The *tactical* use of nuclear weapons, we might say, is to be confined to atomic weapons, and is to exclude even these from use against towns and cities. Their *strategic* use, we might further declare, is to include hydrogen weapons and the mass destruction of targets in towns and cities. We might also state generally that, in order to pursue the moral principle of never using more force than necessary, we would not resort to the strategic use of nuclear weapons unless their employment proved absolutely essential. Thus, without committing ourselves unalterably in advance, or showing our hand too clearly, we would have the option, when threatened with a limited aggression too great for our conventional

[2] *The New York Times,* March 14, 1954.
[3] Dulles, *op. cit.,* pp. 5 and 22.
[4] See Rear Adm. Sir Anthony W. Buzzard, "Massive Retaliation and Graduated Deterrence," *World Politics,* January, 1956, pp. 228–237; and articles by Sir John Slessor and Hanson W. Baldwin in *Bulletin of the Atomic Scientists,* May, 1956.

forces to cope with, of saying to the prospective aggressor: "If you do attack, we will, if necessary, use atomic and perhaps chemical weapons against your armed forces. But we will not, on this issue, use hydrogen or bacteriological weapons at all, unless you do, and we will not use any mass destruction weapons against centers of population, unless you do deliberately." To this statement we might append certain exceptions, such as cities in the front line of the land fighting and those with airfields alongside.

By an announcement of this character we would be modifying our present policy of massive retaliation to one aptly named "graduated deterrence."[5]

In the pre-atomic age, at the time of the *Pax Britannica,* for example, it was sometimes possible to exploit military capabilities in peacetime by threatening other powers with war and possible defeat. The development of atomic and thermonuclear weapons allows for threats of extinction. Such threats can demoralize a whole population, if it values life more than national interest. Threats of unrestricted war, therefore, may move the threatened government either to yield or to react aggressively, and may subject it to pressure from its own population either to defy or to comply with the threats; such threats could even provoke panic or rebellion in a threatened nation. To some extent, the possibility of such developments under threat has always existed, especially in literate societies—in which relatively large parts of the population take an interest in politics—even when war involved less than total destruction. Atomic threats, however, are likely to heighten the probability of such popular pressures; what is more, the probability increases with the degree to which the threat of extinction is understood, and in inverse proportion to the confidence enjoyed at home by the threatened government and to the capability of effective defense.

It may be objected that the last of these three conditions does not apply, in view of the fact that often in history small countries have fought against hopeless odds rather than submit meekly to subjugation by a greatly superior enemy. It should be remembered, however, that in most such cases the weaker power was not threatened with physical extinction; in the few cases in which it was, resistance sprang from a resolution to take a last toll of the conqueror.

[5] Buzzard, *op. cit.,* p. 229.

But, under conditions of thermonuclear warfare, it may not always be possible to exact such a last toll, for it is conceivable that a small country fighting alone might suffer total annihilation without inflicting a single casualty on the more powerful enemy. In such circumstances, resistance is considerably less likely. Any decision not to submit can then be based either on the chance that the threat is a bluff and will not be carried out if the threatened country is staunch, or else on an extremely strong sense of honor that requires a nation to die rather than submit.

As atomic and thermonuclear parity replaces a situation of nuclear monopoly, the threat-value of these weapons diminishes. Threat can now be met by counterthreat, at least as long as the threatened power does not lose its nerve before the specter of reciprocal death and destruction. That is, bilateral threats will tend to neutralize one another. What is even more likely to happen when parity is achieved, however, is that the *explicitness and finality* of unrestricted threats will be avoided; threatening behavior as such is not likely to cease. When war can mean total annihilation, bluff among equals is too dangerous to be tried against a resolute adversary. It is difficult to believe that a country will ever issue an explicit atomic ultimatum to a power enjoying nuclear parity, for the only rational response to such an ultimatum is either compliance or a preventive attack; in the latter case, the ultimatum would defeat its own purpose by giving the enemy the advantage of the first strike. Under conditions of parity of ever-more-destructive weapons, therefore, and with ever-increasing appreciation of that destructiveness among political leaders, it stands to reason that authoritative threats of unrestricted war will in the future become less rather than more explicit and final.

This analysis requires two qualifications, however. First, a country facing invasion may reason that the aggressor has no desire for a nuclear war, and is about to attack in the belief that the war will not be nuclear. In such a situation, the threatened country might conceivably issue a defensive atomic ultimatum in the hope of avoiding both war and political extinction. Second, it does not seem impossible that certain extreme states of the world could lead to explicit and final authoritative threats of unrestricted war, even upon lesser provocation than a threat of extinction. For example, assuming a world in which everything except the Western Hemisphere has fallen under Soviet domination, a further step to force the submission of South America might be seen in the United States as tantamount to direct aggression against itself. In such a "back-to-the-wall" situation, it does not seem inconceivable that the United States might make final and explicit threats of unrestricted war in order to forestall what it judged to be its own political doom. It should be noted that, in contingencies such as these, the atomic ultimatum would be a measure of desperate defense rather than reckless aggression.

Since the end of World War II, nuclear weapons have increased in destructiveness and variety, and have decreased in cost. With the development of warheads of widely differing power, and delivery capabilities differing in range and kind, there has grown a tendency to regard the smaller atomic weapons as already so "conventional" in character as to be virtually indistinguishable in quality from "classical" weapons. Speaking of the development of atomic weapons since the end of World War II, President Eisenhower, in his address on "Atoms for Peace and Progress" before the General Assembly of the United Nations on December 8, 1953, declared that "the development has been such that atomic weapons have virtually achieved conventional status within our armed services." [6] Again at his news conference on March 16, 1955, the President said that, if necessary, we could hit military targets with atomic warheads just as we would "hit them with a bullet." [7]

Such redefinition of conventionality affects the threat-value of nuclear weapons in two ways. On the one hand, references to tactical atomic weapons as conventional may be construed as restricted atomic threats; they imply that such weapons will be used in future local wars, just as "bullets" have been used in the past. The conditions and terms of compliance of such threats involve enemy abstention from local aggression, not merely from employment of nuclear weapons. Hence in the present cold-war situation such threats supplement, with respect to local war, the threat of unrestricted retaliation.

On the other hand, the very possibility of restricted threats implies a differentiation between, and a gradation of, threats. It remains pos-

[6] *The New York Times*, December 9, 1953.

[7] At his press conference on January 23, 1957, the President made a statement which implied that the United States might use small atomic weapons in opposing any communist armed aggression in the Middle East.

sible, after a restricted atomic threat has been made, to specify different, more severe terms of compliance by threatening to use the bigger atomic and thermonuclear weapons. By reiteration, restricted threats may lose some of their effectiveness and become just as conventional as the weapons are supposed to be. In that event, bigger, less restricted threats may be needed to enforce terms of compliance that could originally be exacted by restricted threats, thus once more transcending an enlarged sphere of conventional weapons. It should be noted, however, that the calculations of a potential aggressor are not so much influenced by new definitions of the conventionality of weapons as by estimates of the effectiveness of weapons. Therefore, although calling tactical atomic weapons conventional may strengthen the belief that they will be used in defense, such renaming carries no assurance that bigger "unconventional" weapons will not be used.

Thus any general announcement, prior to the actual outbreak of violence, about the conventionality of tactical atomic weapons can be read in two ways: either as a declaration of intent to extend the old boundaries of wars waged only with high-explosive weapons (that is, as a threat), or as a declaration of intent not to extend the new boundaries of conventionality (that is, as a promise). But the threat is stronger than the promise. The promise would become more credible if precedents supported the definition of conventionality, but no relevant precedents exist. Three conditions must be met before tactical atomic weapons can in fact be viewed as conventional: (1) they must be used in a war; (2) they must be the *only* atomic weapons used in that war; and (3) *the war must end either in a stalemate or in defeat of one of the combatants who did make tactical use of small atomic weapons.* The first and second requirements alone do not suffice to establish the conventionality of small atomic weapons, for victory resulting from their use in a local war would not preclude the possibility that, had the victor faced stalemate or defeat instead, he might have disregarded—or might disregard in the future—the weapons restrictions that, as victor, he had no sufficient reason to ignore.

Hence the third requirement. Prior to the end of a war, it is not certain whether it will end in victory, stalemate, or defeat. Any announcement that precedes its beginning, then, to the effect that *only* less than maximum atomic and thermonuclear power will be used, carries no more conviction than any other declaration of intent.

Since the conditions specified above have not been met, there remains uncertainty as to whether the use of "small" atomic weapons somewhere may not lead to the use of all available kinds of weapons anywhere. We do not know whether it is possible to control the transition from local to general war and from restricted ("conventional") atomic war to unrestricted violence. Several local wars have occurred since 1945 without leading to world war, but these have involved no atomic weapons whatever, so that they do not provide a precedent of control. For this reason, if for no other, the mere threat, not to mention the outbreak, of a restricted local atomic war is likely to arouse deeper apprehensions than would the outbreak of another local war similar to the one in Korea. It may also be predicted that, for the same reason, resistance among the atomic have-not powers to the *use* of tactical atomic weapons will increase as the power and number of atomic and thermonuclear weapons increase. This will be so as long as there are no wars serving to prove that atomic weapons can be controlled and local wars restricted.

Soviet exploitation of the threat-value of nuclear power in peacetime is enhanced by the fact that most of the powers in the Western alliance are atomically destitute. These have-not powers have no protection against a Soviet atomic attack except that which the retaliatory capability of the United States can provide. With the partial exception of Great Britain, that is at present the situation of all the nations with which the United States has common defense arrangements of one kind or another. In fact, the protection by the United States is their only safeguard against conventional as well as nuclear attack; for, given the relative inferiority of the West in conventional armaments, its only hope against a Soviet attack with such weapons in Europe lies in the defensive use of tactical atomic power.

This fact—that our European allies are protected by a coalition that is unable to meet conventional aggression by conventional means —gives the Soviet Union a political advantage in peacetime. For the Red forces could embark upon conventional aggression with good prospects of success, if they could be sure of not meeting with unconventional local defense or all-out retaliation. But the West has no such advantage in its own defense posture. That is why West Europeans tend to view the prospect of an atomic war in Europe as the terrible consequence of U.S. protection rather than of possible Soviet aggression. The Soviet Union may be threatening war, but it is the United States that seems bent on making it an atomic one either by insisting upon unconventional resistance to conventional attack, or, for precisely the same reason, by forcing the aggressor himself to resort to atomic attack. Thus the fear of war in consequence of Soviet aggression turns into a fear of the weapons that will be employed in that war, and the responsibility for aggression becomes less important in European eyes than the responsibility for the nature of the war.

If NATO were politically of one will, this situation might be less serious than it is, but NATO enjoys less than perfect political unity of purpose, and suffers from a military inequality among its members that is accentuated by the virtual U.S. monopoly of atomic power among the Allies. The division of NATO into atomic haves and have-nots was less momentous than it later became as long as the United States enjoyed unquestioned predominance in nuclear weapons over the Soviet Union. With the world balance of atomic power clearly favoring the West, the have-nots in NATO could expect that an American ultimatum of unrestricted retaliation against the Soviet Union itself would effectively counter any Soviet threat of aggression in Europe. The Europeans could hope to be spared the horrors of war, atomic or otherwise; they needed only to assure themselves that the United States, in its own interest, could not permit the Russians to gain control of Western Europe.

Under conditions of nuclear parity, however, with the distribution of atomic capability among the NATO powers remaining unchanged, this reassurance becomes somewhat more labored and dubious, for it presupposes that the United States would be willing to defend Europe even at the risk of suffering nuclear devastation in its own zone of the interior. It is the dubiousness of this presupposition that generates the fear of our European allies that we have discussed.

Therefore Soviet achievement of a respectable nuclear capability offers communist leaders novel opportunities to threaten or cajole the atomic have-nots in NATO. Against a background of fulsome protestations of peaceableness and coexistence, the Soviet Union can suggest that, in the event of war, America's European allies would suffer the horrors of atomic destruction, but that they would be spared that fate if they ended their military support of the United States. As Marshal Zhukov stated at the Twentieth Party Congress,

One cannot fail to note that the governments of states making available their territory for American military bases are playing with fire and sacrificing the national interests of their countries; they are placing their lives in jeopardy. By the logic of armed conflict, these bases must suffer retaliatory blows regardless of upon whose territories they are located.[8]

Threats of this kind have long been familiar in Soviet propaganda. Toward the end of 1954, for example, Soviet leaders countered Field Marshal Montgomery's statements that SHAPE would employ atomic and thermonuclear weapons in the event of a Soviet attack[9] by reminding the British that their islands were especially vulnerable to nuclear destruction. In an article published in *Pravda* and broadcast to the Soviet people on December 4, 1954, Marshal Vasilevsky warned that "the one who would dare to unleash a war would find himself in a most unenviable position." Addressing Field Marshal Montgomery directly, he said:

We both know very well that the atomic and hydrogen bombs are weapons of mass destruction of peaceful populations, weapons of destruction of towns, which are particularly dangerous for countries with a small territory and a large population.

To the extent that unilateral strategic deterrence is replaced by a strategic stalemate, such threats and promises are likely to fall on more fertile ground than they did in the "American-monopoly" phase of the nuclear age. Since the atomic have-nots in NATO lack any strategic deterrent capability of their own, they do not share directly whatever benefits accrue from a strategic stalemate; but they appear particularly exposed to the brunt of the greater destructiveness of war that is inherent in the emerging "conventionality" of tactical atomic weapons.

[8] *Pravda,* February 20, 1956. On January 23, 1957, the Tass news agency, quoting "leading circles of the Soviet Union," mentioned specifically Great Britain, France, West Germany, Italy, Iran, and Japan as countries which have placed themselves "under the threat of retaliatory atomic blows" by allowing themselves to be used by the United States "as bridgeheads for the preparation of atomic warfare" (*The New York Herald Tribune,* January 24, 1957).

[9] Field Marshal Lord Montgomery, "A Look through a Window at World War III," *Journal of the Royal United Service Institution,* October, 1954.

Of course, the Soviet leaders cannot risk an explicit and final atomic threat to any member of NATO unless they are prepared to risk total war, for they must reckon with the possibility that the United States will react to any such unambiguous ultimatum as if it had been addressed directly to itself. It is more likely that Soviet "atomic blackmail" will take forms that will allow for reversals of policy and withdrawals from commitments. Atomic blackmail must be noncommittal, subtle, informal, and casual, rather than binding, gross, authoritative, and solemn. The Russians, therefore, are likely to use indirection, such as warnings of atomic retaliation in the event of Western aggression, and to address their threats to the small and middle powers of NATO.

But the Soviet leaders are likely to observe such precautions only as long as they believe that the United States is determined to come to the support of its allies when they are threatened. In November, 1956, at the peak of the Suez crisis, Bulganin addressed to Eden and Mollet the boldest threat that the Soviet leaders have ever dared to make. He suggested that Britain and France might be subjected to rocket warfare unless British and French forces were withdrawn from Egypt. It is unlikely that Russia would have risked making this threat if it had not been for the deep rift between the United States, on the one hand, and Britain and France, on the other, that had developed at that time.[10] If Russia believed that the United States was prepared to abandon Europe, then it is probable that Soviet threats to the small and middle NATO powers would become more explicit, and perhaps final. Only a strategic nuclear capability of their own would render our European allies invulnerable to Soviet blackmail in such a case.

Under conditions of a strategic nuclear stalemate the United States cannot use strategic threats to counter subtle Soviet tactics against NATO, particularly if the Soviet warnings are accompanied by a smiling and flexible policy of strength and coexistence. Instead, as long as the United States is the only major atomic power in the Western alliance, it has no choice but to press for arrangements making possible an effective use of atomic weapons in the defense of Europe.

But it is doubtful that such plans will be able to provide a strong

[10] See Hans Speier, "Soviet Atomic Blackmail and the North Atlantic Alliance," *World Politics,* Vol. IX, No. 3 (April, 1957), pp. 318ff.

counterweight to Soviet atomic threats. In 1954, for example, the NATO governments agreed to give General Gruenther, the Allied Supreme Commander, permission to proceed with defense plans which included the use of atomic bombs, missiles, and artillery.[11] Yet, shortly before the communiqué announcing this agreement was issued, the press reported that it had become apparent in the meetings of the Military Committee that the Dutch, Belgian, and Danish governments would not agree to the actual use of atomic weapons. And the communiqué of December 18 did indeed state that the approval of planning for atomic defense "did not involve the delegation of the responsibility of governments to make decisions for putting plans into action in the event of hostilities."[12]

In his report to Congress on foreign aid in May, 1956, President Eisenhower announced his desire to hand over armaments with "atomic capabilities" to certain allies. Almost a year later, the United States decided to give to Britain intermediate-range ballistic missiles (IRBM), when they became operational, and to other NATO powers other less efficient advanced weapons. These decisions narrowed but did not close the nuclear-weapons gap between the United States and her European allies. With the exception of Britain, the Western allies will not acquire a strategic deterrent capability. They will receive from the United States only tactical atomic weapons with a range considerably shorter than that of the IRBM. Nor can they be given any atomic warheads, unless the restrictive provisions of the U.S. Atomic Energy Act are changed. In response to the U.S. measures, the Soviet Union embarked upon a diplomatic and propaganda campaign of unprecedented intensity, warning the smaller Western powers of the dire consequences which their association with the United States would entail. It appeared that the Soviet Union was profoundly concerned about the limited sharing of atomic weapons in the Western alliance. Russia again threatened the smaller countries, including West Germany, with atomic retaliation in the event of a Western nuclear attack launched from their territories. The threats were emphatic, but essentially defensive in character. It is possible, however, that the Soviet warnings will strengthen European inclina-

[11] Communiqué of the North Atlantic Council meeting of December 18, 1954, published in *The New York Times,* December 19, 1954.

[12] A German analysis of this NATO decision will be presented at the end of the next chapter, in which German military opinions on the possible outbreak of war are reviewed.

tions to view Soviet nuclear disarmament proposals with greater favor, especially since the British government announced in April, 1957, that the British Isles could not be defended in an atomic war.

In 1954, the question of Soviet "atomic blackmail" was discussed with a number of German military leaders. The situation on which they were asked to comment differed from the peacetime context of atomic blackmail discussed above. In order to probe German views about the probable solidarity of NATO under severe stress, the question was raised by the interviewer in the following form: "Suppose that, after an exchange of atomic blows between the United States and the Soviet Union, the Soviet government were to issue an ultimatum to West European governments to the effect that continued military support of the United States, by permission to use air bases or in other ways, would be followed by Soviet nuclear attacks on London, Paris, Rome, and Bonn, and that such attacks would not take place on the capital of any country that ceased its support of the United States. How would the West European governments react?"

The answers differed widely. They ranged from misunderstanding or evasion of the issue to sarcasm at hysterical American preoccupation with atomic war, but included detailed responses. Most of the answers did come to grips with the problem in one way or another. All in all, the responses can be grouped into three unqualified, negative conclusions.

1. None of the respondents showed any real acceptance of "collective security" as put forth at the time in Secretary Dulles' article on the so-called "New Look" in *Foreign Affairs*.[13] No one suggested that, in the event of war and "blackmail," the NATO powers would stand together because they would be facing a common enemy in common defense.

2. Among those who said that the various governments would react in different ways, none believed that France or Italy would stand up to the threat. Opinions were divided about the probable behavior of the United Kingdom and West Germany.

3. None of the respondents made statements to the effect that Soviet threats would have to be resisted. None of them showed indignation at the suggestion that the Soviet Union would seek to in-

[13] *Op. cit.*

timidate the West. At the time these conversations were held a corresponding inquiry was made in Great Britain.[14] The British responses differed strikingly from the German ones. While the Germans either failed to discuss the issue or gave factual, differential estimates of government response to Soviet "blackmail," the British showed spontaneous indignation and pluck, and all of them agreed that the British would not be intimidated.

The German replies which evaded or misunderstood the question seemed to be prompted by disbelief that an atomic war would start with an exchange of blows between the United States and the Soviet Union. One informant observed that a Soviet attack was conceivable only if the Soviet leaders had reliable intelligence to the effect that an American attack on their country was imminent, "say within a month," or if they wanted to forestall popular unrest in the Soviet Union by resorting to war. The latter assumption revealed that German military leaders still saw a third world war in the image of pre-atomic, conventional warfare.

In the most common misunderstanding of the question, the assumed case of atomic "blackmail" was taken to have occurred in peacetime. It was then observed that the Soviet Union would not dare to issue such an ultimatum to any government in Western Europe, because the Soviet bluff could be called by an American counter-ultimatum to the Soviet government, threatening the Soviet Union with all-out war.

The most pessimistic respondents among those who accepted the hypothetical conditions of Soviet "blackmail" pointed out that the Soviet Union would not need to issue an ultimatum to France or Italy. In these countries, they said, the will to resist would vanish if put to a serious test by atomic war between the Soviet Union and the United States, or, for that matter, by an invasion of Germany. If, in the latter event, the advance were so staged as to permit the British to evacuate their forces from Germany, and if a special Soviet guarantee were offered to the French assuring them of the inviolability of their frontier, the only remaining Soviet concern, it was believed, would be with the question of whether or not the *Americans* would fight. Another respondent pointed out that if the Russians were to use atomic weapons against West Germany, it was

[14] See Harvey A. DeWeerd, "Britain's Changing Military Policy," *Foreign Affairs,* Vol. XXXIV, No. 1 (October, 1955), pp. 102–117.

most unlikely that France or Italy would have to be conquered: "They would fall into the Russian lap like ripe plums."

When the discussion turned to the probable German reaction to the ultimatum, the views expressed were not all favorable to Germany, although most respondents ventured the guess that the Germans would stand up to the Soviet ultimatum, and that they certainly would be more steadfast than the French or the Italians. One informant said he could conceive of the possibility that Soviet commanders would take up radio contact with German army leaders, "say, somewhere in Bavaria," and issue the ultimatum to them. He believed that, in such a case, the German officers would not lay down their arms, even though aware of Soviet capability to demolish the Ruhr industry, or any city in West Germany, by missiles launched in the Soviet Zone of Germany, or even farther east. When asked why he had assumed that the Soviet atomic "ultimatum" would not be addressed to the Bonn government, this informant replied: "Why Bonn? Within a few days after the outbreak of hostilities the heads of the Allied High Commission would have left. The *Bundestag*? It would not be able to deliberate and reach a decision in such circumstances. The federalistic structure of West Germany will lead to a disintegration of political authority in the first few days of war, so that the mainspring of action will be the military officers in command of the fighting forces."

On the whole, then, the replies of German military leaders were pessimistic. It should be added, however, that they did not show signs of personal demoralization. Pessimism was implied in their estimates of the political reactions of others, of governments and people. But these estimates were not recommendations. It is not established that the respondents themselves would yield to the ultimatum if it were submitted to them. Therefore, the replies to the question regarding atomic blackmail may be taken as another illustration of the dissatisfaction felt by German military leaders in 1954 with political conditions in Western Europe.

SIX

The Outbreak of War: 1952–1955

German military opinions on the possibility of a third world war changed rapidly between 1952 and 1955. In 1952 there was general confidence among the German military that the Soviet Union would not dare to attack the West, chiefly because of the relative inferiority of its industrial war potential. The peaceful intent of the United States was not questioned. In the spring of 1954, however, German military leaders were somewhat affected by the popular fear that the United States might resort to preventive war. While they themselves did not advocate preventive war, they seriously discussed the subject in the light of their expectation that the Soviet Union would soon succeed in establishing effective parity with the United States in nuclear weapons. In 1955 doubts about American superiority had risen further; but the interest in the possibility of preventive war had given way to more sophisticated views of the relationship between limited and unlimited war.

Deterrence and Soviet Weakness: 1952

In the spring of 1952, apprehension that Western efforts to rearm Germany might provoke the Soviet Union into violent action against Berlin and West Germany was considerably stronger among the German people than it is today. This fear was openly voiced by the Social Democrats in their fight against EDC. However, some socialist leaders felt otherwise. For example, in a conversation held in 1951 Mayor Ernst Reuter of Berlin dismissed the notion of provocation as naïve, because "Bolsheviks do not permit themselves to be provoked."

In order to assuage the popular fear and to assail socialist criticism, all politicians and journalists who supported the government dealt with the argument of provocation by protesting the defensive character of EDC. They repeated assurances given by Allied spokesmen. Perhaps the neatest, and by no means the least persuasive, argument advanced in this connection was put forth by Erich Mende, a deputy of the Free Democratic Party, in the *Bundestag* debate in July, 1952. He pointed out that the envisioned organization of EDC was so complicated and unwieldy that, for this reason alone, it would be incapable of aggression.[1]

German generals did not believe that the Russians would attack. They agreed with Mayor Reuter that caution would prevent the Soviet leaders from embarking upon an adventurous policy of war, at least in the foreseeable future: "These men calculate the risks of war carefully and soberly." One of the informants considered that 1954–1956 would be the critical years, but added that "Nobody can foresee what is likely to happen in the distant future, so that any estimates beyond 1953 are hazardous." On the whole, military observers agreed with the government that a *weak* Western Europe might invite a Soviet attack, that efforts to make Europe stronger would reduce the likelihood of war, and that progress toward German rearmament was dangerously slow. "EDC will make war less likely" was the general theme.

The generals did not believe that the Soviet Union would abstain from aggression because of peaceful intent. They believed that it was effectively deterred from waging war. But not one military informant attributed the force of deterrence primarily to American superiority in atomic power, or, more specifically, to the capabilities of the U.S. Strategic Air Command. Only during the last three years have German military leaders become aware of the revolution in warfare which the development of atomic and thermonuclear weapons has brought about. In 1952 most of them still looked at the future in the light of the past, and they could not imagine that another world war would differ in nature from the last one. Without exception, they thought of a third world war as a long-drawn-out struggle in which the West would eventually prevail over the alarming strength of Soviet ground forces because of its command of the sea, its exten-

---

[1] The same point was made in an anonymous appraisal of EDC, "Deutsches Soldatentum und europäische Wiedergeburt," *Wehrwissenschaftliche Rundschau*, June, 1952, p. 203.

sive air power, and the economic mobilization base of the United States.

When asked what forces kept Soviet aggressiveness in check, German generals invariably mentioned Soviet weakness and the superiority of the American industrial potential, in that order. Only occasionally did they mention American atomic power, and then only in third place. They believed that the Soviet Union needed time to recuperate from the heavy losses of industrial and human resources suffered in World War II. They argued that the Soviet Union had a weak network of transportation, and lacked adequate manpower in the age groups of highest productivity. They attributed the latter deficiency partly to the effects of the war, partly to demands for administrative personnel and occupation troops in the satellite countries, and partly to the continuous draft upon productive manpower for slave labor in the concentration camps. "The Soviet Union has not yet developed a labor force sufficient to cope with the problems of modern industrial production in a reliable way." In addition, these observers held that the allies of the Soviet Union were unreliable. They believed that unpopular agricultural policies were the major cause of the lack of political cohesion and loyalty in the satellite countries.[2]

For all these reasons, German military experts said that the Soviet Union had much to gain from peace, particularly since it was isolated through encirclement "by the capitalist world" in the form of "bridgehead positions, naval and air bases,"[3] and because the Soviet leaders, aware of American industrial power, would need years of peace to strengthen their defenses and make their country less vulnerable. In the meantime, it was suggested, the Russians would try to weaken the West, particularly in Asia. But they would not go to war, because their country was weak and they had "too much to lose." No one who was interviewed in 1952 suggested that the Soviet Union might catch up with, or overtake, the United States in total military strength. Indeed, that suggestion was very seldom heard anywhere in the West at that time.

Only one military informant alluded to the possibility that the United States might embark upon war. But the suggestion was not

[2] See also Günther Blumentritt, *Deutsches Soldatentum im europäischen Rahmen,* Giessen, 1952, pp. 50ff.

[3] Leo Freiherr Geyr von Schweppenburg, *Die grosse Frage,* Berlin [n.d.], p. 22.

explicit; he merely said that "many people" in Germany were convinced "that the Americans would go to war some day, to exploit their arms superiority, and that German rearmament merely served as preparation for war." In general, however, the military were not, in 1952, concerned about the possibility of preventive war. They did not believe that the United States had the intention or the Soviet Union the ability to unleash another world war.

Two years later, the picture had changed.

Preventive War: 1954

In the spring of 1954, prompted by Secretary Dulles' doctrine of "massive retaliation," by the possibility of American intervention in Indochina, and, to a lesser extent, by a number of American statements on preventive war, apprehension that war might break out was more intense and widespread in Germany than it had been at any time since the communist invasion of South Korea.[4] Soviet designs to expand the domain of communism were held to be a lesser danger to world peace than the American interest in arresting the communist drive for world power. Opinions of this sort were by no means confined to communist fellow-travelers or to observers predisposed to underrate the danger of communism. They were shared by many Germans with anticommunist and pro-Western sentiments. Except for some on a "lunatic" fringe, no German accused the United States of aggressive intent, yet many judicious observers believed that American foreign policy was jeopardizing peace. This danger was attributed to the emotionalism of American policy, to its moralistic bent, and to American carelessness in calculating the risks and consequences of war.

All the qualities in which American foreign policy was found wanting were held to be characteristic of Soviet policy. While inher-

[4] On May 15, 1954, John Cowles proposed in a speech at Rochester, New York, that the United States should proceed to war in case the Soviet Union were to reject complete disarmament. Beginning on May 24, 1954, Stewart and Joseph Alsop published a series of articles in their syndicated newspaper column to the effect that the United States had lost strategic leadership and military superiority to the Soviet Union; soon the United States would have to choose between capitulation, preventive war, and a forced struggle for survival, they said. On May 25 the Alsops wrote that the possibility of preventive war was being seriously considered in high government circles. A speech generally understood as advocating preventive war was given by Adm. Robert B. Carney, Chief of Staff of the Navy, on May 27, 1954. While the speech had not been approved in the White House, the State and Defense departments had examined the text and had raised no security objections.

ently more noxious, the latter was deemed a lesser menace to peace because of the constraint and aversion to adventurism reflected in it. It was feared that United States policy might plunge the world into war as a result of adventurism and emotionalism rather than by rational design, whereas communist caution and rationality were considered to be reliable safeguards against any precipitate execution of admittedly worrisome long-range plans. Given their concern with the preservation of peace, therefore, many Germans were terrified by their strongest ally. In public discussions of world affairs in Germany in 1954, the Western coalition was pictured as an arrangement in which the United States was the most powerful but the least reasonable ally, while the undeniable weakness of the Western European powers was balanced by their superior political wisdom. There was no certainty, however, that the United States would avail itself of this wisdom. In some sensational publications, the fear of American rashness reached hysterical proportions.

Members of the military class did not fall prey to this hysteria. Quite a few of them, however, spontaneously raised the issue of preventive war in conversations, and discussed it without passion, if not without bias. Their views on preventive war were, of course, not expressed in public. This is another major illustration of the divergence of private from public opinion on military issues in Germany.

To those German generals who are well read in the literature of their profession, the subject of preventive war is less repugnant than it is to many civilians. Neither advocacy nor rejection of preventive war is necessarily associated in their minds with strong moral feelings. Preventive war seems to them, rather, a technical problem of warfare.

The greater the ignorance of the destructiveness of modern weapons, the easier it is to discuss dispassionately the advantages and disadvantages of preventive war. From a purely military point of view, preventive war deprives the enemy of the advantage of surprise by striking before he is optimally prepared to strike himself. Several German officers remarked that European history contains many useful lessons on the subject of preventive war, and occasionally they referred to the opinions of the elder Moltke on the subject. Most of them, however, were aware that the age in which grand strategy was a purely military concern had passed, and that technology had changed since Moltke's day. They felt, if only dimly, that preventive atomic war presented problems that differed from those that had accompanied the preventive wars of the past.

Those who expressed opinions on preventive war in conversation usually began by saying that the United States was faced with the prospect of losing its decisive superiority in the weapons of mass destruction. Thus it was not the American superiority in unconventional weapons, but, precisely, the impending *loss* of that superiority, that prompted their interest in the subject. No informant considered that the Soviet Union might resort to preventive war, partly because the Soviet Union was still held to lack the requisite strength, and partly because it was believed that it could attain its political ends by other means. All the comments revolved around the possibility of an American surprise attack.

The discussions were about the possible origins of preventive war, rather than about its political or military consequences. Popular fear and executive action were singled out as possible causes of a preventive attack by the United States. It was pointed out that the American people's confidence in the efficacy of deterrence might fade if they realized fully the danger of growing Soviet strength in unconventional weapons. One informant recalled standing on top of the Empire State Building sometime in 1952 and thinking how easily New York could be destroyed by an atomic attack. "These are facts to be reckoned with. Once they are fully appreciated in the United States, and as Soviet capabilities increase, it will be difficult to find fault with a policy that seeks to remove this terrible danger."

Preventive war might also be triggered by purely executive action, some thought. Some incident in the cold war might exhaust American patience. An "ultimatum" might be issued by the United States government which would lead to war. It is interesting to note that this observer believed that an ultimatum would precede an actual attack; even in fear or anger the United States would not act with unmitigated rashness.

But these views were not firmly held. Later in the conversation, the same informant who had spoken of the ultimatum considered it quite conceivable that the United States and the Soviet Union might eventually attain some kind of thermonuclear balance, "a state of mutual deterrence which might buttress peace, just as the two pillars of a Gothic arch support a tremendous weight." But specifically on the subject of preventive war, he agreed with others that the strongest incentive to it was not the possession of overwhelming superiority, but rather the impending loss of American preponderance in the field of nuclear armaments and the mounting realization of the American people that they were exposed to the danger of suddent, violent death and terrible destruction.

Another informant found it difficult to discover grounds for hope that the United States could hold communism in check and continue to exercise the power of unilateral deterrence. "Perhaps it is best to throw all available A-bombs upon the Soviet Union now, before it is too late," he said, to which a participant in the conversation replied, "You will have to abolish Christianity in America first."

A high-ranking general considered it possible that the President might inveigle the United States into preventive war. He agreed that it was necessary to consider soberly the consequences of the developing atomic parity between the United States and the Soviet Union. In the past, the American monopoly in atomic weapons was rightly regarded as a guarantee of peace, he said, though it was not the sole one. But the growing strength of the U.S.S.R. in this field favored preventive war by the United States before parity was attained. "This is only logical," he said, "but consider what tremendous responsibility rests upon those who have to act."

He held it unlikely that any president of the United States could "simply push the button" to unleash war. Then he added that "in the future, a president might imitate President Roosevelt's political performance that led to Pearl Harbor." Influenced by some American writings on the subject, this general believed that President Roosevelt had intentionally provoked the Japanese into striking at Pearl Harbor, thus making it possible for him to put on them the onus of the war which he secretly desired. The general believed that Roosevelt had manipulated the outbreak of the war and succeeded in concealing its essentially preventive nature, though he did not explain why, if that was the case, Pearl Harbor was not alerted to the danger in any way. In the future, he went on, it might be neither possible nor necessary to invite an atomic Pearl Harbor; a lesser incident might suffice to carry the nation into a war in which American preventive action would appear as defensive retaliation. In expressing this view, the general was not advocating preventive war; but, by ascribing Machiavellian statecraft to the U.S. government, he managed to combine the moral comfort of dissociating himself from Machiavellianism with the intellectual satisfaction of appreciating its working. The conflict between the United States and the Soviet Union thus gave him a double opportunity to nurse his anti-American feelings. So long as the United States did not embark upon preventive war, he could regard its position as precarious; if it should be embroiled in such a war, he could hold it to be immoral. In either case, the United States was saddled with the dilemma of power, which Germany, the loser in two world wars, could watch with innocence and yet with a superior knowledge of the need for amorality in foreign policy.

The view that America might exploit some minor incident or even fabricate one in order to launch a preventive war was not an exceptional one in 1954. A high official in the Blank Office, holding pro-Western views, at least on the surface, expressed the same opinion and added that "quite a few people" in Germany thought this way. Thus he attributed a view which implied grave doubts of American political morality to an anonymous "quite a few"—a rhetorical device frequently used by those who seek to disguise their own hostile or unpopular feelings.

In general, none of the military observers were well informed about, or especially interested in, the constitutional checks upon presidential decisions in the United States. Compared to "the President" and "the people," Congress seems to lead a shadowy existence in the German military mind. Just as the role of Congressional resistance to American intervention in Indochina was virtually overlooked in favor of Eden's and Churchill's caution on that issue, so the role that Congress might play in supporting or checking any popular trend or Executive inclination toward preventive war did not come into view in these conversations.[5] Perhaps this blind spot indicates that, to the German military mind, the conduct of foreign affairs is not affected by the character of domestic political institutions: whether or not a government is democratic, foreign policy is made, it seems, by the happy few who have power.

One civilian, however, a leading German theologian, did inquire about the Congressional resistance that an adventurous president

[5] A former German general asked the interviewer whether it was true that Congress had played no role in preserving peace, and that, had it not been for Churchill and Eden, there would have been a world war.

might encounter. He wondered whether, under the impact of atomic developments, traditional American abhorrence of preventive war might vanish. His question was prompted by the controversy then going on in the United States over the so-called "Bricker Amendment," which sought additional constitutional safeguards against the possibility of unrestrained foreign-policy moves by an American president. The informant felt that, if the President could act independently of Congress in an emergency, the gate might be open to preventive war. In any event, under modern technological conditions, he added, it would not be possible to distinguish between aggressive and defensive war; the concepts familiar from past moral theology and international law no longer applied.

German officers did not seem to give much thought to the political consequences of preventive war upon allies and neutrals. This omission cannot be attributed altogether to narrowness of professional interest, since on many occasions these officers freely expressed their private opinions on politicians, policies, and political issues. Probably the omission was due to a deeply rooted professional belief that in war, force supersedes politics. The political or psychological repercussions of preventive war were not disregarded in all the conversations, however. When they were mentioned, they were deemed disadvantageous to the aggressor, much as he might benefit militarily from surprise. Thus the relationship of military and political factors was presented as a dilemma. One informant expressed it neatly: "If the United States starts World War III, it has half lost it psychologically. If it does not start World War III, it has half lost it militarily."

The theme of preventive war did not recur in any of the conversations held in the autumn of 1955, just as it had not arisen in 1952. In 1955, with growing awareness of the destructiveness of thermonuclear weapons, considerations of preventive war had receded into the background. Coexistence, rather than unilateral deterrence, was now viewed as the mark of the age.

Limited and Unlimited War: 1954–1955

The reaction to the policy of massive retaliation announced by Secretary Dulles on January 12, 1954, was more favorable among the German military than among most civilian observers, because the former welcomed American firmness vis-à-vis the Soviet Union, while the latter feared war. Several former German officers commented that the New Look was "not really so new," inasmuch as the United States had been relying all along on its strategic air power instead of building up its ground forces as well. Others simply regarded the policy of massive retaliation as sound in view of the deplorable and dangerous Western weakness in ground forces and of United States strength in naval and air power. However, in one way or another, all of them indicated that they considered the policy to be a cold-war move rather than a grand strategy for war. When the crisis in Indochina did not lead to U.S. intervention, it became still more apparent to them that American foreign policy labored under considerable national and international difficulties, and that its deeds were more restrained than its words.

Thus the relation between limited and unlimited war remained in the center of German military attention, despite the fact that the policy of massive retaliation, at least in the form in which it was originally announced, had implied restriction of American freedom of action to the choice between peace or all-out war. Some German military observers suggested as early as 1954 that, with the approaching parity in nuclear weapons, the danger facing the West was that of a series of peripheral wars "waged by proxies [of the great powers] or in some other way, permitting the two main powers to ration their participation in war so carefully as to avoid total war between them." A young former staff officer suggested that, for Germany, too, the real danger might lie in a possible satellite attack, by the forces of East Germany, Czechoslovakia, or Poland, rather than in a direct attack by Russia, and he added that in that case the Western reaction might well be less than massive.

But this view, and the doubt it implied about the seriousness of American intentions, was exceptional. Most military observers believed that communist aggression against Western Europe, by whatever nation, would lead to all-out war. The closest some informants came to the young staff officer's question regarding the U.S. resolution to defend Europe was in inquiring about the possibility that American isolationism would be revived, and in differentiating between the trigger effect of local aggression in various areas of the world. For example, one of them, who did believe that a communist attack on Western Europe would lead to general war, doubted that an aggression on Iran would have the same result.

War may be limited, among other respects, according to the area of conflict or according to the weapons used. If the former be called "localized war," and the latter, arbitrarily, "restricted war," it may be said that German military observers in 1954 were concerned about the possibility that unrestricted, global war might come about by an extension of a localized and restricted conflict, because the United States lacked the forces to fight peripheral wars with conventional weapons. In fact, they considered it more probable that a global war would come about in this way than as a result of an American preventive attack against the Soviet Union. Civilian observers, however, often failed to see a difference between these two possible ways in which unlimited violence could originate, since in either case, they held, the United States would in fact be initiating unrestricted world war. But whereas many civilians were quick to interpret such possible action as resulting from American *lack of concern* about the horrors of war, military observers attributed it rather to a *weakness* of the American defense posture, which permitted the United States no choice other than between localized war, with the odds against it, and the holocaust of war, unlimited as to both weapons and area.

Toward the end of 1955, the relation between limited and unlimited war continued to interest German military observers. Speculation about the outbreak of unrestricted global war, however, had changed in three important respects since 1954: the possibility that the United States might embark upon preventive war appeared considerably less likely and "realistic" than it had eighteen months earlier; it was no longer taken for granted that only conventional weapons would be used in a limited war; and, with new weapons developments, it became possible to distinguish between tactical and strategic use of nuclear weapons.

Between 1954 and 1955 there had been much talk about the so-called "relaxation of tension" in the cold war, and the possibility of preventive war appeared to recede. In addition, the possibility that the United States might seek to forestall imminent Soviet achievement of nuclear parity had vanished in the belief that, for all practical purposes, parity already existed. When, in 1955, the subject of preventive war came up at all in conversations with the military, it did so in the new context of "mutual deterrence" and with the substitution of the term "surprise" for "preventive action."

It was pointed out that the historically unprecedented importance of the first strike to the outcome of unrestricted global war had rendered the question of aggressive *intention* less meaningful than ever before. In two world wars it had been possible to take the offensive, attain resounding victories, and yet be defeated in the end, years later. In the future, however, the first offensive action might well decide the outcome of the war, so that the power that was not, morally, the aggressor "must yet attack and strike the first blow if it wants to be successful." Thus, once the outbreak of unrestricted global war appeared close, "it would hardly matter whether a nation was criminally imperialistic or peaceable"—it would have to try to strike first in any case.

Even so, the attacker would run risks infinitely greater than those usual in the past, because the enemy might survive the surprise attack with a reduced yet still fearful power to retaliate in kind. As one informant put it, "war has become impractical." In short, while in 1954 preventive war was viewed with interest and held to be morally reprehensible but militarily effective, in 1955 it was considered less interesting, morally indifferent, and extremely hazardous—hazardous, indeed, to the point of ineffectiveness. The concept of preventive war had changed into that of pre-emptive action—that is, an action designed to exploit the advantage of surprise, without assurance, however, that the military benefits of surprise would in fact attend it.

German military observers saw the need for pre-emptive action in case of imminent war as a technical military, rather than as a moral, problem. They judged the issue in terms of capability rather than intention. Some of them noted, in this connection, that Soviet military writers were apparently revising their old military doctrine, according to which surprise was judged to be less important in war than were "permanently operating factors" such as military organization, economic strength, morale, and so on.[6] In July, 1955, an article appeared in the *Frankfurter Allgemeine Zeitung* which

[6] For a discussion of this doctrine, see R. L. Garthoff, *Soviet Military Doctrine,* The RAND Corporation (Santa Monica, California), Report R-223, May 1, 1953 (out of print); also published in book form by The Free Press, Glencoe, Ill., 1953.

argued that the Soviet leaders no longer seemed to adhere to their classical defensive strategy which had, in the wars against Charles XII, Napoleon, and Hitler, used the fierce Russian winter and vast, roadless Russian expanses to exhaust and defeat the invader. Soviet military writers, too, were discussing surprise. The author of the article reviewed statements by Isayev, Shatilov, and Rotmistrov.

At the beginning of 1955, Isayev had warned the British and French of the fate their countries would suffer in the event of atomic war. In view of Soviet capabilities in intercontinental jet bombers, American strategists as well, Isayev added, would be ill-advised to expect their country to remain safe. Shatilov had "for the first time" criticized "widespread [Soviet] military thinking in merely defensive categories," and had taken to task "some comrades" who refused to consider defending the Soviet Union by military activity "in enemy space." Finally, Marshal A. Rotmistrov had publicly criticized the wisdom of defending the Soviet Union by sacrificing its own territory, which, according to the idealized Soviet picture, was the plan that had been followed in the first period of the war against the Germans in 1941 and 1942. The author of the German article reviewed these statements and concluded: "It cannot be judged how long this new spirit of a quick reaction against American strategic formulae has been cultivated among Soviet leaders"; it should be taken for granted, however, he added, that prior to the publication of these statements in the Soviet press careful consideration was given to the momentous issues discussed.[7] It was characteristic of the German daily and professional press at the time that it paid little further attention to these matters.

In addition to the change in emphasis on preventive action, the views on the outbreak of unrestricted global war differed in 1955 from those of 1954 in two other respects. These can be considered together. In 1955 military observers no longer took it for granted that only conventional weapons would be used in limited wars, and they had become aware of the development of nuclear weapons to a point that required differentiation between "small" and "large" warheads, and between "tactical" and "strategic" weapons. This distinction still left much to be desired, but it led to novel appraisals of the relationship between local and global wars, and to more sophisticated

[7] Arthur W. Just, "Auch die Russen sprechen von Überraschung," *Frankfurter Allgemeine Zeitung,* July 9, 1955.

speculations about the way in which unrestricted global war might break out. This increased sophistication was due, in part, to additional information on nuclear weapons that German readers had obtained in 1954 and 1955. In large part, however, the change was induced by events that had dramatized the problems of atomic and thermonuclear warfare: by the official announcement in December, 1954, that NATO would plan for the use of atomic weapons in the defense of Europe; by the atomic exercise CARTE BLANCHE of June, 1955; and by the fierce public criticism of NATO strategy by Colonel von Bonin.

Several informants observed that "small atomic weapons" now had to be included in the category of conventional weapons in the sense that their use in the future would have to be taken for granted in both local and global wars. This belief was based on the opinion that the outcome of the restricted peripheral wars that had occurred after World War II had been disappointing to all belligerents, and that the big powers were engaged in adapting their conventional forces to the conditions of atomic warfare; the latter process was referred to as "transarmament" (*Umrüstung*). The first Soviet announcement in 1955 of a reduction of their armed forces by 640,000 men, for example, was generally regarded not as a step toward disarmament, but as a measure to *strengthen* the Soviet army by such transarmament.[8]

The only distinction, then, that it seemed meaningful to make with regard to weapons was between the use and nonuse of "*large* atomic and thermonuclear warheads" in *global* war. The types of war were thus reduced to three: (1) global war without use of large atomic and thermonuclear weapons; (2) global war including use of large nuclear weapons; and (3) local war (in which *small* atomic weapons would be used). Without exception, "local war" meant war outside Europe; any war in Europe was regarded as a phase of global war.

Very few informants believed that another global war fought only with classical and small atomic weapons was likely. In 1954 German civilians had sometimes expressed the opinion that, in another world war, the belligerents might refrain from using thermonuclear weapons, just as they had refrained from the use of poison gas in

[8] See Erich Dethleffsen, "Atomwaffen und Ost-West Konflikt," *Offene Welt,* January, 1956, pp. 10 and 12.

World War II. Even in military circles this possibility had not been entirely dismissed at the time, although, upon reflection, military observers usually subscribed to Field Marshal Montgomery's view that while the hydrogen bomb had increased the fear of war and thus made peace more secure, its use in global war, if one occurred, was certain. The latter view had become fairly general by 1955.

Also in 1955, as a result of political efforts at coexistence under conditions approaching or constituting nuclear parity, it was judged less likely than in previous years that a global war would break out without being preceded by a local war. The concern was no longer that the peace would be suddenly broken by global war, but rather that a world war might develop out of a peripheral conflict. This danger would have appeared particularly great to those who assumed that the big powers would not abstain from using "small" atomic weapons in local wars, had it not been tempered by their belief that this very probability would deter communist aggression in peripheral areas as well as in Europe.

It was generally felt, however, that the United States might lose control over the course of events if it got involved in another peripheral war. The source of this feeling was never fully revealed, but the feeling could be inferred from various contradictory expectations that were expressed. For one thing, German military observers believed that if the United States were drawn into another local war as a result of Soviet aggression, American nuclear strength would have lower deterrent power than it had had in the past. By the very decision to attack in a peripheral area, the Soviet Union would be showing disrespect for the American deterrent capability; such a decision might indicate that the Soviet leaders were confident of their ability to neutralize the threat of strategic retaliation by a corresponding counterthreat of their own. In addition, German observers intimated that, for two reasons, the United States itself would find it difficult not to enlarge the scope of a local war in which it was a belligerent. In the first place, it was likely to lack the military resources to win the small war, and might therefore be driven to enlarge it in the hope that its strategic capability would decide the issue. The second reason given was more emotional in nature, and might have been interpreted as expressing an anti-American attitude were it not for the probability that it had some deeper source associated with avalanche fantasies. The argument was that, by employing tactical atomic weapons in a local war, the United States would in effect be lowering the barrier to the use of bigger, even more destructive, weapons. Once this was done, the temptation to go on to the hidden perils of chaos would be great, if not irresistible. This fear may be linked to the feeling that man has overreached himself by harnessing the new, fearfully destructive, and ultimately uncontrollable forces of nature to his purposes. By an inexorable logic, according to this premonition, nature might revenge herself by depriving man of his own self-control. Having challenged fate by venturing into its forbidden recesses, man would be ruled by fate.

There were a few military observers, however, who doubted that small atomic weapons would be regarded as conventional, or that their use in future local wars could be taken for granted. One of them pointed out that "if a power wanted to reach limited objectives without running the risk of pulling the trigger of unrestricted global war, it would impose upon itself constraints in the use of weapons. The dividing line between tactical and strategic atomic weapons is fluid. Once a conflict started with the use of any atomic weapon, there would be danger that it would spread, not only geographically, but also by resort to more powerful atomic weapons." The few informants who argued along this line concluded, therefore, that the likelihood of local *atomic* wars had *decreased* in proportion to the increase in availability and destructiveness of the "large" thermonuclear weapons possessed by both sides.

Another conclusion that can be drawn from the near-achievement of nuclear parity, and from the developing conventionality of tactical atomic weapons, was not fully considered by German military observers, regardless of the view they held on the likelihood of local atomic wars. It would have been possible to argue that, since both the Soviet Union and the United States had to reckon with the possibility of their own destruction in case of unrestricted global war, the United States would seek to avoid getting itself involved directly in future local wars. But German military observers failed to distinguish between peripheral wars, such as that in Korea, in which the United States was a belligerent, and local wars, such as that in Indochina, in which the United States did not participate. They also failed to detect the possibility and examine the impact on the East-West struggle of a third kind of local war, such as one, say, between

Egypt and Israel, in which neither the Soviet Union nor the United States participated. It may be surmised that not even the occurrence of the second and third types of local war was readily imagined by German officers because it would have betokened isolationism on the part of the United States, the prospect of which aroused dormant apprehensions.[9]

This review of German military opinions on the relation of restricted to unrestricted war may best be concluded by presenting in some detail a German analysis, published in the leading German military monthly early in 1955, in which the relation between limited and unlimited war was examined with special attention to the situation in Europe.[10] The article dealt with the resolution of the NATO Council of December, 1954, which authorized SHAPE to *plan* for the atomic defense of Western Europe, but which reserved the decision to *use* these weapons for the Allied governments, that is, for the political authorities rather than for the Supreme Allied Commander.

The author of the article, Joachim Ruoff, distinguished between the use of (1) "strategic atomic weapons," (2) "tactical atomic weapons in Western Europe," and (3) "tactical atomic weapons elsewhere in the world." The NATO decision of December, 1954, was relevant only in the second case (although Ruoff acknowledged that the employment of strategic nuclear power from bases located in Great Britain and North Africa would require the consent of the British and French governments, respectively). In the author's view, Soviet superiority in ground strength was a compelling reason for employing tactical atomic weapons to defend Western Europe in the event of Soviet attack, regardless of whether or not the Red forces themselves used atomic weapons in their attack. The older Western strategy of December, 1952, which underlay the ambitious Lisbon force goals for NATO, had envisioned a nonatomic, conventional defense of Europe, but this plan had had to be changed in 1954, for it was realized that only the atomic weapons of the West, rather than any increase in its ground strength, could tip the military balance of East and West in Europe. Realistically viewed, then, given

[9] See also Frido von Senger und Etterlin, "Eine neue Form der Kriegskunst," *Aussenpolitik,* January, 1956, pp. 25–32.
[10] Joachim Ruoff, "Atomwaffeneinsatz mit Vorbehalt," *Wehrkunde,* February, 1955.

any Soviet attack on Europe, the West's choice lay between atomic resistance or defeat; it no longer had freedom to choose between use and nonuse of atomic weapons.

Ruoff distinguished further between the *right* of governments to decide whether or not their countries were at war, and their *prerogative,* once in a war, to stipulate that the only suitable defensive weapon could or could not be used. He acknowledged the right, but declared that the claimed prerogative was "a novelty." He attributed insistence on this unprecedented prerogative to the fear of European governments that "the use of atomic weapons in defense may lead to retaliatory atomic attacks [by the Soviets] upon industry and population centers"; but, he remarked, the decision of the NATO Council "simply ignored the fact that there is no alternative to defense with atomic weapons other than capitulation."

Ruoff then proceeded to examine the argument that the use of atomic weapons in a local conflict would enlarge that conflict and lead to world war. He asserted that, generally, the danger of enlargement was independent of the kind of weapons used in a local conflict, and that, specifically, in Europe, nonatomic as well as atomic war might lead to global conflict. "The danger resides not in the use of atomic weapons, but in the deliberate decision to extend the local conflict," and this danger, he added, had not been removed by the resolution of the NATO Council to make the defensive use of atomic weapons dependent on governmental decision.

Ruoff pointed out that the political prerogative of the NATO governments to decide what weapons should be used in defense only after an attack has occurred has been justified also on the ground that it would keep the Soviet leaders in doubt about the character of any war they might initiate. Uncertainty as to whether or not atomic weapons would be used in the defense of Europe, this argument runs, might induce them not to employ atomic weapons in their attack. Ruoff regarded this argument, too, as "unrealistic." He argued that the aggressor

must in any case take account of the possibility that the West will employ atomic weapons tactically and strategically, though possibly after some delay, whenever the comprehensive nature of the conflict has been recognized. Hence, the aggressor does not need to decide whether the whole war will be waged without atomic weapons, but only whether or not it is advantageous for him to abstain from immediate strategic and tactical use of atomic weapons. Such abstention renders operations with numerically superior conventional forces against a weak opponent possible only until such time as the defense resorts to atomic weapons. The advantage to the stronger land power of such an initial conventional phase is counterbalanced by the considerable risk involved in permitting the defense to employ its strategic atomic power undamaged, and at a time of its choosing.[11]

Evidently Ruoff based his analysis on the assumption, which was ignored in the December, 1954, decision of the NATO Council, that the Soviet Union could not attack Western Europe unless it was prepared to embark on world war, even though it could not be *certain* in advance that war in Europe would in fact lead to world war.

He refined his analysis by examining the implications for European defense of a Soviet decision to wage war under three different assumptions regarding the balance of power between East and West: (1) Soviet superiority in weapons of all kinds; (2) Soviet superiority in classical arms and equality with the United States in atomic armament; and (3) Soviet superiority in classical arms and inferiority in atomic weapons.

In the first case, Ruoff argued, no successful defense would be possible. A Soviet victory by conventional means would be assured, provided that the Soviet superiority in atomic weapons was so great "as to prevent reliably the defensive use of atomic weapons which would invite [Soviet] retaliation."

The second case would put a premium on surprise at the very beginning of the war, for the objective would be to destroy the Western atomic potential. If the aggressor failed to resort to sudden surprise attack, he would risk having his own nuclear power destroyed, which might in turn neutralize or reverse his superiority in conventional weapons.

The same reasoning would apply to the third case. Since the aggressor would now run a higher risk, however, due to the atomic superiority of the defense, he would have to strike even harder at the atomic potential of the enemy to transform his inferiority into superiority.

Thus the author of the article again reached the general conclusion that "once the possibility is excluded that the defense is initially ready to capitulate, the aggressor must employ at least [*sic!*] his

[11] Ruoff, *op. cit.*

strategic weapons in sudden attack at the *outbreak* of war. He is compelled to act thus not by the resolution of the defender to employ [tactical] atomic weapons in defense, but by the fact that the defender *possesses strategic* atomic weapons." [12] In other words, considering the threat of an American strategic nuclear capability from the viewpoint of the Soviet leaders, the author concluded that only a successful surprise blow against the United States would meet the strategic prerequisites of a Soviet conquest of Europe.

What, we may ask, if these requirements were disregarded by the Soviet leaders? We have already seen that, in Ruoff's view, any other strategy would be hazardous and disadvantageous for the Soviet Union. Ruoff did not consider whether a reduction of risk and disadvantage sufficient to justify a different Soviet strategy might result from American withdrawal from NATO. Nor did he consider the possibility that, in certain circumstances, the Soviet leaders might think it unlikely that the United States would be willing to unleash nuclear war in response to a local communist attack in Europe. He argued that the Soviet leaders would face the irreducible risk of a strategic strike at Soviet targets, if ever they attacked any NATO power in Europe. This risk would force the Soviet leaders either to abstain from aggression altogether, or to be prepared to strike at the United States as well as Europe. Third, the author did not examine the specific political or military circumstances in which the Soviet leaders might believe that the United States would not be willing to initiate a total war for the sake of Europe. For example, if the Soviets expected a swift collapse of European resistance, they might conclude that the chances of a successful attack on Europe would be heightened rather than lowered if they abstained from a simultaneous nuclear strike at the United States. He only discussed the consequences, *for Europe,* of the opening phase of a war in which the Soviet Union would employ conventional arms and the NATO powers would delay the defensive use of atomic weapons in accordance with the Council's decision. He pointed out that, in such a case, Western inferiority in ground forces would lead to loss of territory at the beginning of the war. In particular, West Germany would be overrun quickly, and the effective defense of other European countries would be jeopardized, because warfare under such conditions "would inevitably lead either to retreat of the NATO

[12] Ruoff, *op. cit.;* italics added.

forces without battle, or to their quick disintegration. In either case, the essential prerequisites for the defense of Western Europe would be lost, and no later approval of the use of atomic weapons could compensate for that loss."

Hence Ruoff's conclusion: "In these circumstances it appears more practical from the first to give the Supreme Commander of the NATO forces a free hand to use these [atomic] means of war."

In conversations held in 1955, several German military leaders elaborated this weighty conclusion without endorsing it explicitly. They pointed out that, once the Supreme Commander were given authority to use atomic weapons, there would remain the task of delegating this authority to lower echelons in the air, ground, and naval forces. Several informants observed that the decision to use atomic weapons could not possibly be left to lower commands. In part, this view may have reflected resistance to the trend of conventionalizing atomic weapons, and in part it may have been inspired by the conviction that the relative destructiveness of weapons must correspond to the military rank of the men entitled to use them: the more powerful a weapon, the higher the rank requisite for its employment. Otherwise, order in both the zone of battle and the military hierarchy might be endangered.

The evidence at our disposal does not suffice, however, to state with assurance that German military leaders as a group wished to see the Supreme Commander of the NATO forces, rather than civilian governments, entrusted with primary responsibility for employment of atomic weapons in the defense of Europe.

SEVEN

The Character of World War III

During the early fifties, the views of former German military leaders about future wars appeared to be inspired by their World War II experiences. They envisaged another world war as a long and far-flung struggle in which the Western coalition would start out by being inferior in ground forces, but which it would win in the end because of its vast war potential, its command of the seas, and its domination of the air. The German generals had doubts about the effectiveness of atomic strategic bombing, and, to the extent that they did not ignore it, they held the tactical application of atomic power to be impractical. They assumed that conventional forces would ultimately determine the outcome of World War III.

These views have been slow to change under the impact of nuclear developments, but former officers in the younger age groups and military critics outside the Defense Ministry have begun to attack the strategic notions inherited from the past. The older generation have continued to stress the importance of conventional arms, but they have confined themselves in recent years to arguing for the importance of conventional armament in terms of *German* security needs. Questions of *global* strategy have receded into the background.

As late as 1954, the concern of German military leaders about German security centered around the danger of a Soviet tank assault. Although they did not believe in the imminence of war, the army generals were prone to dramatize the exposure of West Germany to the Soviet threat by talking about the time that it would take Red armored forces to reach West German cities. They did not measure the threat in minutes of advance warning or flying time, but in "tank-hours." "Hamburg is only one tank-hour away from the Iron Curtain, Frankfurt only two tank-hours." They thought that the forced crossing of the Rhine, perhaps in the neighborhood of Bingen or Worms, might be an early objective of the Red forces. The decision in Europe would thus be reached somewhere between the Iron Curtain and the Rhine.

Once the Rhine was crossed, according to this opinion, the Russians would have little difficulty in rolling on to the Atlantic coast, from which "it would take years to drive them off." Hence not only the defense of West Germany but the course of the whole war was expected to be determined by the ability of the Western ground forces to defend German territory in the early stages "with the highest degree of mobility." [1] The first phase of the war was envisaged as a replica of early tank battles in World War II, while the image of the later phases appeared to be modeled after the reconquest of Western Europe by Allied forces.

Since Germany was unarmed in the early fifties, the estimates of successful defense of West German territory in the event of an early outbreak of war were anything but reassuring. However, when the issue of German rearmament was raised, most German military leaders abstained from carrying their concern to the public, with the major exception of Heinz Guderian, who attacked and ridiculed Western defense plans. Some of his colleagues characterized Guderian as a firebrand whose *political* views should not be taken seriously; others adopted an ambivalent attitude toward him, praising his past military accomplishments and deploring his defiant opposition to German rearmament plans. As one of them put it in 1952, "Guderian is worth reading. He should not be read by the Germans, however, but by the Americans."

The poor prospects for the defense of West Germany in the event of war did not, on the whole, lead German generals to make defeatist or pessimistic predictions about the outcome. For a number of reasons, they believed that a successful strategy of Western European defense was not beyond reach. Since they were confident that war was not imminent, they saw all time gained as an opportunity to increase the strength of the West. They believed that every Ger-

[1] For an authoritative public statement of this view, see A. Heusinger, "Die Verteidigung Westeuropas," *Bonner Hefte*, October 15, 1953.

man division put under arms would somewhat reduce the danger of Soviet occupation and enable Allied military leaders to defend Germany farther to the east.

The generals also believed that, with twelve German divisions and Allied assistance, it might be possible to halt a Soviet advance in Europe. They remembered that even toward the end of World War II German soldiers had fought at the eastern front with dogged determination, had not panicked, and had often scored local successes against formidable odds. Moreover, high-ranking staff officers put much stock in the possibility of winning a campaign against an enemy superior in manpower by outmatching him in generalship. Their confidence in the quality of German military leadership had not been shaken. Some former generals believed that a Soviet pincers might be cut off by well-trained, competently led German and Allied armor, according to a plan of highly mobile defense.

Such hopes were heightened by certain estimates of Soviet strategy.[2] Soviet leaders were not assumed to be adventurers, as Hitler was. If they decided on war, they were expected to be cautious enough to choose a strategy that would involve the least possible risk of ultimate defeat. Their approach to military as well as political problems was also assumed to be "more global" than that of other powers. The German strategists, therefore, did not believe it likely that Soviet forces would begin a war by attacking Central Europe without guarding their flanks. They thought the Soviet Union would consider itself ringed by Western air bases from which air power could attack the most vital Soviet targets—"railroads running from east to west through Poland, the traffic center of Moscow, the oil at Baku, and the industrial centers around Krivoi Rog and at the Donets"[3]—and dominate the long flanks of a Soviet advance in Central Europe. Since Western control of Asia Minor, North Africa, Spain, England, Greenland, and Okinawa was viewed as balancing in great part the Bolshevik superiority in land forces, the generals did not believe that the Kremlin could afford to launch a thrust

[2] See especially the views of Generals Dethleffsen, Blumentritt, and von Sodenstern and of Admiral Heye, in Adelbert Weinstein, *Armee ohne Pathos,* Bonn, 1951, Chap. I; Erich Dethleffsen, *Das Wagnis der Freiheit,* Stuttgart, 1952 (of which an English version was published in *Foreign Affairs,* April, 1952); and Georg von Sodenstern, "Strategische Gedanken zur Gegenwart," *Wehrwissenschaftliche Rundschau,* May, 1951.

[3] Erich Dethleffsen, in Adelbert Weinstein, *Armee ohne Pathos,* p. 23.

against the West German and French industrial areas without first securing the Mediterranean area. Nor did they think that the Russians could bypass Scandinavia.[4]

According to this view, the Russians would realize that a decision could be reached only if they succeeded in occupying and staying in Scandinavia, Germany, Holland, Belgium, France, Italy, Spain, the North African coast, the Suez Canal, the Balkans, Arabia, Turkey, and Persia.[5] Thus, in the opinion of these German observers, even a successful Soviet drive to the Atlantic would not guarantee the Russians final victory unless they first secured the Scandinavian and Mediterranean flanks. Such a drive could not therefore be the sole objective in the Soviet war plan, so that Soviet military action on the flanks of Europe would help equalize the balance of forces facing each other in Western Europe.

The German generals who engaged in these various speculations concluded that the superior Soviet strength in ground forces was not sufficient to make up, in a world-wide contest, for Western superiority in air and sea power. Rather than attack in Europe,

. . . if Russia were to believe that she had to create better starting conditions for a war that she either deemed inevitable or that she intended to wage, then she would try to do so by aggression in Asia Minor with a push to the Suez Canal.[6]

These views met with some criticism. An important military official in the Blank Office pointed out that the kind of strategic reasoning imputed to the Soviets represented only the way the German General Staff would approach the problem. He added, "One can only hope the Russians would approach it the same way." Another defense official seemed to miss the point of the argument somewhat by remarking that possession of Middle Eastern oil would be of little use to the Soviets as long as they lacked tankers to ship it. Some former generals who were critical of "the land-bound strategy" of the former German General Staff pointed out that victories on land are no longer decisive in war. The last world war, they said, had shown clearly that mobile mass armies could maintain themselves on the conquered parts of a continent only if they could rely on the

[4] Sodenstern, op. cit.
[5] Dethleffsen, in Weinstein, op. cit., Chap. I.
[6] Ibid., p. 25.

support of naval power. Domination of the sea had become the primary aim of strategy.[7]

While the emphasis on the importance of the Middle East was correct in the opinion of most German military leaders who talked about the strategic problems of another world war, some of them believed that Soviet possession of the Atlantic coastline would constitute a most serious threat to the Allied command of the sea. This view was held in particular by naval officers, of course, but a former German commander of armored forces also regarded the establishment of Soviet submarine and air bases on the Atlantic coast, or in Scandinavia, as the greatest threat to the West as a whole, even greater than "the destruction of the whole string of Western European capitals, such as London, The Hague, Brussels, Paris, Bern, from Russian rocket bases on the Rhine. . . ."[8]

Despite these differences of opinion, German strategic thinking in the early fifties had five outstanding general characteristics:

1. The defense of West Germany was envisioned as part of the more general problem of the defense of the West in a global war. The possibility of local war in Central Europe was disregarded. This attitude reflected confidence in the solidarity of the West based on common interests. West Germany was judged to be so important that the Soviet leaders would not dare regard it as a suitable theater of localized war (as they would Asia Minor in the aforementioned analysis); correspondingly, Germany was held to be too crucial an area to be surrendered by the West (as Czechoslovakia had been) or to be defended by the West merely on a local scale (as in Korea).

2. No serious doubts were entertained that the West would win a global war in the end.

3. It was believed possible, but not inevitable, that German forces would have to yield German territory at the beginning of the war and continue fighting for victory elsewhere. This grim prospect was faced calmly by German generals when the conversation turned to the subject; occasionally it was alluded to even in professional military writings.

Thus General Günther Blumentritt, who publicly supported EDC

[7] See also Frido von Senger und Etterlin, "Von Schlieffen zur Europa Armee," *Aussenpolitik,* March, 1952.

[8] Leo Freiherr Geyr von Schweppenburg, "Will They Attack?" in *The Western Defenses,* ed. Brig. J. A. Smyth, London [n.d.; probably 1951], p. 31.

from the beginning, pointed out in 1952 that in case of a withdrawal according to plan not only German territory but also other areas might be lost.[9] General von Sodenstern wrote in 1952 that the defense of Europe

can always be understood only as a part of the strategic task of the Anglo-Saxon general staff. What weight is to be attributed to it . . . will not be determined by the need for security of the Europeans but by the prevailing total situation. . . .

It goes without saying that an American or British-American "strategic concept," in view of the fronts to be guarded, must attempt to hold together the forces and means of combat for use at a central point. . . . It is possible that this central point will be located in Europe. But it need not be so.[10]

4. It was widely though not generally believed that armies would continue to play a decisive role in the future. Naval and air forces were held to have merely important supporting functions. While the importance of air power in future war was recognized, no occasion was lost to point out that air power would not *decide* the war. Importance was attributed to the interdiction of ground operations by air power and to the reduction by air bombardment of the enemy war potential. But when the subject of war in the air was discussed in conversation, speaker after speaker emphasized that air power was "not war-decisive."

This view was held despite the fact that both the American industrial potential and the advanced bases of the United States ringing the Soviet Union were considered indispensable for winning the war in the end. Relatively little attention was paid, and little importance attributed, to air bases in the United States, or to intercontinental bombing. It appeared that the phrase "not war-decisive" meant that air power could not break the will of the Soviet leaders to continue the war, could not force a cessation of war by crippling the Soviet war-making capacity, and was unable to occupy and hold enemy territory.

5. These views, often justified by reference to the experience of the last world war, were not modified in the light of the superiority of the United States over the Soviet Union in atomic weapons.

[9] Günther Blumentritt, *Deutsches Soldatentum im europäischen Rahmen,* Giessen, 1952.
[10] Georg von Sodenstern, "Die strategische Lage der Welt," *Wehrwissenschaftliche Rundschau,* March, 1952.

In the early fifties, very few German military observers attributed to atomic weapons any revolutionary influence upon warfare.[11] On the contrary, quite a few German experts of high military standing doubted or belittled the effectiveness of atomic weapons. They thought atomic weapons unsuitable for "tactical" purposes because of their radiation effects, and they belittled their strategic significance because of a general bias against strategic air power.

Some of the opinions expressed in the early fifties make strange reading today. For example, Felix M. Steiner, a former SS general, wrote in 1951:

[In 1945] the A-bomb appeared to be the invention of a decisive weapon. But had the [last world] war not really been decided already when it was released? For Germany had capitulated and the Japanese were so cornered in their island [sic] that they were incapable of any liberating operation. World public opinion, however, attributed the ending of the war to the A-bomb and has grown used to considering its possession the recipe of victory. If the bomb can be thrown by both sides, all unilateral hopes disappear suddenly. Is it not even possible *that both sides will anxiously refrain from employing it again?*

The author added:

Incidentally, the conditions which prevailed when the A-bomb was used in 1945 have been decisively altered.[12]

After some vague references to efforts at measures of "thorough" protection against atomic warfare which industrialized countries had allegedly made by dispersing their industries and relocating them in relatively inaccessible areas, Steiner concluded blandly, "It appears that under special conditions of [geographical] space the A-bomb has already lost its decisive importance in war." [13]

Steiner argued in all seriousness that the efficiency of the atomic weapons was too low to warrant their use. In his opinion, neither A-bombs nor rockets could contain or neutralize "the marching

[11] Exceptions to these views were taken by Leo Freiherr Geyr von Schweppenburg, one of the few army generals who said in 1951 that the outcome of the next war would be decided by long-range air forces carrying atomic warheads ("Will They Attack?" *op. cit.*, p. 31), and by naval officers who emphasized that another global war would be an encounter between the Soviet Union as a land power and the Western coalition which commanded the sea.

[12] Felix M. Steiner, *Die Wehridee des Abendlandes*, Wiesbaden, 1951, p. 46; italics in original.

[13] *Ibid.*

potential" of the enemy. This could be done in the future, as in the past, only by ground forces, that is, by relatively small, highly mobile, armored units (rather than by motorized divisions). Supported by integrated tactical air forces and complemented by airborne troops, these mobile forces, he said, would be "the standard arm" of the future.

General Halder, former Chief of Staff of the German army, stated his opinion on the subject of atomic weapons in a book, written in the form of a conversation between himself and two young visitors who sought the opinion of the aged general on the past history of the German army and the future of Germany. When Halder was asked, "What about the atom bomb or the hydrogen bomb? Could it not be that it will not be used at all?" he answered,

Be that as it may . . . one can throw atom bombs—insofar as their effect can be judged from news in the press—only in places where forces will certainly not meet in combat. One can throw them only on targets one does not want to occupy. The A-bomb can therefore be used for purposes of denial; e.g., the Russians can use it to blockade the south of England, to cause inundations at the coasts in south England, north Germany, and Holland; the Americans to cut off Russian reserves. . . . We could have used it to neutralize the almost uninhabited and to us almost inaccessible area of the Pripet marshes. . . .[14]

General Guderian, another former Chief of Staff of the German army, spoke in a similar vein. Like General Halder, he believed that atomic weapons could not be used in the vicinity of one's own troops because of the fallout danger.[15] While Guderian admitted that the effect of atomic and hydrogen weapons would be especially great on "mass targets," it appeared "more than doubtful" to him "that the effect of these weapons will be sufficient [sic] against the extensive space of Eurasia."[16]

Thus the gist of these opinions was that atomic power would not decide a future war; that atomic weapons were primarily area-denial weapons and could not directly influence the result of combat; and that the Soviet Union would be well prepared to meet the danger of these weapons. In conversations, in which the last argument was further explored, it transpired that the Soviet Union was

[14] Peter Bor, *Gespräche mit Halder,* Wiesbaden, 1950, p. 248.
[15] Heinz Guderian, *So geht es nicht,* Heidelberg, 1951, p. 23.
[16] Heinz Guderian, *Kann Westeuropa verteidigt werden?* Göttingen, 1950, p. 61.

quite generally considered less vulnerable to atomic attacks than was the United States because of the larger size of its territory, the wider dispersal of its industrial capacity, and because of the greater hardiness and lower living standard of its population.

Ever since the spring of 1952, German military observers could have realized, had they wished, that the old NATO strategy based on the Lisbon goals for ground forces was likely to be revised in favor of plans for an atomic defense of Europe. The first "tactical" atomic bomb, with ground soldiers near the site of explosion, was tested in Yucca Flats, Nevada, on April 22, 1953. The event was widely reported in Germany.[17] The previous September, Winston Churchill had suggested to the United States that "with increased air power and atomic weapons a considerably smaller number of ground forces than the ninety-six divisions originally envisaged would be sufficient to defend Europe."[18] In February, 1953, British General Sir Richard Gale discussed in public the possibility of the tactical use of atomic weapons,[19] and in testimony before the Senate Foreign Relations Committee on April 1, 1953, General Gruenther did the same in considerable detail.[20] The first battery of atomic guns was stationed in Germany in September, 1953,[21] and three months later President Eisenhower spoke of the "conventional" character of tactical atomic weapons.

By 1954 it became clear that SHAPE was seeking NATO authorization to use atomic weapons in the event of war. An army-air force atomic exercise, under the facetious code name BATTLE ROYAL, was held in the British Zone of Germany in October. In the same month, Field Marshal Montgomery, in a lecture widely commented on in both the West and the Soviet Union, expressed his firm belief that air power would be the dominant factor in future war, and that atomic and thermonuclear weapons would be used in the event of a Soviet attack. Early in December, 1954, SHAPE was authorized

[17] It should be noted, however, that the German press missed the possible implications of this event for European defense. Of more than thirty of the most widely read West German daily papers that reported the news, only one, *Süddeutsche Zeitung,* carried an editorial, and it merely criticized the fact that the test had been televised in the United States.

[18] *The Economist,* November 22, 1952, p. 539, quoted in Wing Cmdr. J. D. Warne, *N.A.T.O. and Its Prospects,* New York, 1954, p. 41.

[19] *The New York Times,* February 25, 1953.

[20] Testimony of Gen. Alfred M. Gruenther, *Hearing before the Committee on Foreign Relations,* U.S. Senate, April 1, 1953.

[21] *Manchester Guardian,* September 19, 1953.

to base its military defense plans on the use of tactical atomic weapons.

As to the development of strategic nuclear capabilities, the increase in the destructive power of unconventional weapons that had taken place since the end of World War II was no secret to the average newspaper reader in Germany, let alone to the professional soldier. President Eisenhower's statement of December, 1953, that the new weapons were twenty-five times as efficient as the bombs exploded at Hiroshima and Nagasaki was soon made obsolete by announcements of new tests. At the time the President spoke, Malenkov had already claimed Soviet possession of the H-bomb and the breaking of the American monopoly, and Vishinsky had declared that the idea of the atomic superiority of the West was nothing but a fairy tale.[22] Perhaps the latter claim could have been dismissed as propaganda at the time, but ever since the beginning of 1954 German military observers had known of various authoritative American statements, such as that by Secretary Dulles, to the effect that the Russians could succeed within a few years in eliminating the American lead in unconventional weapons.[23]

The acquisition of a tactical atomic capability by NATO clearly was a challenge to German military observers to re-examine the traditional doctrines of conventional arms and their military worth. The strategy of global war also had to be re-examined, as the stockpiles of atomic and thermonuclear weapons grew on both sides of the Iron Curtain. Most of the older German military leaders, however, were very slow in appreciating these massive facts and rapid developments in the field of unconventional armaments.

In conversations in 1954 it appeared sometimes that these military leaders were simply uninterested in informing themselves about the new developments. One of the best summaries of American, British, and German information on the development of atomic power and "the revolution in modern warfare" was written by a younger former German officer and published in easily accessible form in the spring of 1954. Yet it was unknown to all but one of the generals, inside and outside the Blank Office, visited by the present author a month after it appeared.[24]

[22] Malenkov's statement was made on August 8, 1953; Vishinsky's, on November 27, 1953.
[23] John Foster Dulles, "Policy for Security and Peace," *Foreign Affairs,* Vol. XXXII, No. 3 (April, 1954).
[24] "Atombilanz 1953," anonymous article in *Das Parlament,* April 21, 1953.

Most surprising was the response of some older German military leaders to the H-bomb test at Bikini on March 1, 1954. The fate of the Japanese fishermen on the "Lucky Dragon," who had suffered from the fallout of the Castle test, created a major sensation in all of Europe. In the German press, the treatment of this disaster and the fantasies induced by it about the American threat to the future of mankind were surpassed only by the press comments on the NATO atomic exercise CARTE BLANCHE more than a year later. Former German generals did not appear to share the excitement. It seemed at first that their attitudes reflected professional detachment and sobriety, but upon closer investigation it became evident that many older leaders regarded the whole affair not as an event from which military lessons might be derived, but rather as something illustrating the sensational character of the press.

One of the generals, who in 1950 had minimized the military value of atomic weapons, now said:

There are two schools of thought in the United States concerning atomic and thermonuclear weapons. One school, composed of pacifists, creates fear by exaggerating the effectiveness of these weapons. The other school tries to give the impression that the effect of these weapons is less terrible than the alarmists claim it is. The truth, of course, is secret. It probably lies somewhere in the middle.

He agreed with some other generals that the development of modern weapons required a unified civil defense on a supranational scale, but as he amplified his view it appeared not to be taken specifically in the light of that development:

If another war were to break out, millions of people would take flight blindly toward the West. They would clog the highways and no military movement would be possible. Your tanks would not operate, and all military movement would be seriously disrupted. The Russians would not care. They would strafe the highways to clear them; you would not do so.

Opinions such as this differed from those of the Social Democrats who, in view of the development of atomic power, urged adoption of civil-defense measures for political and humanitarian reasons. The general insisted on civil defense mainly as a way of avoiding obstacles to the military conduct of war on the ground. The lesson he drew from the development of atomic weapons was only that like other weapons they would strike terror into the hearts of civilians.[25]

Interestingly enough, the few former German officers who were better informed than their colleagues about the development of nuclear weapons were generally skeptical about the stability of *military* morale under conditions of modern combat. One of them considered it possible that the morale of Soviet ground forces would collapse in Western Europe, if their homeland was devastated by the American Strategic Air Command. Older German military leaders who tended to regard only *civilian* morale as unstable rejected this idea: military forces could not be demoralized. This difference in the assessment of the morale effects of atomic power in times of war, like the differential interest in atomic weapons, appeared to be a function of service as well as of age. The older generation of army officers expressed the most traditional views and were most strongly at variance with younger officers of the former *Luftwaffe*.

In 1954 it was hard to escape the conclusion that, as in 1950 to 1952, many older German military leaders still approached the subject of atomic and thermonuclear air power with certain prejudices formed in the past which prevented their appreciation of the nuclear revolution in warfare. They had not forgotten that the former army General Staff had rejected Douhet's doctrine that air power could win wars. Perhaps past interservice rivalries and social, political, and military criticism of the German *Luftwaffe* under Göring still colored their views of modern air power. Probably their belief that German military prowess had been humbled at the western front by the sheer weight of American industrial might was readily associated with resentment of the idea that industrial power, rather than generalship, could determine the shape of war in the future. And certainly there was professional reluctance to admit that weapons outside the jurisdiction of one's own service might lower its military worth in relation to that of other arms.

The conservatism of the older leaders was undoubtedly strengthened by the younger military critics, who spoke about the nuclear revolution of warfare, attacked the rearmament policy of the Bonn

---

[25] In some other instances this expectation was justified by military observers in their attributing a lasting damaging effect on the morale of German civilians to Allied bombing of German cities in the last war.

government, assisted the Social Democratic opposition in their political fights, and came up with some absurd conclusions concerning
the worthlessness of conventional arms. This became evident in the
summer of 1955, at the time of NATO atomic exercise CARTE
BLANCHE, in which the second and fourth Allied Tactical Air Forces
and other air force units participated.

The exercise was held in Holland, Belgium, northeastern France,
and West Germany. It lasted from June 20 to June 28. Before it
was completed, Adelbert Weinstein, a former General Staff officer
with the rank of major, had formed and spread his opinion that
the NATO doctrine of using tactical atomic weapons to compensate
for Western inferiority in ground-force strength had rendered all
former military theories of defense invalid. Since the Soviet Union
as well as the United States had atomic weapons, he said, there
would not be any classical warfare in Europe, but a "classical
atomic war" with the terrifying prospect of "automatically rendering
the whole Federal Republic a combat zone." [26]

Colonel von Bonin, too, characterized CARTE BLANCHE as "the
last warning" to the Germans:

The NATO leadership has resolved to turn Germany in the event of
war into an atomic battlefield. . . .
Have we become so cynical that we remain unmoved by the figures
of 1.7 million dead and 3.5 million wounded Germans, that would have
resulted [if CARTE BLANCHE had been a wartime action rather than a
maneuver] according to the cautious and certainly far too conservative
estimate of the men in command of the exercise? [27]

Weinstein pointed out that, as atomic weapons became more
abundant, they would entirely replace conventional arms. He characterized the planning activities in the Blank Office under General
Heusinger as hopelessly out of date and did not spare German
military traditions at large:

German military history belongs to the past and will not be continued, because the atomic weapons are revolutionizing everything. . . .

[26] Adelbert Weinstein, "So stellt man sich den Krieg der Zukunft vor," *Frankfurter Allgemeine Zeitung,* June 22, 1955. A journalist told the interviewer that Weinstein left the
maneuver on the first day because he believed he had a story and had nothing further to learn.
[27] Bogislav von Bonin, *Atomkrieg—unser Ende,* Düsseldorf, 1956, pp. 22ff.

We are not sure that at the present our Defense Ministry has any advisers who recognize the change in strategy which the atomic development has brought about.[28]

Weinstein's arguments were repeated by many other journalists. If these critics had confined themselves to urging a revision of German defense planning so that the new ground forces could meet the conditions of atomic warfare, or if they had merely warned that the projected armament for the German forces would delay the adaptation of German defense to those conditions, they might have encountered a kinder reception, at least among officers outside the Blank Office. Many of the generals supported the Defense Ministry in December, 1955, when a revision of German defense plans in the light of atomic developments was officially announced. But Weinstein and other journalists went much farther. They joined the neutralist camp and advanced anti-American and defeatist arguments which at least by implication questioned whether NATO had any value for Germany, and whether conventional rearmament made any sense whatever. Weinstein contended that even forces organized and trained for atomic warfare could not meet German security needs: the entire effort to protect German security had better be devoted to passive civil defense, he concluded. Moreover, he suggested that there was no safety for Europe in the possible destruction of the Soviet long-range air force by SAC, since the Soviet Union, though crippled and unable to strike back at the United States, might still be able to attack U.S. advanced bases and to devastate Europe.[29]

German military leaders thought little of Weinstein's competence. They said that his opinions were subject to frequent and erratic changes, and they deplored the attention given him by high American civilian and military authorities who granted him interviews both in the United States and in SHAPE. Whatever merit Weinstein's arguments had was almost entirely lost on German officers in consequence of his attacks on conventional rearmament at large. While the military leaders refrained at the time from publicly

[28] Adelbert Weinstein, in a symposium on "The German Soldiers," *Der Monat,* August, 1955, p. 432.

[29] Adelbert Weinstein, "Wir müssen umdenken," *Frankfurter Allgemeine Zeitung,* July 7, 1955.

expressing their own opinions about atomic war in Europe, they sided with the government in insisting that civil defense alone would never meet German security needs.

The best German account of CARTE BLANCHE was published anonymously in the military monthly *Wehrkunde,* the organ of the *Gesellschaft für Wehrkunde,* which supported the government armament policy. It summed up the lessons of the maneuver as follows:

1. Atomic defense has become an "irrevocable fact" in NATO plans.

2. CARTE BLANCHE has confirmed the thesis "which of course is neither new nor entirely uncontroversial" that "the preponderant role" in future war will be played by air power.

3. Missiles are not likely to replace air power, "since they do not allow such rapid changes in target choice and such a wide range of destructive effects as does air power."

4. CARTE BLANCHE was not intended to demonstrate and did not demonstrate that ground forces would be "superfluous and without value or outdated in the future"; but "it appears necessary to give new thought to their organization, armament, training, and use on the battlefield, and it is indeed true that these ideas will deviate considerably from traditional conceptions."

5. In view of the relatively small maneuver area, it would be "hasty" to conclude from CARTE BLANCHE that "every war in the future would last only a few days."

6. It is probable, however, that in the initial phase of a future war both sides will attempt to attain domination of the air "in order to destroy the air power of the enemy and to gain freedom in the full use of atomic weapons."

7. CARTE BLANCHE demonstrated certain weaknesses of NATO's air defense with regard to the operations of all-weather fighters, in the employment of fighter craft for bombing missions, and in respect to the vulnerability of air bases in Western Europe. The latter would be "ideal targets" for the enemy because of the dependence of present aircraft on runways.

In conclusion, the author of the article reassured his readers, somewhat less than cogently, that "the 400 bombs whose drop was simulated in Western Europe did not prove that in the event of war West Germany would be reduced to 'shambles and ashes.'

For these 400 bombs were bombs from the arsenal of NATO; their use is planned for countering aggression from the east. The meaning of their employment [in CARTE BLANCHE] lay undoubtedly in demonstrating to a possible opponent the superiority [of NATO] in quantity and in the art of employment [of atomic bombs] and in spoiling his taste for any aggression." [30]

It is impossible to say to what extent German military leaders outside the government subscribed to these conclusions. Weinstein's arguments were used by the socialists in the *Bundestag* when the lessons of CARTE BLANCHE were debated. General Heusinger, Theodor Blank, and the former army officers among the *Bundestag* deputies who defended NATO and the government policy did not fare too well in that debate.[31] In describing the role of atomic power they were less specific, and in estimating its relation to conventional forces less open-minded, than the anonymous author of the article on CARTE BLANCHE had been. It is possible, however, that the parliamentary fight in which military officials and parliamentarians rushed to Adenauer's defense forced them to exaggerate their conservative views.

In any event, by the end of 1955 it appeared that all professional officers regarded the tactical atomic weapons available to NATO as an integral part of Western defense, but neither the German government nor former German officers showed any interest at that time in the equipment of the *Bundeswehr* with such weapons. Tactical atomic firepower was held not to replace but to improve conventional armament; small tactical atomic weapons were thus accepted as "conventional." "Unconventionality" now attached principally to large warheads or to hydrogen bombs and to their strategic employment.

Some generals also qualified the doctrine they had held in the early fifties that nuclear air power would not be "war-decisive." They now admitted that "atomic attacks" could have a decisive effect in certain circumstances. For example, General Blumentritt,

[30] "Luftmanöver 'Carte Blanche' im Kommandobereich Mitteleuropa," *Wehrkunde,* July and August, 1955. The quotations are from the August issue, p. 352. (The figure of 400 simulated bombs dropped in CARTE BLANCHE as given in *Wehrkunde* was higher than that mentioned in the parliamentary debates on the exercise and elsewhere in the German press.) Another somewhat more propagandistic attempt to draw lessons from CARTE BLANCHE in support of German rearmament in NATO was made by A. W. Uhlig, *Atom—Angst oder Hoffnung? Die Lehren des ersten Atommanövers der Welt,* Munich, 1955.
[31] See Chap. 10.

in a booklet entitled *Impact of Atomic Technology on Politics and Economics,* continued to express uncertainty as to whether atomic and hydrogen weapons would be used *strategically* in another world war. He still doubted that strategic bombing of Soviet targets could force a decision, because of the vastness of Russia, the indifference of her peoples to death, and the dictatorial nature of her regime. He added, however, that the effect of strategic bombing on areas densely populated by "softer and more sensitive" people than the "robust" Russians would "certainly be an annihilating one." "We need only think of our small Western Europe or of the British Isles. There the effect could be decisive." [32]

The official views of the German government on the grand strategy of the West remained unchanged. They continued to be based on the conviction that the interests of German and European security were integrally connected with those of the United States, and that a Soviet attack on Germany would lead to U.S. thermonuclear strikes against Russia. As late as September, 1956, Theodor Blank reaffirmed this opinion before the German public. In describing the unconventional aspects of modern war, he used the familiar symbols of ancient combat. He referred to long-range thermonuclear weapons as "the sword" and called European defense, geared to tactical atomic warfare, "the shield." Thus the picture of global war faded into the image of a duel between two Homeric warriors. In this image, it was difficult to identify the nature and conduct of the enemy, who was called "the aggressor." Against him "the sword" would be wielded under the protection of "the shield," whether the enemy attacked with classical or modern weapons, and whether he was Russian or not. Finally, Blank's image of future global war was quite hazy on the wounds that the enemy might be able to inflict with his own "sword" in the event of a nuclear duel:

NATO strategy rests on the basic idea of sword and shield with reference to the large area on both sides of the Atlantic which is to be defended jointly. The sword consists of the modern nuclear and long-range weapons. These are primarily in the hands of that country which possesses sufficient financial means and possibilities for their development and production. That country is the U.S.A. The sword serves pri-

[32] Günther Blumentritt, *Einwirkung der Atomtechnik auf Politik und Wirtschaft,* Schriftenreihe zur Wehrpolitik, No. 9, Bad Godesberg, January, 1956, p. 5.

marily to deter every possible aggressor and is therefore a decisive means for maintaining the peace. Should aggression occur nevertheless, the sword weapons [*sic*], by a powerful counterstroke, can prevent the aggressor from continuing the combat. This sword is in need, however, of protection by the shield on the European continent. This shield protects the radar stations, the instruments of command, and the gun positions (*Abschussbasen*) of the modern weapons. At the same time it protects our own territory against the quick grasp of enemy forces. Carriers of the shield are the ground forces, the means of air defense, and, for the Federal Republic, light naval forces for the protection of the exits from the Baltic Sea. Sword and shield condition and complement one another. Beyond a certain measure, neither can be weakened at the expense of the other.[33]

To what extent did Germany's military leaders subscribe to these views in the fall of 1956? In July, they still insisted on Germany's need for conventional ground forces, and they supported the government, which claimed in the parliamentary debate on conscription that a German contribution of conventional forces to NATO would render unconventional war less likely.[34] But it will be remembered that as early as the spring of 1954 there were German military leaders who believed that the approaching parity in nuclear weapons favored the Soviet Union rather then the United States in the *peacetime* struggle for power. Even then, they feared that the flexibility of U.S. foreign and military policy in areas *outside Europe* would be restricted by increasing American reliance on unconventional weapons.

It is certain that in 1956 this concern was heightened, shortly after the *Bundestag* cast its vote in favor of conscription, by the public disclosure of the Radford Plan, which implied the possibility that American manpower *in Europe* would be reduced in the future.

Finally, by 1955 at the latest, some military observers had begun to re-examine on military grounds the value of the United States as a military ally of Germany and Europe. These observers viewed the nature of global war and American grand strategy in a way that was at variance with the notions they had entertained in the early fifties, and they disputed the government's ideas about "sword"

[33] "Bundesverteidigungsminister Theodor Blank über Probleme der Umrüstung" (in an interview for the West German Broadcasting Network, September 23, 1956), *Wehrkunde,* October, 1956, p. 511.
[34] See Chap. 11.

and "shield" in the coalition. Specifically, some German military leaders began to consider seriously that American grand strategy might either want or be forced to move in the direction of a disengagement from European affairs in peacetime, and to concentrate instead on long-range defense of the United States in the event of global war.[35]

The disintegration of, or a lasting crisis in, the NATO alliance would create circumstances in which these views could become prevalent not only in the German military class, but also in Germany at large. Such a development would appear to be independent of the outcome of the next German election in the fall of 1957 and of the complexion of the German government thereafter, because German military policy will continue to be influenced more strongly by world events, and particularly by the balance of power between the United States and the Soviet Union, than by the number of German people who vote the socialist ticket.

[35] See Chap. 13.

Part II

The Views of the Politicians

EIGHT

From EDC to WEU: 1952–1954

Although the socialists have voted against ratification of all treaties on German rearmanent, and have opposed many legislative measures designed to enable the Federal Republic to honor its international obligations, the Social Democratic Party does not reject rearmament in principle. The pacifists in its ranks or among its leaders have never determined the policy of the party. Nor did the *Sozialdemokratische Partei Deutschlands* (SPD) always claim that the reunification of Germany must take precedence over rearmament. Socialist pressure for reunification assumed importance in German politics only when EDC was put forward as a compromise substitute for the original American proposal to create a national German army. EDC, which it was hoped would mollify the French and yet satisfy the Germans, was accepted by the German government parties but aroused the socialists, because they believed that rearmament in the context of a Western alliance would eliminate chances of reunification.

Under the forceful leadership of Kurt Schumacher, the original socialist policy on rearmament had only two main tenets. The socialists wanted adequate protection of West Germany against the danger of Soviet aggression, and they were opposed to rearmament so long as Germany remained in any way under the tutelage of the victors in World War II.

According to Schumacher, adequate protection of German security required the stationing of very large forces in Germany. For that reason, Schumacher proposed that the United States prove the seriousness of its concern about the Soviet danger by sending many more divisions than Congress had yet authorized to stand guard against aggression. This view was shared in 1950 by General Guderian and other high-ranking German officers. Remembering the large number of German divisions that had fought on the eastern front in World War II, these generals considered the addition of a mere ten or twelve German divisions to the ground forces of the West a woefully inadequate measure.

Socialists and some generals at that time also joined in urging greater national independence for Germany. At the beginning of the debate on rearmament in November, 1950, when the price the West would pay for German participation in European defense was not yet certain, Guderian rushed into print to denounce the "bankruptcy" of Yalta and Potsdam, and to insist on freedom and equality for Germany. He ridiculed the military posture of the West, which in his opinion was so weak that it did not even merit the name of defense. He advocated a Western European union that was to include Great Britain and the Scandinavian countries, and he urged expansion of the Western European "base of operations" by the integration of "the African space" into the European defense system. In a later pamphlet, published in 1951, Guderian attacked Adenauer, and insisted that re-establishment of a free, unified, and neutralized Germany was more urgent than the formation of West German contingents for European defense.[1] Many of Guderian's political arguments have since been repeated by the Social Democrats.

Schumacher believed that Germany would have to be defended at the Vistula instead of at the Rhine. In order to protect West Germany against Soviet attack and occupation, and in order to render liberation in a later phase of the war unnecessary, he held that defense would have to take the form of a counterattack, which would require ground forces sufficiently strong to take the offensive. Again, at that time, many German officers found Schumacher's reasoning basically sound.

Yet Schumacher's ideas must be considered demagogical, since he must have realized that the U.S. government would regard his force goals as utopian. He could hardly have failed to see that an American attempt to meet his demand would have put the United States on a war footing and might have induced the Soviet leaders

[1] Heinz Guderian, *Kann Westeuropa verteidigt werden?* Göttingen, 1950; *idem, So geht es nicht,* Heidelberg, 1951.

to embark upon preventive war. Franz-Josef Strauss, in the July, 1952, debate, still scoffed at the socialists for Schumacher's suggestion that the West should launch an attack in the area of the Vistula and the Niemen in the event of war. The government never tired of claiming that German rearmament would have a purely defensive and deterrent character. Rearmament, they said, would avoid war. But from the beginning, the government failed to inform the *Bundestag* and the German public precisely what form the defense of Germany would take, if deterrence should fail.

There was some German discussion of this issue in 1952, but it was limited to a small circle of military experts who derived their ideas from the experiences of World War II and from doctrines cherished by the former German General Staff. The ideas centered either on the defensive strength of so-called "hedgehog" positions or on small, highly mobile armored forces that were to harass and cut off the pincers of an enemy advance. Some military critics thought little of these ideas. One general commented sarcastically in an interview, "Of course, according to the tradition of the German General Staff, no military task is insoluble. Mass can be neutralized by mobility, and the most powerful enemy be defeated by superior German generalship."

Other German military observers pointed out in conversation that parts or all of West Germany might well have to be surrendered to the enemy at the beginning of a war, but that it was important not to lose sight of the larger strategic objectives: the defense of Europe as a whole, and eventual victory. It is perhaps understandable that the government did not wish to discuss in public the disconcerting possibility of a retreat toward the West, but by remaining silent it beclouded the strategic aspects of German rearmament. There is some evidence from interviews conducted in the spring of 1952 that these aspects were not faced squarely in the Blank Office itself.

Schumacher's early conception of defense by counterattack in Europe was one of the few genuine military alternatives to retaliation by the American Strategic Air Force that had been advanced in the German public debate on the defense of Germany. It soon vanished from the debate, however, because public discussion focused on the political aspects of rearmament. By July, 1952, most of the socialists warned that rearmament within EDC might provoke the Russians, would render reunification impossible, and would leave Germany a victim of political discrimination by the Western powers. With few exceptions, former German generals now supported the rearmament policy of the government, not because they preferred EDC to a national army, but because they preferred rearmament to continued demilitarization.[2]

Schumacher's views about the effect of German rearmament on relations with the Western nations proved to be almost entirely wrong. Until his death in August, 1952, he took a rigidly defiant attitude toward the participation of West Germany in the defense of Europe, because he held that by occupying Germany the Western powers had assumed the responsibility for protecting Germany against aggression. If they now found themselves in conflict with the Soviet Union, Schumacher argued, they would have to settle this conflict without the support of occupied Germany, or else first restore Germany's sovereignty and then explore her interest in contributing to the common defense of Europe against Bolshevism. In the opinion of the socialists, any other procedure was tainted with intolerable indignity and left uncertain the question of whether the Western powers would relax their grip on Germany.

As in the earlier case of its fight against German participation in the Schuman Pool, the SPD attacked the government for its submission to the Western policy of granting Germany certain limited political rights in order to exact commitments from her in exchange. They pictured participation in EDC as a price to be paid for abolition of the Occupation Statute, referring to this "tie-in" procedure as the U.S. policy of the *"junctim."* [3] Carlo Schmid wrote:

Each time the occupying powers decide to discontinue some regulation which has become unbearable, they make the action, entirely appropriate on its own merits, subject to the assumption by the Germans of obligations which a free nation would not normally be asked to accept.[4]

Evidently this socialist view was moralistic rather than political in character. It disclosed a feeling of righteousness on the part

[2] The exceptions are illustrated in the book by Hugo C. Backhaus, *Wehrkraft im Zwiespalt,* Göttingen, 1952.

[3] See the report which Willy Brandt gave to the *Bundestag* on December 3, 1952, about the position taken by the Social Democratic minority in the *Bundestag* Committee for the Occupation Statute and Foreign Affairs, *Bundestag Record,* December 3, 1952, p. 11111.

[4] Carlo Schmid, "Germany and Europe—The German Social Democratic Program," *Foreign Affairs,* July, 1952, pp. 535–536.

of the opposition, but showed little understanding of the distribution of power among victors and vanquished. CSU Deputy Franz-Josef Strauss said in a *Bundestag* debate that the Social Democrats wanted "all or nothing"—that they overlooked the fact that the only alternatives open to Germany were "the possible or nothing."[5] And again, with effective sarcasm—

One cannot demand either of the Federal Government or of Dr. Adenauer that seven years after the war he should win . . . the second World War.[6]

From the beginning, Adenauer and his party promoted the idea of German rearmament because they believed that by meeting the wishes of the Western powers West Germany could further her own interests. She could rid herself of the shackles of occupation, gain the confidence and the protection of the Western allies, and banish forever the age-old conflict with France. As late as February, 1955, Adenauer revealed to a British journalist that his political imagination owed much to the prewar spirit of Locarno:

I first expressed my ideas on European integration and a conciliation between France and Germany in 1925, and I pleaded the same ideas before the Reich Cabinet of Marx, which was in office at that time. I was motivated by the conviction that it was essential for Germany and France—and for Europe—to make an end to senseless strife. I have championed this cause since that time in my various offices and as a private person, and I have also dedicated my policy as Federal Chancellor to its service. In a Franco-German understanding I see the essential prerequisite for the unification of Europe. . . .[7]

Since the Germans were not anxious to bear arms again, and since the socialist opposition to rearmament was extremely vocal, the Bonn government was able to drive a hard bargain with the Western powers in the negotiations about EDC. This was revealed in Strauss's statement in the July, 1952, debate:

One cannot discuss what has been accomplished in Paris [by the government] . . . because this would lead to the most severe attacks upon the French government in Paris.[8]

[5] *Bundestag Record,* July 10, 1952, p. 9863.
[6] *Ibid.,* p. 9852.
[7] Quoted in Alistair Horne, *Return to Power*, New York, 1956, p. 405.
[8] *Bundestag Record,* July 10, 1952, p. 9860.

German participation in the EDC could be attained by the West only at the price of changing her political relationship with the Western powers. The Occupation Statute was superseded by the Contractual Agreement, and the so-called "Germany Treaty" defining the altered political status of the Federal Republic was signed along with the EDC treaty on May 27, 1952.

In his statement to the *Bundestag* on July 9, 1952, the Chancellor stated the terms of the bargain that had been concluded. He said that the Western powers could not be expected to change the Occupation Statute and thus "give up the rights which flowed from the unconditional surrender of Germany so long as the Federal Republic failed to integrate itself with the West," that is, so long as it failed to rearm.[9] He urged the deputies to consider the two treaties concerning Germany and EDC together, and to do so in the light of Germany's postwar history. Describing the road which Germany had traveled since the days of the four-power agreement at Potsdam in August, 1945, he told a dramatic story of West Germany's rapid resurrection within the power system of the West. The *Bundestag* had to decide, he said, whether or not the treaties were appropriate instruments for integrating West Germany into Western Europe. Whoever approved of the treaties would approve of the new place which West Germany could occupy as an equal partner in Western Europe. Whoever opposed them would in fact make a decision in favor of the neutralization of West Germany in the East-West conflict, and in favor of surrendering Germany's lot to the Soviet Union. Similarly, Strauss warned that the United States would withdraw from Germany, politically and militarily, if the treaties were not ratified—a warning that was sounded again in many later debates.

The government and its supporters were profoundly gratified that West Germany had ceased to be an outcast among the nations, and had acquired not only the support of the Western powers but also the prestige that went with that support. In the future, said another CDU deputy, there will be neither victors nor vanquished, but only allies.[10] Strauss said that the Germany Treaty served to liquidate the old policy of the occupation powers, while the treaty establishing EDC was part of the new policy which recognized

[9] *Ibid.*, July 9, 1952, p. 9790.
[10] Eugen Gerstenmaier, in *ibid.*, July 9, 1952, p. 9802.

the Federal Republic as a partner of the West. He regarded EDC and the Schuman Pool as steppingstones toward the pacification of Western Europe and toward a politically united Europe. To be sure, West Germany was not yet a member of NATO, but the government was confident that partnership in EDC would necessarily lead to membership in NATO, with which EDC was connected by an arrangement providing for mutual assistance. It was useless to insist, Strauss said, that the victors had assumed "total responsibility" for Germany's safety by winning "total victory": Germany herself had to assume responsibility for her future.[11]

The socialists, however, opposed the treaties venomously. In May, 1952, when the signatures were finally affixed to the treaties, Schumacher intimated that an act of treason had been committed by the Chancellor. Many Germans were evidently confused. Some politicians made headlines by calling the treaties a "super-Versailles." The opposition denied passionately that a new phase of international relations would begin for West Germany with the ratification of the treaties.

Concentrating their attack on the then unresolved Saar issue, on the failure of the Western powers to accept West Germany as an equal member in NATO, on remaining economic restrictions, and on the restrictive nature of EDC, which did not provide for the membership of Great Britain or any other Protestant power in Europe, the socialists interpreted the political meaning of the treaties as the crowning event of the occupation period. Herbert Wehner spoke of the exchange of the shackles of occupation for the shackles of alliance.[12] Instead of acknowledging the political gains that the Federal Republic had made under Adenauer's leadership, he exclaimed that through the treaties "German policy has become a function of other powers,"[13] and that there now was an increased "risk of the Koreanization of Germany."[14] With the collusion of the government, the two Germanies had been converted, another Social Democrat said, into "fortresses of the two power blocs."[15]

Regarding the strategic aspects of rearmament, the opposition charged that Germany's security would not be safeguarded by the

[11] *Ibid.*, July 10, 1952, p. 9853.
[12] Herbert Wehner, in *ibid.*, July 10, 1952, p. 9875.
[13] *Ibid.*, p. 9873.
[14] *Ibid.*, p. 9874.
[15] Fritz Erler, in *ibid.*, July 10, 1952, p. 9906.

proposed arrangements. They suspected that the rest of Europe would be favored by NATO planners at the expense of West Germany. Fears that Germany might be considered expendable and that German soldiers might be called upon to defend France rather than their own country were stimulated by Frenchmen in responsible positions and by American popular magazines. General Juin caused a stir in Germany when he was reported to have said, in December, 1952, that the Soviet forces could be in Paris in twenty-three days after the beginning of war. This statement conflicted strikingly with beliefs which the German government professed to hold. General Ridgway refused to comment on Juin's estimate at a press conference in Paris; he merely declared that he regarded the progress of the Western defense organization as "encouraging," but that he had never considered it "satisfactory." [16]

Popular and illustrated accounts in American magazines showing alleged plans for the defense of Europe at the Rhine played into the hands of the German opposition. So did popular articles on the possible use of atomic weapons. Such articles did political harm in Germany. For example, on December 5, 1952, the SPD deputy Fritz Erler, in a major speech on EDC in the *Bundestag,* embarrassed the government by saying:

> The participation of German contingents in the common armed forces makes no sense militarily, as long as the Germans cannot participate precisely as others in the political and strategic conception of the total organization, and as long as deeds do not prove that Germany is to be spared the fate of scorched earth. I ask you to read an entirely new document, the military analysis published in the *Saturday Evening Post* of November 29. . . . It is pointed out there that probably not even the line of the Rhine can be successfully defended; that one would have to consider for Europe a strategy stressing the flanks; that, so far as Germany is concerned, it will be important to retard as much as possible a Russian advance; that this will have to be done by means of a maximum of demolitions which are listed in detail, by using underground partisans and all the other means with which we have concerned ourselves before in this house. Furthermore, it is pointed out very amicably that one could of course also explain to the Russians, "If you, the Russians, cross the border, then we will just destroy your army by the hydrogen bomb, even if the civilian population of this region will un-

[16] *The New York Times,* January 8, 1953.

fortunately die too." This looks somewhat different from the offensive toward the east which has been announced to us here today.

The Federal Republic cannot genuinely participate in work on a strategic plan. Germany is no member of NATO.[17]

The government could not afford to dismiss such criticism lightly. Several speakers in the *Bundestag* who supported Adenauer's policy insisted that NATO planners would have to spare Germany the perils of becoming a battleground in the event of war:

We expect of the Federal Government that it will press successfully for a strategic conception according to which Germany cannot become the theater of a conflict.[18]

What distinguished the government speakers from the opposition was not any lack of concern about NATO strategy, but their confidence that NATO planners would surely take account of West Germany's exposed position.

It should be remembered, however, that despite occasional references by both the opposition and the government to the danger of Germany's becoming "an atomic testing ground," the image of war was shaped by recollections of World War II. In 1952, any fear of war was fear of an attack by Soviet ground forces. When German politicians referred to nuclear bombing, they thought of strategic bombing, and the possibility that tactical atomic weapons might be employed in the defense of Europe did not enter their minds.

In addition, World War II experiences dominated the thinking of the German military experts in 1952. The experts agreed with the government that German membership in NATO would be attained in due time, and they favored acceptance of EDC even though it did not provide for such membership. The military experts differed with the politicians, however, pointing out, mainly in personal conversations, that strategic plans could not and should not be discussed in public. The parliamentary debate on this aspect of the issue appeared to them as the kind of civilian folly in which parliaments habitually indulged, and, privately at least, they talked about the strategic issue in a way which suggested that their respect for the professional military planners in NATO

[17] *Bundestag Record,* December 5, 1952, p. 11478.
[18] Franz-Josef Strauss, in *ibid.,* July 19, 1952, p. 9858.

was stronger than was their deference for the Bonn government.

There is inferential proof that the socialist protest against the exclusion of Germany from NATO was not really born of concern for the security of West Germany. In 1954, Germany did become a member of NATO, and was thus able to safeguard her security interests in precisely the way that the socialists had demanded ever since 1952. But the socialists failed to acknowledge that their own demands had now been met: beginning in 1954, they opposed German rearmament, even within NATO.

In August, 1954, when the French Assembly rejected EDC, Adenauer's policy of European integration collapsed. The Chancellor never quite recovered from the blow. German nationalistic and neutralist tendencies were strengthened by the French move, as Heinrich von Brentano pointed out in the *Bundestag* on October 7, 1954. Adenauer himself interpreted the failure of EDC as the biggest tactical success of the Soviet talk about the reduction of international tensions and the possibility of coexistence.[19]

At the London Conference of the Western powers, held from September 28 to October 3, 1954, new international defense arrangements quickly replaced the plans for EDC, and they were signed in Paris on October 23. The Chancellor was gratified to be able to tell the *Bundestag* on October 7 that the London Conference had been the first since the end of World War II in which a German delegation had participated along with representatives of the great powers. In the October and December debates on the new agreements, Adenauer stressed the political gains that West Germany had made as a result of substitution of WEU for EDC. They were important gains, particularly from the viewpoint of the Social Democrats. Many of the old socialist demands had now been met. The tie-in between the restoration of German sovereignty and the German defense contribution was removed: the Federal Republic became sovereign before it joined WEU. West Germany became a member of NATO. The rights of the former occupation powers to meet any emergency in Germany with whatever measures they deemed necessary were virtually rescinded. Adenauer pointed out that the Allies had now agreed to take emergency measures for the protection of their troops only if the federal government re-

[19] *Ibid.*, December 5, 1954, p. 3121.

garded them as necessary. Nor could the number of Allied troops in Germany be increased without German concurrence.

WEU was an alliance without any anti-German features. Both Germany and Italy were assured, as were the other members of WEU, of mutual assistance in the event of aggression. The United Kingdom had committed itself to participation in the European defense system, and the possibility remained that other free powers, such as the Scandinavian countries, would join WEU. From the socialist point of view, this last feature was of major importance. EDC had been conspicuously weak in representation of Protestant powers, and the socialists had strenuously objected not only to the restrictions of EDC but also to its Catholic complexion. Adenauer added that Germany was free to engage in civilian atomic research and to exploit atomic energy for peaceful ends. She was free to produce many of the weapons that the German contingents would need, including particularly fighter aircraft.

Despite all these attainments, the Chancellor had to face the fact that his original policy of European integration had failed, for WEU was a much looser arrangement than EDC had promised to be. Heinrich von Brentano said on October 7 that his political friends regretted that they were forced to follow a road different from EDC toward the political co-ordination of European politics. Adenauer was quite eloquent in pointing out that WEU did not mean lowered aspirations for a united Europe.[20] This assertion, although undoubtedly sincere, was of small solace to those among his supporters who felt discouraged at his defeat. The replacement of EDC by WEU had shocked many members of Adenauer's own party who were ardent believers in the political promise of European integration.[21]

The FDP, the second largest party of the coalition, was satisfied with the change from Adenauer's policy of European integration to a traditional military alliance; so were many of the former generals. They preferred WEU to EDC, but Thomas Dehler, the chairman of the FDP, irritated the Chancellor by advocating the socialist line that the West should negotiate with the Soviet Union

[20] Konrad Adenauer, in *ibid.*, December 15, 1954, p. 3124.

[21] These deputies included Eugen Gerstenmaier, Chairman of the Foreign Policy Committee. Gerstenmaier was reported to have been reassured by the Chancellor's declaration of October 5, 1954, to the effect that the achievement of European unity remained the aim of the government. (*Frankfurter Allgemeine Zeitung*, October 6, 1954.)

before the treaties were ratified. Only slightly less ominous, from Adenauer's viewpoint, were the remarks made in the debate of October 7, 1954, by Hans-Joachim von Merkatz, another party leader of the coalition and chairman of the right-wing German Party, who viewed the London treaties in the light of a third-force movement in Europe. Thus the failure of EDC set into motion forces against Adenauer's policy which have been gaining momentum since. They curtailed the majority that the Chancellor commanded in the *Bundestag,* and they are almost certain to lead to substantial losses for the CDU in the elections of 1957.

In the debates of October and December, 1954, the Social Democrats celebrated the demise of EDC. They acknowledged that many of the features of EDC that they had found unacceptable were now eliminated and replaced by more desirable arrangements. But they did not go on to support rearmament within NATO. They continued to oppose the government, though partly on different grounds. They now derived one of their main arguments against rearmament from changes in the world situation. In a speech on October 7, 1954, Erich Ollenhauer advanced the thesis that the need for a German defense contribution was no longer urgent, and that the *Bundestag* could therefore await all the more patiently the outcome of negotiations with the Soviet Union on the issue of German unity, which, he said, was now more pressing than ever.

Ollenhauer's view that the danger of Soviet aggression had lessened was shared by a large part of the German people. This was the result of various events, including Stalin's death, the anti-communist uprising in East Germany on June 17, 1953, which had electrified the Germans, and, probably, the simple fact that, despite four years of Western talk about rearmament and four years of Soviet protests and attempts at intimidation, no communist intervention had occurred. According to German opinion polls, German expectations of war had steadily declined since 1950. In answer to the question, "Do you believe that there will be a new world war within the next three years?" the percentage of the respondents who considered war "probable" had dropped from 35 in 1950 to 7 in 1954, while the percentage of those who thought war "improbable" had risen from 17 to 48 in the same period (see Table 1).

TABLE 1

GERMAN ESTIMATES OF THE PROBABILITY OF A NEW WORLD
WAR WITHIN THE NEXT THREE YEARS *
(In percentages)

	1950	1951	1952	1953	1954
Probable	35	18	16	8	7
Possible	48	56	47	39	45
Improbable	17	26	37	53	48
	100	100	100	100	100

* *EMNID-Informationen,* Vol. VII, No. 1 (January 1, 1955).

In arguing that the danger of war had diminished, Ollenhauer
mentioned, among other things, the end of fighting in Korea, new
Soviet moves for control of armaments, and President Eisenhower's
proposal to establish an international agency for the peaceful use
of atomic energy. The socialist leader declared that the tendency
toward relaxation of international tensions was now far stronger
than the danger of a violent conflict between the two big power
blocs. Hence it was necessary to examine anew any German contribution to the defense of the West.

On October 23, the Soviet government proposed an international
conference on Germany, but, in the light of the failure of the
meeting of foreign ministers in Berlin early in 1954, the United
States and its major Western allies opposed a top-level conference
prior to the ratification of the London treaties. On November 29,
1954, the Western powers replied negatively to the Soviet
notes. A few days before the December debate in the *Bundestag,*
the Soviet government declared in yet another note to the Western
powers that it would not assent to holding a four-power conference
on Germany after the ratification of treaties that provided for
West German rearmament and membership in NATO.

The *Bundestag* sessions of December 15 and 16 were held under
the impact of these events. The socialists pressed the government
to work for an East-West conference at an early date. Herbert
Wehner quoted George Kennan, who had warned against membership of the Federal Republic in NATO.[22] Like Kennan and Nehru,
Wehner pointed out that the division of Germany, situated as she
was in the heart of Europe, was the greatest menace to peace.

[22] See George Kennan, "For the Defense of Europe: A New Approach," *The New York
Times Magazine,* September 12, 1954.

He added that the peaceful unification of Germany, rather than rearmament in NATO, was the prerequisite of Western security and avoidance of war. Thus the socialists, who had demanded German membership in NATO as long as the EDC arrangement precluded it, now argued that attainment of such membership, through the Paris agreements, was a danger to peace and unification.

The government stood fast. It insisted that the reunification of Germany remained a fundamental aim of the signatory powers of the new treaties. Believing in the political value of a policy of strength, Adenauer predicted that the Soviet Union would be willing to negotiate not in spite of the treaties, but because of them. Several speakers took issue with the opposition on its estimate of the Soviet menace. Heinrich von Brentano on October 7, 1954, and Adenauer himself on December 15, insisted that the free world was still in mortal danger of Soviet aggression. Adenauer and deputies from all the government parties said that communist talk about coexistence was nothing but a tactical trick of the new Soviet leaders, who were facing difficulties in both their domestic and foreign policies.[23] The difference on this point between the opposition and the coalition was well characterized by Kurt-Georg Kiesinger, who mentioned a conversation he had had with a socialist:

In the last analysis [the Social Democrat had said] what separates us is probably the expectations we Social Democrats and you [members of the CDU] entertain. You consider the Soviet Union more dangerous than we do.[24]

Former German officers differed with both the government and the opposition on the danger of war. They had not considered war imminent in 1952, and they had not revised their views in 1954. But although fluctuations in the international climate did not, in their view, affect the need for rearmament, they agreed with Adenauer that Soviet talk of coexistence was a political maneuver, beyond which the basic conflict between the Soviet orbit and the West remained an enduring fact.

[23] Konrad Adenauer, in *ibid.,* December 15, 1954, pp. 3121 and 3134; Horst Haasler, in *ibid.,* December 16, 1954, p. 3178; Hans-Joachim von Merkatz, in *ibid.,* p. 3184. Thomas Dehler, too, spoke against "coexistence."

[24] *Ibid.,* December 15, 1954, p. 3152.

By December, 1954, almost two years had passed since the United States had tested its first tactical atomic bomb at Yucca Flats. General Gruenther had testified before a Congressional committee on April 1, 1953, that NATO was looking to such weapons to neutralize its inferiority to the Soviet bloc in ground forces. Except for passing references, however, the 1954 debates in the *Bundestag* did not reflect these developments. Ollenhauer did point out that atomic and hydrogen weapons had reduced the military worth of any contribution Germany might make to European defense. The balance of power between the United States and the Soviet Union, he said, would not be affected decisively by twelve German divisions.

Characteristically, the German press failed to attach any military significance to this argument, but interpreted it, as it did Ollenhauer's charge that rearmament was less important than social insurance, as an attempt to appease those elements in the SPD that opposed rearmament on principle. On the whole, the parliamentary debate continued to center around the *political* implications of German rearmament. To the extent that its military aspects were mentioned, it was still rather generally implied that another war in Europe would follow the pattern of the last.

For example, socialist deputy Fritz Baade questioned the military value of German rearmament with unprecedented sharpness. He compared what he called the "symbolic value" of Allied troops in Germany with their real military worth. Baade acknowledged their "symbolic value" (which he used as a pejorative term for the deterrent function of the Allied forces), since their presence reminded the Soviet Union that an attack upon Western Europe would mean the outbreak of World War III. He likened their value to that of the very small Allied contingents stationed in West Berlin. Their real military value, however, was negligible, he said. If deterrence were to fail, these troops could not prevent Germany from becoming "a twice-scorched earth" [25]—once by Soviet conquest and a second time by Allied reconquest.

Reviving in part Schumacher's early argument against German rearmament, Baade then pointed out that the addition of German divisions to existing Western strength would not change the fact that the Soviet Union would still be able to overrun Western

[25] *Ibid.,* December 16, 1954, p. 3196.

Europe. What difference did German rearmament really make, then? Baade answered maliciously that German divisions would make it possible for Allied troops to execute an "orderly retreat" to the Atlantic coast, while without German help the retreat would get out of control. German troops would serve only as a "shield" to prevent losses and disorganization among the retreating British, American, and French formations. Baade claimed that General Gruenther himself had openly spoken of the fact that German troops would be a "shield" for Allied soldiers—an allegation which was, of course, promptly denied by a CDU deputy.

The speakers for the coalition met Baade's challenge without much fervor. They spoke about the military function of German rearmament in general terms, in a way that bordered on triteness. It was said that defense "must be common"; that the common forces of the free world would prevent totalitarianism from leading free nations into slavery; that WEU would be "an efficient system of collective self-defense"; that the coming European coalition could be "the instrument of a strong peace"; that the new treaties would prevent any European "fratricide" in the future; and, repeatedly, that the defensive character of the new arrangements was evident and guaranteed.[26] Such general protestations appeared far more important to the deputies than the need to explain in some tangible manner how the alliance would perform its tasks in the event of a showdown. In particular, the government expressed no military views on the problems of the nuclear age.

WEU was ratified in February, 1955. In the crucial parliamentary debate, Adenauer quoted General Gruenther, who had given a well-timed speech in North Dakota on February 22, 1955, three days before the *Bundestag* vote. Gruenther had outlined the "forward strategy" of NATO to allay German apprehensions that, despite rearmament, the defense of the West would take place at the Rhine or even farther west. Adenauer simplified Gruenther's ideas in a surprisingly crude way, making a statement which the opposition scornfully threw back at him later in the year, when the German debate finally came to focus on the atomic strategy of NATO. Said Adenauer:

[26] See the statements by Adenauer, in *ibid.*, December 15, 1954, pp. 3124–3125; Hasso von Manteuffel, in *ibid.*, December 16, 1954, p. 3199; Will Rasner, in *ibid.*, pp. 3189 and 3196; and Horst Haasler, in *ibid.*, p. 3179.

So long as we don't belong to NATO, we are the European theater of war in case of a hot war between Soviet Russia and the United States, and when we will be in NATO, then we will no longer be this theater of war.[27]

[27] Adenauer, in *ibid.*, February 25, 1955, p. 3736.

NINE

Reunification: 1950–1955

The issue of the reunification of Germany kept the government and the opposition locked in an irreconcilable conflict. Subscribing to the vague American thesis that negotiations with the Soviet Union were possible only from a position of strength, Adenauer was unwilling to yield to the socialist demand that he prevail upon the Western powers to negotiate with the Soviet Union before the treaties on rearmament were ratified. This conflict over the timing of negotiations with Russia became acute during the debate over the EDC treaties, particularly after the publication of the Soviet proposal of March 10, 1952, for the neutralization of unified Germany,[1] and it reached another climax in January, 1955, shortly before the treaties on Germany's membership in WEU and NATO were ratified by the *Bundestag*.

Since Adenauer could never indicate just when a position of sufficient strength would be attained, and since the Western powers found it impolitic for a long time to say what price they would be willing to pay for reunification, neither Adenauer nor the United States could ever convince the German socialists that there was as much interest in ending the partition of Germany as in West German rearmament.[2] As early as 1952, an adviser to the Ministry for

[1] All German critics of Adenauer's policy have emphasized ever since that the West, by treating this proposal as an attempt to prevent agreement on EDC, missed the opportunity to unify Germany and secure for her the neutral status eventually attained by Austria. See especially Paul Sethe, *Zwischen Bonn und Moskau*, Frankfurt, 1956.

[2] The haziness of the American position was most evident in the thesis that EDC and the progress of German rearmament would "enhance the prospects for the peaceful unification of Germany by increasing the attractive power of this prosperous Western Germany vis-à-vis the Soviet Zone" (President Eisenhower in a letter to Chancellor Adenauer dated July 23, 1953, *The New York Times*, July 26, 1953).

All-German Affairs wrote that the formula "negotiations from positions of strength" was merely another instance of American inclination to suspend foreign policy until military objectives were reached, an inclination that had also been evident in the earlier American policy of unconditional surrender.[3]

In December, 1955, when Molotov had made it unmistakably clear once more that the Soviet Union would accept unification only of a communist Germany, some Social Democratic leaders still blamed the West for the impasse that had been reached. One of them said at that time, "The man in the street does not believe that the Adenauer government really wants unification. As a matter of fact, he is not convinced that the United States wants it."

Adenauer probably recognized the vagueness of the American position on German unification, but no doubt felt that he could not force the hand of Washington. He certainly was always convinced that Germany could never attain peaceful unification on acceptable terms without the support of the three major Western powers. It was therefore imperative first to secure some general declaration from the Allies. In 1952, both the Chancellor and other prominent members of his party pointed out that, as long as EDC was not ratified, the occupation powers (including the Soviet Union) could reunify Germany without consulting her. But in consequence of the signing of treaties that provided for a rearmed and independent West Germany, this prerogative of the occupation powers ceased to exist; it now became the obligation of the West to seek Soviet consent to peaceful unification in collaboration with the Federal Republic.

The government never stopped warning the opposition that Germany could not count on Western support for reunification if, by delaying rearmament, she failed to prove that she was a reliable ally. When, after the failure of EDC, Adenauer pressed for ratification of the WEU treaties, deputies who supported his policy reminded the opposition that the Chancellor had established his "credibility," a most precious political asset for the Federal Republic, and that the admission of Germany to WEU had to be regarded as "a prepayment of confidence made by the free world."[4] The impli-

---

[3] Wilhelm W. Schütz, *Deutschland am Rande zweier Welten*, Stuttgart, 1952.
[4] Will Rasner, in *Bundestag Record*, December 16, 1954, pp. 3189 and 3195.

cation was clear: German efforts at unification without that confidence made no political sense.

In January, 1955, Adenauer again described the basis of his policy in a letter to socialist leader Ollenhauer:

the undertaking of the Western powers to pursue together with us the reunification of Germany in peace and freedom was not made unconditionally; it is linked to the ratification of the treaties. . . . If we now in spite of that ask the three Western powers to approach the Soviet Union they will refuse the request, pointing to their note of November 29th [1954], which the Soviet Union has not answered. We would be in danger that the ratification of the Paris Treaties would not take place, and that therefore the obligation of the three Western powers to pursue together with us reunification in peace and freedom would not become effective—while, on the other side, the Soviet Union would not undertake any such obligation. In short, *Germany, as so often in recent decades, would find herself without a friend between two stools.*[5]

Thus the issue of reunification necessarily receded into the background of Adenauer's policy, and insistence on the merits of the policy of strength only served to keep it there.

The Social Democrats, on the other hand, believed that in its own national interest the United States could not possibly afford to abandon West Germany, and that German efforts to ensure American support were therefore unnecessary. They claimed, accordingly, that unification rather than rearmament was the prime objective of the federal government, and that it could be pursued with audacity and impunity. They regarded Adenauer as unduly subservient to the United States, and they never hesitated to say so.

The Social Democrats sensed that German rearmament had been proposed originally not at all as a means to unification of Germany, but in order to retain West Germany within the Western camp and thus increase the likelihood of successful defense of Western Europe in case of a Soviet attack. They did not deny that the United States shared West German wishes for unification, but they realized that American expectations that reunification would be achieved were less hopeful than their own. For the American problem would have been considerably easier had it been possible for the United States to talk to the French—who at the time feared German re-

[5] Quoted in *The Times* (London), January 31, 1955. Italics supplied.

unification—only about moderate expectations and to the Germans only about ardent wishes.

The Social Democrats justified their policy in pathetically unrealistic terms, particularly after Schumacher's death. They claimed that Soviet intentions regarding Germany were obscure and had to be ascertained in negotiations before the Federal Republic assented to rearmament and alignment with the West. Their pressure for unification was based on blindness to the Soviet Union's daily rejection of German unity in the Allied Control Council, as well as in several conferences of foreign ministers from 1945 to 1948. The socialists seemed unaware that it was just this Russian policy that had led to the formation of the Federal Republic in the first place. Moreover, in every conference with the Soviet Union after 1948, it continued to be clear that no terms of unification satisfactory to the West were acceptable to the communists.

In the debate of July, 1952, Carlo Schmid said:

> If the Russians show unmistakably that they do not want the unity of Germany—except in the form of a Russian province—well, then a new situation will have been created. Then, one will have to consider what must be done.[6]

Contentions of this sort were repeated by the socialists in virtually all debates on foreign policy in the years that followed, as if time had not made the Russian position unmistakably clear.

Even in December, 1955, after all the German parties had been stunned by Molotov's brutally frank insistence at Geneva that the communist institutions of East Germany would have to be preserved, Ollenhauer still suggested that a clarification of Soviet intentions was necessary. He proposed that Germany, reunified as a democratic country, become a member of a European security system acceptable to both East and West. He admitted that the Soviet leaders might not accept such a solution, but argued that, if they rejected the proposal, at least the situation would have been clarified.[7] Again, Fritz Erler, addressing an audience of British and German politicians and military experts in the spring of 1956, declared that

> now that diplomatic relations between Bonn and Moscow have been established, this connection may be of additional help if used not as a

---

[6] *Bundestag Record*, July 9, 1952, p. 9818.
[7] *Ibid.*, December 2, 1955, p. 6157.

special line, but as one of the Western lines of communication to Moscow intended *to find out what the Russian position is.*[8]

The socialists never sought an answer to the question of why the Soviet Union should find it in its interest to surrender East Germany, either to the West or to a necessarily uncertain state of neutrality.

There is no simple explanation for the parochial failure of the socialists to appreciate the role of power in international affairs. When pressed for such an answer, Social Democrats have been either evasive or naïve. Evasiveness was inherent in their notion that Soviet intentions were obscure. Their naïveté was particularly evident in their opinion about the price the West might have to pay for reunification. For example, they occasionally suggested in conversation that the United States might make concessions to the Soviet bloc in Asia in order to achieve German unification, but they never indicated the conditions under which it would be to *American* interest to make such concessions. Their view of Soviet intentions also blinded the Social Democrats to the fact that the weakening of the NATO alliance—to which they themselves contributed—was in the declared interest of the Soviet Union. Yet the socialist position on foreign affairs has accrued to German and Western advantage to the extent that it has prevented the issue of unification from being usurped by political adventurers in the struggle for power in Germany. After the end of World War I, the German Social Democrats had been called traitors by the extreme right for supporting the Weimar Republic and the peace treaty of Versailles. They remembered this when, after World War II, excluded from government responsibility, the Social Democrats became the champions of national unity at a time when government and many traditional nationalists supported West German rearmament and collaboration with the victorious Western powers. Unlike nationalists at the extreme right in German politics, the Social Democrats respect democratic institutions. Their foreign policy must be understood in the light of their long anticommunist history. They fought the communists long before the United States adopted the policy of containment. Soon after the conclusion of World War II, General Lucius

---

[8] *News from Germany,* published by the Executive Committee of the SPD of Germany, International Department, Bonn, May, 1956 (italics supplied).

Clay told Kurt Schumacher, "Don't forget that the Soviets are our allies," and the socialist leader replied, "General, don't forget that the Soviets are our enemies." [9] The courage and determination of the socialists in resisting communist maneuvers cannot be doubted. They fought staunchly for the freedom of Berlin during the blockade of 1948, before they could be sure of American support. And it was primarily the workers—from whom the Social Democrats have traditionally drawn much support—who participated in the uprising against the communist authorities in East Germany in 1953.

In the July, 1952, *Bundestag* debate on EDC, the moderate CDU deputy Ernst Lemmer pointed out that when the Versailles treaty was debated in the German *Reichstag* in 1919, the leaders of the opposition declared solemnly that they did not doubt the patriotic motives of the SPD and the Center Party, which voted for the treaty. Lemmer impressed the *Bundestag* by recalling this incident, and by reminding the SPD deputies that the old German National Party had disqualified itself for participation in the government of the Weimar Republic by not living up to the spirit of that declaration. He appealed to the Social Democrats to recognize the patriotic motives of those who favored EDC, and thus to offer a token of national solidarity despite their opposition. Lemmer's appeal had no effect.

Socialist intransigence was partly the consequence of Adenauer's lack of interest in giving the opposition a fair deal. When the Chancellor took office in 1949 by a margin of one vote, it did not appear likely at first that he could easily afford to dispense entirely with socialist co-operation. Economic prosperity and the course of the cold war, however, made it possible for him to treat the opposition in an autocratic manner. He claimed all success for himself and for those who followed him. In the elections of 1953 the West Germans endorsed his rule with an overwhelmingly strong vote.

The differences between the Christian Democrats and the socialists on the issues of rearmament and unification may have been aggravated by the greater political self-assurance of the SPD. Christian Democrats have derived their political self-esteem from their power and success, and from American support and praise. The so-

[9] Mentioned by Fritz Kühn at a meeting of the German-English Society (*Deutsch-Englische Gesellschaft*). See *Deutsch-Englisches Gespräch 1955*, Königswinter, April 14–17, p. 74.

cialists, to be sure, have had only their past to fall back on, but their anti-Nazi record may have lessened their need for American praise and approval. A close reading of the parliamentary debates during the fifties gives the impression that the Christian Democrats felt more strongly than the socialists the need to emphasize Germany's political reliability and to appear publicly concerned about some stigma of Hitler's rule. They often spoke as though Germany did not deserve the confidence of the West unless she made a special effort to gain it. Such moral preoccupation suggests feelings of guilt and remorse. The socialists, evidently possessed of greater self-assurance, rarely spoke in this vein.

This difference cannot be attributed entirely to the rhetoric of parliamentary debate. Personal conversations with deputies of the two parties revealed the same difference in attitude. Socialists appeared less preoccupied with the role they had played under the Nazi regime than did deputies of the government parties. While many members of the CDU were apt to remark in private, and without provocation, that they had of course never been Nazis, most socialists remained silent on this point, seeming to take it for granted that they could not possibly be suspected of such affiliation.[10]

Similarly, American opposition to Nazism never appeared to have meant to any socialists that American standards of political morality were superior to their own. Efforts to ascertain that the American interviewer did not hold such a presumption with regard to German politicians were made only by deputies of the government parties, particularly during the late forties and early fifties.

Such differences in self-assurance may be related to personal experiences during the Nazi period. Germans who actively fought against, or suffered much from, the Nazi regime are able to face the present without disconcerting memories of personal compromise in their political conduct. Such compromise, however subtle, often enabled others to survive Hitler's rule with less physical risk, which was the reward of prudence; but it may also have tried the conscience—a price often paid for prudence.

An indication of past compromise with the Nazis is a personal history free of the grosser forms of persecution, although it is a crude

[10] The question of political affiliation under the Nazi regime was never raised in the interviews, but it is perhaps of some interest that only one of the former Nazis included in the sample voluntarily identified himself as such.

indication, since many anti-Nazis were never persecuted. An analysis of the autobiographies of CDU and SPD deputies in the 1953 *Bundestag* shows that 30 per cent of the socialists, but only 5 per cent of the CDU/CSU deputies, spent time in Nazi concentration camps or prisons. If emigration and persecution other than arrest and imprisonment are added to these percentages, they rise to 53 for the socialists and to only 18 for the government deputies (see Table 2). The autobiographies of the deputies also show that other less

TABLE 2

INDICATIONS OF DEPRIVATION DURING THE NAZI PERIOD OF CDU/CSU
AND SPD DEPUTIES IN THE GERMAN BUNDESTAG, 1953 *

	CDU/CSU (250 Deputies)	SPD (162 Deputies)
(1) Dismissal, resignation for political reasons, or persecution other than imprisonment	12.4%	13.8%
(2) Emigration	0.4	8.8
(3) Concentration camp or imprisonment	5.2	30.6
Total percentage	18.0%	53.2%

* The table is computed from the autobiographies of the *Bundestag* deputies published in *Amtliches Handbuch des deutschen Bundestags. 2 Wahlperiode, 1953* (as of July, 1954). No double counts were made. Persons falling under more than one of the categories listed in the table were counted only under the category bearing the highest number, that is, the category of most severe deprivation. More Christian Democrats than socialists failed to give precise information on their careers during the years of Nazi rule.

severe career upsets under the Nazi regime were experienced by the socialists more frequently than by their colleagues who now support the government.

The figures thus indicate that the incidence of suffering under the Nazi regime was both relatively and absolutely higher among the Social Democrats than among the deputies of the government parties,[11] but it should be stressed that the figures are given here only to support the suggestion that the differences in political self-assurance vis-à-vis U.S. policy between Christian Democrats and socialists have been accentuated by personal experiences at the time when Hitler was master of Germany. The figures do not prove anything whatever about the relative attachment to Nazi ideas at the present time of members of the two parties.

[11] The incidence of deprivation of deputies of other government parties is not shown in Table 2; it is considerably lower for all of them than for the CDU/CSU or the SPD.

Socialist attitudes toward American policy were probably influenced also by various postwar events. Disappointment with the early punitive policy of the occupation powers was intense among those Germans who believed, however unrealistically, that their own anti-Nazi records entitled them to expect at least the trust of the victors. But during the early period of occupation confidence was withheld from all Germans, and it later began to appear that American confidence and support went to those who aided the postwar aims of American policy, not exclusively to those who had been active anti-Nazis. The socialists, therefore, were shocked and disappointed.

Leaders of the opposition still frequently complain, at least in private, that the political representatives of the United States in Germany do not maintain the contacts with them that a parliamentary opposition has a right to expect. That kind of resentment reached a peak when it was believed that Secretary Dulles tried to influence the 1953 election in Adenauer's favor,[12] and again when the American press chided the Germans for alleged Nazi leanings after the Saar plebiscite of 1955. In that plebiscite, a large majority of Germans, including Adenauer's own party, cast their votes against France, that is, against the Chancellor's policy. German socialists noticed that, while the vote was misread in the United States (even more than in France) as proof of Nazi leanings, little alarm had been shown by the American authorities at the conspicuous rise, since 1953, of the number of former Nazis in Adenauer's cabinet and government.

Socialist views about foreign policy were thus colored by the personal bitterness of the relations between government and opposition leaders, but it is also likely that past political experiences—at the time of the Weimar Republic, under the Nazi regime, and in the early postwar period—influenced the political conduct of the SPD.

It must not be overlooked that the socialists' insistence on reunification has been primarily the form in which they expressed their

[12] On September 3, 1953, Secretary Dulles said that failure to retain the coalition government under Chancellor Konrad Adenauer "would be disastrous to Germany and to the prospects of reunification." "Such a failure would create a state of confusion that could postpone indefinitely a rational solution of the German problem in the interests of the Germans." The SPD promptly accused the United States government of "a vicious attempt" to influence the outcome of the elections. Fritz Heine, press chief of the SPD, issued a statement which said, "The socialist party protests in the most decisive manner against the unbelievable attempt of the USA to deceive the German voters with perversion of facts" (*The New York Times,* September 4, 1953).

opposition to rearmament. To the majority of West Germans, unification has not been as pressing a concern as has the issue of rearmament. Frequent contacts with East German visitors and refugees are often only a source of embarrassment to West Germans. Refugees from the East discover that the sweet liberty in West Germany has a bitter taste of complacency. An independent writer said in 1954 that the West German spirit of condescension toward "the eighteen million slaves in the Soviet Zone" had become strong, although "in many cases it rested only upon a higher standard of consumption of butter, meat, and textiles." [18]

With the passage of time, the gulf separating the social and economic structures of the two Germanies has deepened, and some Social Democrats admitted privately in 1955 that there was little evidence of willingness on the part of the West Germans to sacrifice any of their comforts in the interests of reunification. Some observers suggested that Germany could have achieved reunification if the federal government had expended as much energy on that task as it has on rearmament. They overlooked, however, not only the conflict of interests on this issue between the East and the West, but also the upsetting effect that reunification would have on the West German economy.

The Social Democrats have gained few supporters from among the former German military class, despite their position on unification. As of the end of 1955, most of the former German generals had nothing but scorn for socialist views on foreign policy. They tolerated Adenauer's policy on unification on the assumption that his publicly expressed confidence about its effectiveness was partly forced on him by domestic political considerations. They did not share the Chancellor's hope that the Soviet Union would ever voluntarily surrender any communist part of Germany to the West, but they appreciated Adenauer's need to justify rearmament to the voters in terms of the nationalistic issue which the socialists, of all people, presented as their main concern. To the generals, rearmament seemed the main prerequisite of any German foreign policy worthy of the name, and they therefore found less fault with the Chancellor's policy than with that of his opponents.

[18] Margret Boveri, "Die Deutschen und der *status quo*," *Merkur*, June, 1954; reprinted under the title "Schuld oder Verrat" in Hermann Rauschning, Hans Fleig, Margret Boveri, J. A. v. Rantzau, *Mitten ins Herz*, Berlin [n.d.], pp. 26ff.

After the Geneva Conference of July, 1955, socialist naïveté with respect to Soviet intentions was no longer exploited by the Soviet Union, but simply ignored as politically irrelevant.[14] At the Geneva conference of foreign ministers in October–November, 1955, the Bolshevik leaders made it ruthlessly clear that their new diplomacy of smiles and flexibility did not extend to the German issue. Stalin's successors treated this issue with Stalinist hardness, thus crushing the hopes of the socialists and making the unrealistic character of their policy evident to all.

At the same time, however, the Chancellor's protestations that a Western policy of strength would eventually lead to the peaceful unification of Germany were shown up by Soviet intransigence as the rhetoric they had always been.[15] The fact that Adenauer had reiterated American expectations did not save him from standing revealed, after the middle of 1955, as the champion of a policy which had failed to improve the chances of reunification.

Foreign Minister von Brentano said that the second Geneva Conference was "a profound and bitter disappointment" to all Germans. In his speech of November 8, Molotov had not even attempted to present the Soviet position on reunification in a form corresponding to the much-cited "spirit of Geneva" of the Summit Conference of the previous July. Brentano said that Molotov's speech indicated that ten steps would have to be taken to satisfy the Soviet Union before reunification could be seriously considered:

1. A European security system would have to be established on the basis of the *status quo,* that is, on the basis of the division of Germany.
2. The military coalitions existing in Europe—NATO, WEU, and the Warsaw Pact of the Soviet satellites, but not the bilateral Soviet-satellite arrangements—would have to be dissolved.
3. A reunified Germany would have to be obliged not to join any

[14] This contemptuous disregard of the socialist opposition did not prevent the Soviet Union, after August, 1956, from citing the outlawing of the Communist Party in the Federal Republic as a principal obstacle to unification, thus again strengthening the Social Democratic opposition to Adenauer's policy.

[15] On December 2, 1955, Adenauer redefined the policy of strength by saying quite weakly that "it must consist of expressing one's point of view clearly also when facing an opponent" (*Bundestag Record,* p. 6163). Franz-Josef Strauss redefined "policy of strength" more interestingly with a neutralist undertone. He said that it meant "being so strong that one's own freedom of decision could not be influenced by pressure from friend [*sic*] or foe or be turned into its opposite" ("Sicherheit und Wiedervereinigung," *Aussenpolitik,* March, 1957, p. 145).

coalition, or become a partner of any military alliance; that is, Germany's neutrality would have to involve a restriction of its sovereignty.

4. Allied troops would have to be withdrawn from Germany, the Americans across the ocean, the Russians beyond the border.
5. Germany would have to be demilitarized.
6. The relations of the four major powers with both German governments would have to be normalized.
7. An All-German Council would have to be formed, equalizing the influence of the Pankow and Bonn governments.
8. The political, social, and economic "achievements" of the working population in the East German Republic would have to be safeguarded in a reunified Germany.
9. The influence of the "Junkers, monopoly capitalists, and militarists" would have to be eliminated in West Germany.
10. The two governments of Germany would have to collaborate in preparing specific proposals for reunification.[16]

All these measures were unacceptable to the Bonn government, and the last five were unacceptable to the German Social Democrats as well. The eighth proposal shocked the socialists most. Molotov had made no attempt whatever to exploit the conflict on foreign policy between Adenauer and Ollenhauer, but had brusquely scoffed at both of them.[17]

[16] These ten points are summarized from Brentano's speech in the *Bundestag*. See *ibid.*, December 1, 1955, pp. 6106*ff*.

[17] At least one German commentator offered an interesting explanation of Molotov's speech of November 8. Shortly before delivering it, Molotov had been called back to the Kremlin to report on the progress of the Geneva Conference. He said to reporters at the Moscow airport that he was flying back to Geneva with better baggage. After he had given his speech, Dr. Silex wrote in *Deutsche Kommentare* (December 3, 1955), "The world knows now what was in the bag. Molotov had been informed that the series of [Soviet] atomic tests, begun in September, had been so successful that the date for 'the most powerful H-bomb explosion of all times' [as Khrushchev was to call it] could be set. . . . Molotov's better baggage was nothing but his knowledge of the imminent explosion of the superbomb."

TEN

The Atomic Exercise "Carte Blanche": 1955

Preoccupation with the danger of thermonuclear war gave the German debates on rearmament an entirely new character in 1955. Nuclear developments had been dramatized in Germany by the atomic exercise CARTE BLANCHE, held by SHAPE in June, 1955, and to a lesser extent by the dismissal of Colonel von Bonin from the Defense Ministry.

CARTE BLANCHE stirred the German press and the *Bundestag* far more than had any previous maneuver involving atomic weapons, or any public statement on the atomic defense of Europe. It furnished emotionally powerful ammunition to the parliamentary opposition, which treated it as a rehearsal for war. Colonel von Bonin's dismissal was less spectacular, but his criticism of the Defense Ministry was reported widely. Through him and other journalists, notably Adelbert Weinstein, the impact of atomic weapons upon European defense became for the first time the concern of a wide public in Germany. The *Bundestag* debates on CARTE BLANCHE in July and December, 1955, in which the opposition used many of Bonin's and Weinstein's arguments, were broadcast to millions of Germans.

The Social Democrats repeated their old argument that German soldiers were intended merely "to replace American soldiers and [that] this shift would entail no addition to Western strength,"[1] but they refrained from wild attacks on the military capabilities of the Allied ground forces similar to those made by Deputy Baade in 1954. Instead, the socialists concentrated on three issues: atomic

[1] Peter Blachstein, in *Bundestag Record,* July 16, 1955, p. 5599; also Fritz Erler, in *ibid.,* p. 5611.

warfare in Europe, the alleged incompetence of the German Defense Ministry, and the failure of the government to inform the German people of the horrors of atomic war.

None of the Social Democrats concerned themselves with the military worth of atomic weapons. They seemed entirely indifferent to the question of whether employment of tactical atomic weapons would improve the chances of victory for the West in the event of war. Nor did they address themselves in any way to the deterrent effect of these weapons. They regarded atomic war as "collective suicide," [2] and its military or political aspects did not seem to them worth discussing. They apparently were unaware or unconcerned that their approach to nuclear war constituted a political attack on NATO that was welcome to nobody but the Soviet Union.

The socialists viewed CARTE BLANCHE exclusively as a horrible threat to the civilian population. A few days before the first socialist interpellation on CARTE BLANCHE came up for debate, Erich Ollenhauer led off by exclaiming that the employment of tactical atomic weapons would have an annihilating effect upon German civilians. [3] A few days later, it was mentioned in the debate that if the 335 atomic bombings simulated in the exercise had occurred in reality, 1.7 million Germans would have been killed and 3.5 million incapacitated, to say nothing about numerous additional victims of radioactivity. In CARTE BLANCHE there had been "sixty operational targets" on German soil, the socialists said, and these were not remote from cities. "How would . . . the civilian population react? How would the political and military leadership look the day after?" [4] One socialist deputy asked what would happen if "big" rather than tactical bombs were to be dropped on Germany, [5] and another spoke of H-bombs with cobalt coating "which, everybody knows, can extinguish all life on earth within a short time." [6]

The opposition went on to accuse the government of negligence in not providing for adequate civil defense, or for a radar warning system in the Federal Republic. Ollenhauer repeated without qualification Adelbert Weinstein's sensational demand that the federal

[2] Fritz Erler, in *ibid.*, June 28, 1955, p. 5285.

[3] *Ibid.*, p. 5231.

[4] Peter Blachstein, in *ibid.*, July 16, 1955, p. 5599; similarly Fritz Erler, in *ibid.*, December 7, 1955, p. 6213.

[5] Peter Blachstein, in *ibid.*, July 16, 1955, p. 5598.

[6] Wilhelm Mellies, in *ibid.*, p. 5586.

government reallocate to civil defense all of the nine billion marks projected for rearmament.[7]

From the fact that German civilians would be exposed to mass slaughter in the event of atomic war in Europe, the socialists concluded, without apparent logic, that any German contribution to the forces of NATO would be useless. In the atomic age, said Ollenhauer, neither 6,000 volunteers nor 12 army divisions would contribute anything worth while to German security; "everybody knows this."[8] Even in the more temperate speech he made after the conference of foreign ministers in Geneva, Ollenhauer repeated: "The military value of the rearmament of the Federal Republic is still more dubious than it used to be."[9] And Fritz Erler, implying that German ground forces had no value unless they rendered *atomic* war less likely, asked the government:

is it not true, to speak soberly, that the Western plan of defense aims at compensating for the superiority of Soviet ground forces by means of atomic weapons in any event, whether or not there are German divisions . . . ?[10]

Since in the opinion of the opposition NATO plans for the employment of tactical atomic weapons in the event of a European war would lead "as it were, inevitably to a general war of destruction,"[11] the socialists implied that a German defense contribution to NATO would not only be useless but would also constitute moral collusion in the preparation of unspeakable horror. One deputy characterized as a danger the very presence of Allied air bases in Germany.

Although the socialists thus claimed to be concerned with German security, they gave no evidence whatever that they were concerned about the Soviet threat to security. The enemy was held to be a lesser menace than the nature of nuclear war itself. They believed even more firmly than they had in 1954 that the danger of Soviet aggression had abated. At the same time they believed that, if war did occur, it would be far more horrible than previous ones because of NATO's intention, so dramatically demonstrated by

[7] Adelbert Weinstein in *Frankfurter Allgemeine Zeitung*, June 28, 1955.
[8] *Bundestag Record*, June 28, 1955, p. 5232.
[9] *Ibid.*, December 2, 1955, p. 6162.
[10] Fritz Erler, in *ibid.*, December 7, 1955, p. 6213.
[11] *Ibid.*, p. 6211.

CARTE BLANCHE, to use atomic weapons. While, in the eyes of the socialists, the Soviet Union seemed twice vindicated—by a more conciliatory policy since Stalin's death and by its demand for a ban on atomic weapons—American lack of aggressive intent was apparently held to be irrelevant in view of the American intention and ability to resort to nuclear weapons if war should break out.

If the socialists had believed that a stronger Western defense posture would have increased its deterrent effect and rendered the outbreak of war less likely, they would have had to criticize themselves for having retarded German rearmament. Since they considered German rearmament superfluous, they criticized Theodor Blank and his Ministry instead, for failure to appreciate the realities of the nuclear age. They exclaimed that the ideas of the Defense Ministry were hopelessly out of date, based as they were on the premise that traditional forms of warfare would recur in the event of another conflict. The government acted, the socialists charged, as though nothing had happened since 1952: Ollenhauer called Bonn's defense plans "eerie." [12] The Germans heard similar charges from abroad. For example, on September 30, 1955, *Die Welt* reprinted a comment (originally published in *The Manchester Guardian*) on the lessons of CARTE BLANCHE, which said that in the opinion of Sir Richard Gale each of the new NATO divisions could hold a front 25 km in length with the support of atomic weapons. *The Manchester Guardian* observed that this would require some thirty active divisions for the defense of Germany, more than General Gruenther had, or in all probability could ever hope to have, in Central Europe. The British paper concluded that there seemed to be an element of unreality in the existing military plans.

Thus the German opposition challenged, for the first time, the professional competence of the older generation of the former military class on a strategic issue connected with German rearmament. The criticism hit General Heusinger as much as Minister Blank, and the socially displaced, inactive members of the military profession no less than their colleagues who occupied positions in the Defense Ministry. Most of the older members of the military class were united with the military personnel in the Defense Ministry in their reluctance to revise traditional ways of thinking in the light of nuclear armament. Or so at least it appeared, since neither the gov-

[12] *Bundestag Record,* June 28, 1955, p. 5232.

ernment nor the former German generals had spoken in public, until the CARTE BLANCHE debate, about any change in the military worth of conventional arms.

Angry replies by Theodor Blank and others in his Ministry to the effect that the press was incompetent to deal with such issues only made matters worse. If the press could not deal with the issues competently, asked the opposition in rebuttal, why had the government experts been silent? Churchill, Eisenhower, and many scientists had warned the people of other countries about the strategic implications and dangers of nuclear war. Why, then, had the German Chancellor failed to stand up before the German people and tell them the truth? [13]

Nobody has taken the occasion of the maneuvers [i.e., CARTE BLANCHE] to set forth the consequences [of atomic war] for the population of the affected areas.[14]

All the speakers of the opposition referred scathingly to the statement that Adenauer *had* made in February, 1955: had he not said that, as a member of NATO, Germany would not become a theater of war? [15] By implication, one deputy compared that statement to Göring's wartime boast that bombs would never fall on German cities.

In July and December, 1955, Adenauer and his supporters neither replied to the taunts of the opposition nor amplified the meaning of the February statement. They also found it surprisingly easy to parry the argument that German troops were meant merely to compensate for the reduction of the U.S. Army by 450,000 men (the figure quoted at the time). That argument had little effect in the public German debate. The government met it either with unembarrassed silence or with the answer that the reduction, like that of the Red forces by 640,000 men, was the result of structural changes required by the process of adapting the ground forces to the demands of atomic warfare.[16]

[13] Peter Blachstein, in *ibid.*, July 1, 1955, p. 5601.

[14] Fritz Erler, in *ibid.*, December 7, 1955, p. 6212.

[15] Erich Ollenhauer, in *ibid.*, June 28, 1955, p. 5232; Peter Blachstein, in *ibid.*, July 16, 1955, p. 5599; Fritz Erler, in *ibid.*, December 7, 1955, p. 6212. Adenauer's statement is quoted at the end of Chap. 8.

[16] Erich Mende, in *ibid.*, December 7, 1955, p. 6218. Erich Dethleffsen expressed himself similarly in a public speech on "Atomwaffen und Ost-West Konflikt" at Frankfurt/Main, January 20, 1956, published in *Offene Welt*, January–February, 1956, p. 10. The same argument was advanced in the July, 1956, debate by Fritz Berendsen.

As to CARTE BLANCHE, deputies of the government parties pointed out that it would take time to evaluate its lessons, and that the hasty conclusions which the opposition had drawn made no military sense. Except for elaborate protests that they had not been neglecting civil defense, the government supporters avoided discussing the dangers to which the civilian population would be exposed in an atomic war. They concentrated instead on proving that conventional ground forces were still useful. In doing so, however, several spokesmen belittled the military worth of nuclear weapons and advanced strategic notions that were indeed dated, as the opposition had charged. This does not necessarily mean that the government was acting disingenuously in order to assuage the public anxiety of which the opposition had made itself spokesman; rather is it likely that the government speakers were sincere in what they said. Thus the government was defending the sound cause of German conventional armament on shaky grounds, while the opposition attacked it without logic but from a firmer premise. Blank tried to defend his Ministry against the charge that it entertained outdated strategic ideas, but the limitations of his own views were perhaps most strikingly revealed in his remark on July 16, 1955, that atomic weapons were still so expensive "that their use must be confined to targets that are militarily worth while." [17]

In June, 1955, when CARTE BLANCHE took place, a German booklet was published in Bonn entitled *On the Future of the German Soldier*. It contained prefaces by Adenauer and Blank. All the arguments in favor of German rearmament were recapitulated, but none of them was carefully reviewed in relation to the possibility of atomic war. The booklet would not have read very differently if nuclear weapons had never been invented.

It was suggested in the booklet that if, contrary to expectations, the deterrent effort of the West should fail, the outcome of war would end in victory for the West, because

in the long run the total military and economic strength of the free world will be superior [to that of the Soviet block].[18]

The military importance of the economic mobilization base was assumed to be as great as it had been in the last two world wars, an

[17] *Bundestag Record*, July 16, 1955, p. 5589.
[18] *Vom künftigen deutschen Soldaten*, Bonn, 1955, p. 16.

assumption that was also often made by German generals in private conversations in 1952 and 1954.[19] It was further pointed out in the booklet that German rearmament would reduce the danger of a successful surprise attack on Western Europe by communist forces:

> After the formation of German forces the balance of power will be such that the danger of a surprise attack will be largely removed. An aggressor would then have to make larger preparations which could not be hidden and which would offer time to the West for taking further measures.[20]

The government parties entered the debate on CARTE BLANCHE with exactly this same strategic viewpoint about the importance of German rearmament. Their case had been stated most succinctly in a speech by Fritz Berendsen, the military expert of the CDU, which had been intended for delivery in the foreign-policy debate of February, 1955, and which was published in May, one month before CARTE BLANCHE. Once Germany was rearmed, Berendsen said, the Soviets would need to bring up new forces from the interior for an attack on the West, and this "would take several weeks"; hence time would be gained through German rearmament "for political negotiations as well as for countermeasures by the West." [21] Blitzkrieg in Central Europe would be impossible. The Soviet forces could attack in the center only if they struck simultaneously at the northern and southern flanks of Europe, at Norway, and at Italy; this would require in turn attacks on Greece and Turkey. Berendsen concluded:

> A large-scale attack by Soviet forces on Central Europe is connected with such a number of auxiliary operations that it is questionable whether the Soviet armed forces, strong as they are, are capable of undertaking it.[22]

A month later, CARTE BLANCHE so stirred the German public that General Heusinger and Minister Blank had to make special efforts to reassure the people that disaster was not imminent, and that despite the advent of tactical atomic weapons ground forces were

---

[19] In 1955, however, some younger former German officers doubted the validity of this assumption in view of the speed with which atomic weapons might force a decision in the future.

[20] *Vom künftigen deutschen Soldaten, loc. cit.*

[21] Fritz Berendsen, "Die Pariser Verträge im Blickfeld des Soldaten," *Wehrwissenschaftliche Rundschau,* May, 1955, p. 193.

[22] *Ibid.,* p. 195.

still needed to protect West Germany from being overrun by Soviet land forces.[23] But most of the deputies who spoke along these lines in the *Bundestag* appeared to be less sure of themselves than they had been before, and they now expressed their beliefs with some reservations. Ground forces had become "not useless" or "not super-fluous," or were considered to be "still meaningful"; this was a far cry from the assertion that "with German formations at the disposal of the West for the defense of Europe, the defense of the Federal Republic becomes possible."[24]

The government and its supporters advanced two main arguments: (1) If, in view of nuclear parity, the giant powers abstained from the use of unconventional weapons, as Churchill had considered possible, ground forces would remain—or, rather, once more become—important. (2) However, if unconventional weapons were used in a future war, ground forces would still have important functions to perform.

In presenting the first argument, the supporters of the government took the position that with the advent of nuclear parity the balance of power in the East-West conflict was determined by conventional armament. This argument brought the German government into conflict with the strategic views held by the U.S. government under the policy of the so-called "New Look." Not until August, 1956, did Dr. Adenauer indicate in public that he was aware of this conflict.

In the debates of 1955, Kurt-Georg Kiesinger insisted that "despite the possession of the H-bomb [by both sides], or perhaps because of it, the danger of military conflict with conventional weapons is by no means excluded"; hence the importance of German rearmament is "extraordinarily great";[25] it is of "utmost importance."[26] Western Europe and the rest of the free world "have no other choice but to counter the tremendous Soviet superiority in conventional weapons by equally strong forces."[27] Blank said that Germany would be "completely defenseless" if it failed to rearm.[28] Minister Strauss

[23] General Heusinger on the North West Radio, June 30, 1955; Theodor Blank in the *Bundestag*, *Bundestag Record*, July 16, 1955, p. 5589.

[24] *Vom künftigen deutschen Soldaten, loc. cit.*

[25] *Bundestag Record*, December 2, 1955, p. 6166.

[26] *Ibid.*, June 28, 1955, p. 5294; Erich Mende and Franz-Josef Strauss expressed similar views in the same debate.

[27] Kurt-Georg Kiesinger, in *ibid.*, December 2, 1955, p. 6166.

[28] *Ibid.*, July 16, 1955, p. 5589.

insisted on the great importance of ground forces precisely because in two years atomic parity and mutual deterrence might become effective. General von Manteuffel simply pointed out that other nations, too, had conventional weapons.[29]

The second argument in favor of conventional armament was derived from the belief that the military value of unconventional weapons was problematical. While there was no agreement as to the relative value of conventional and unconventional arms, the government speakers were agreed that nuclear weapons could not replace conventional forces. This view was also held at the time by almost all former German generals outside the government. Regardless of the specific form given to this idea, it was meant to convey the impression that the opposition exaggerated the military value of nuclear weapons. By implication, all those who concentrated on the horrors of nuclear war to the exclusion of other considerations were charged with military incompetence.

Some spokesmen, especially older members of the military class, warned that never in the past had any single weapon been decisive in deciding the outcome of war—an argument that appealed to the inclination of Germans to ascribe special authority to history. When General Heusinger used this argument in his broadcast on CARTE BLANCHE, he weakened its persuasiveness by juxtaposing his certainty regarding the indecisiveness of any single weapon with his uncertainty about the future of unconventional weapons. Since nobody knew how the latter would develop, he said, conclusions on military strategy and tactics in nuclear war had to be drawn with great caution. Other former generals pointed out in private in 1955 that conventional weapons should not be regarded as altogether obsolete. One of them said, "After the invention of gunpowder it took five centuries until the bayonet and the lance were abandoned." A deputy of the *Bundestag* mentioned in conversation that two leading German military officials had defended the strategic value of German rearmament to a parliamentary committee in the summer of 1955 on the ground that "the army would come into its own after atomic blows had been exchanged." In a similar vein, former General von Manteuffel said of CARTE BLANCHE in the *Bundestag* that the "wear and tear of the air force" had been very great on

[29] Hasso von Manteuffel, in *ibid.*, p. 5591.

both sides,[30] which he adduced as proof that ground forces were irreplaceable. Fritz Berendsen simply said that since radioactivity could be more destructive to one's own troops than to the enemy's,

the use of tactical A-weapons is thoroughly problematical. . . . The renunciation of classical military contingents would be tantamount to rendering the country defenseless.[31]

The argument that "ground forces have not become superfluous despite nuclear weapons, airplanes, and missiles"[32] was occasionally refined in an attempt to meet the doubts of the opposition. In particular, it was claimed that air force bases needed protection by ground forces,[33] or that only the army was capable of occupying enemy territory: the war could not be *finished* without armies.[34]

Only younger parliamentarians unencumbered by the traditions of the German army were ready in 1955 to concede in public that the value of conventional forces had been reduced by the advent of nuclear weapons. Franz-Josef Strauss said in the July, 1955, debate that the modern weapons of mass destruction had created a strategic revolution in consequence of which land forces no longer had the classical importance they had had in the past, and in December Erich Mende introduced a speech on the development of missiles with a statement rarely heard from any former officer in the German army:

In Germany we still think too much in terms of the technology that prevailed in World War II, without knowledge of that which in the last ten years has begun to revolutionize political, economic, and even cultural thinking.[35]

In December, 1955, Blank replied to the Social Democrats that his Ministry did have conceptions, ideas, and plans on how to adapt

[30] *Ibid.*

[31] Berendsen, *op. cit.,* p. 196.

[32] Theodor Blank, *Bundestag Record,* July 16, 1955, p. 5589.

[33] *Ibid.;* see also Frido von Senger und Etterlin, "Eine Neue Form der Kriegskunst," *Aussenpolitik,* January, 1956.

[34] Blank, in *Bundestag Record,* p. 5589.

[35] *Bundestag Record,* December 7, 1955, p. 6216. Mende's colleague, Hasso von Manteuffel, too, conceded that a revolution of warfare was taking place, but he concluded, more conservatively, that conventional weapons "have maintained their military value" although army divisions "will probably no longer be the decisive weapon" (*ibid.,* July 16, 1955, p. 5591; also *ibid.,* July 6, 1956, p. 8801).

the ground forces to the requirements of nuclear war. He pointed out that these German ideas "have always been considered in NATO"; he had heard much praise of his military experts in NATO, he said, but never the criticism that their ideas were antiquated.[36] Thus Blank resorted to the authority of NATO in order to intimate that those Germans who differed with NATO were uninformed and incompetent. It is characteristic of the low confidence of the opposition in its own military judgment that, until 1955, such appeals to the authority of Allied military leaders were never challenged in parliament, and hardly ever in the press. Speakers for the coalition quoted General Gruenther as a "crown witness" to the truth of the claim that West Germany could be defended,[37] and while the opposition dissented passionately from this estimate, it refrained from attacking General Gruenther or any other American or British military leader.

By the fall of 1955, the press campaign against the antiquated planning of the Defense Ministry that had been led by Weinstein and Bonin had temporarily subsided, although some commentators in the daily press and in military magazines continued to discuss the optimal size of the projected German divisions. For the general public this was too technical a question to be of much interest, but in private conversations there was some bewilderment that the British and Americans at SHAPE should disagree on this point.

On December 29, 1955, the public debate of this particular issue came to a halt. The German press published a release of an *American* news agency to the effect that, on the basis of experiences gathered in the exercise CARTE BLANCHE, the future German divisions would be so organized as to meet the requirements of atomic war. These plans were attributed to the Defense Ministry of the Federal Republic and to SHAPE. The lessons derived from the atomic maneuver were described as follows: The total strength of the division would be as small as possible to ensure the highest degree of mobility and to reduce vulnerability to atomic attack. Regiments would be abolished as divisional units. The basic units would be battalions equipped with strongly increased firepower (double that of World War II in the case of the projected six armored divisions). These basic units were to be highly mobile and capable of in-

[36] *Ibid.*, December 7, 1955, p. 6216.
[37] Berendsen, *op. cit.*, p. 193.

dependent action, so that they could be readily detached from their own divisions or combined with units of other divisions. The divisions would be freed from their own logistic support; such support would be given them by special troops.

Adelbert Weinstein attributed these changes of mind on the part of the traditionalists in the Defense Ministry to the criticism of military writers, to acknowledged military leaders of the last war who would not join the new forces, and, above all, to the evaluation of the atomic maneuvers. He quoted Montgomery's warning that, when there is conflict between tradition and progress, tradition should yield.[38]

[38] The reference was to Field Marshal Montgomery's speech, "The Global War of the Future," delivered at the Royal United Service Institution on October 12, 1955, and published in German translation in *Aussenpolitik,* December, 1955, pp. 755–769.

ELEVEN

Conscription: 1956

Although the Social Democrats had voted against the Paris Treaties in February, 1955, they recognized that, as a result of ratification, the Federal Republic was bound by them. On December 2, 1955, in the *Bundestag* debate on the Foreign Ministers Conference in Geneva, Erich Ollenhauer had stressed that his party appreciated, of course, that West Germany would have to meet her international commitments. In conversations, Social Democratic deputies pointed out that, in deference to democratic procedures, no other position was possible, but that that was not generally accepted by the rank and file of their party. One of them said, "Opposition to rearmament among our members remains strong. Many of them do not understand why the SPD should stop fighting rearmament merely because it has been outvoted in the *Bundestag*."

The leaders of the party had to find a way out of the dilemma of either alienating their followers or failing to abide by the majority decision of the *Bundestag*. They did so by pointing to the stipulations in the treaties which provided for the possibility of changing them by negotiation. Immediately after he had affirmed socialist acceptance of Germany's treaty obligations, Ollenhauer said:

I should like to add that considerations of treaty changes or of adjustments of the treaties to the changed situation [in the world], which the treaty itself explicitly provides for, have nothing whatever to do with loyalty to the treaties.[1]

Similarly, when, in 1956, the socialists contested Germany's obligation to put up a force of 500,000 men, they claimed that their do-

[1] *Bundestag Record*, December 2, 1955, p. 6160.

ing so was not a defiance of Germany's international commitments. They maintained, against the protests of the government, that the figure of 500,000, which had first been mentioned in the *Accord Special* of the defunct EDC treaties and had been reiterated in Protocol II on the Forces of the West European Union, constituted a maximum rather than an obligatory force goal for Germany. For that reason, the opposition felt free to advocate a substantially smaller contribution to NATO—200,000 to 250,000 men—to be supplemented by a compulsory militia for home defense.

The question of the size of the German contribution to NATO was connected with that of the most efficient and most economical method of raising the armed forces. A smaller force could conceivably be constituted by volunteers rather than conscripts. Thus conscription versus voluntary service became an important political issue in the spring and summer of 1956. And since those who agreed on conscription could disagree on the terms of service, there was introduced a third, subsidiary, issue into the debate of 1956.

In March, 1956, the *Bundesrat* recommended twelve months of military service instead of the eighteen months stipulated in the government bill on conscription. What is more, the representatives of the four *Länder* of the Federal Republic in which the Social Democrats were the leading coalition party did not commit themselves on the principle of conscription. Finally, reluctance to support the plans of the government was no longer confined to the opposition alone. Influential *Bundestag* deputies of the CDU/CSU also favored a short, one-year military service. These men included Richard Jaeger, the CSU Chairman of the Defense Committee.

Theodor Blank had not foreseen all these obstacles to his plans. Only toward the end of March did he state in public the arguments for a military establishment of 500,000 men consisting largely of conscripts serving a term of eighteen months. He said that with a force of 200,000 or 250,000 men the German contingent would be proportionately lower than that of the other NATO powers.[2]

A reduction of the German force goal to 250,000 men, or 0.5 per cent of the population, Blank argued, would mean that the German contribution would be proportionately less than Italy's force of 280,-000 men, which represented 0.6 per cent of her population. One could

[2] Theodor Blank's release was carried in many German newspapers, for example *Frankfurter Allgemeine Zeitung*, March 28, 1956, and *Deutsche Kommentare*, April 7, 1956.

then no longer speak of an adequate German contribution to the common defense. To support his argument further, Blank published the following figures:

	Peacetime Military Strength in Thousands	Percentage of Population
United States	2,865	1.8
United Kingdom	772	1.5
France	850	2.0
Belgium	145	1.65
Netherlands	125	1.2
West Germany	500	1.0

As to the method of raising the required force, Blank pointed out that all countries "which play a role militarily" [3] had compulsory military service, and West Germany could neither raise 500,000 men on a voluntary basis nor create the indispensable reserves for home defense in that manner.

At the time of the debate, the Federal Republic had only a few thousand men under arms. Six thousand of them had started their service on the basis of the Volunteer Law, which had been passed in the summer of 1955, and which limited the first contingent of the future German *Bundeswehr* to that number. An additional few thousands had been hastily drawn from the Border Security Force (*Grenzschutz*) in 1956. There had been opposition to that measure, which at the time was favored by American authorities. In November, 1955, some German observers had pointed out in conversation that if the Border Police were turned into a regular military force any small international incident might develop into a conflict involving NATO, because Germany would lack troops outside the NATO machinery.

In any event, expectations that the 18,000 men of the Border Security Force would apply for transfer to the *Bundeswehr,* when a law authorizing them to do so was passed early in 1956, were disappointed; only a few applied. The Blank Office had been receiving applications for voluntary service for many years. Their number totaled 210,000 by early April, 1956, of whom 50,000 were young men without prior military service. But it had been impossible to process

[3] *Ibid.*

the applications prior to the passage of the Soldiers' Law (which authorized the government to raise 150,000 volunteers). Following its enactment on March 6, 1956, the Defense Ministry hoped to have 96,000 men under arms by the end of 1956, using the Border Police as a base and adding to them untrained volunteers after appropriate processing of their applications by screening boards.

Yet Blank pointed out that this procedure, while filling the needs for 1956, would not enable the Defense Ministry to dispense with conscription in the years thereafter, if Germany wanted to bring the *Bundeswehr* up to 500,000 men. Besides, a force composed entirely of long-term volunteers would be inordinately expensive, he argued, because volunteers who periodically returned to civilian life after completing their term of service would, as a group, have intolerably large claims on the treasury. Finally, Blank insisted on eighteen months of service as the minimum period required for adequate training.

In July, 1956, when the bill on conscription was presented to the *Bundestag* for a vote, it contained no reference whatever to the length of service. For this reason, the opposition called the bill a torso, but it was the only way its passage could be ensured. CSU Deputy Jaeger said in the debate that keeping the decision on the length of service in abeyance would make it possible to judge later on the basis of events whether a sufficient number of volunteers ready to serve at least three years were available. The required length of service for the conscripts could then be determined in the light of those facts.

As late as March, 1956, it was widely expected that the Social Democrats would favor conscription, since opposition to professional armies had been a socialist tradition from Bebel to Schumacher. It was assumed that the SPD would continue to reject a professionalized *Bundeswehr* that could become a state within the state capable of meddling in politics, as the *Reichswehr* had been in the days of the Weimar Republic. From 1952 to 1955, the Social Democrats had indeed viewed the institution of voluntary military service with deep suspicion. In the latter year, a socialist youth leader remarked in conversation that the volunteers registered in the Defense Ministry were "either adventurers or young men who had difficulty finding something useful to do, the second sons of farm-owners, refugees from the East, or boys who are good for nothing."

Shortly before the second and third reading of the government bill on conscription on July 6 and 7, 1956, however, the SPD decided against conscription in favor of a small force of volunteers. There can be no doubt that this decision was taken with a view to gaining votes in the general election of 1957, especially among the youth and the women. It was so interpreted by the government parties and in the German press. Thus the government parties, which advocated conscription, became the spokesmen of the more democratic form of military recruitment, whereas the SPD found itself in the strange company of the right-wing German Party which sympathized with the idea of a professional army, although it voted for the government bill in the end.[4]

Deputies of the government parties insinuated in the debate that securing votes in the forthcoming election by opposing conscription seemed to concern the Social Democrats more than anything else. In reply, the socialists pointed to their record of safeguarding the democratic character of the *Bundeswehr*. They had collaborated with the CDU in this respect, both in the Defense Committee and on the floor of the *Bundestag*. For example, against the opposition of the government, but with the support of many CDU deputies in the *Bundestag*, they had taken the initiative in forming the Personnel Selection Board, which had caused the Defense Ministry no little embarrassment by passing judgment on the suitability of incumbents in leading military positions, as well as of candidates for such positions. The socialists had also strongly supported the creation of a Parliamentary Defense Counselor (*Wehrbeauftragter*) to safeguard the basic rights of German soldiers, and above all to assist the *Bundestag* in the parliamentary control of the armed forces. The establishment of this new office was inspired by a Swedish precedent that had been studied by two members of the Defense Committee.[5] Finally, the Defense Committee of the *Bundestag* itself has permanent investigatory authority in relation to the Defense Ministry. These three agencies—the Personnel Selection Board, the Parliamentary Defense Counselor, and the Defense Committee—thus restrict

[4] Ludwig Schneider, the military expert of the German Party, had originally favored a professional army, according to *Frankfurter Allgemeine Zeitung*, April 17, 1956. The FDP abstained from voting on the bill on July 7, 1956, although Erich Mende, its military expert, had declared himself in favor of conscription only a few days before the vote was taken.

[5] One of them was the CDU deputy Karlfranz Schmidt-Wittmack, who, like Otto John, defected to Communist Germany, but who, unlike Otto John, did not return to West Germany.

the power of the executive over defense in favor of public political control. It so happened that in 1957 the government succeeded in preventing the appointment of a Parliamentary Defense Counselor who would have the confidence of the opposition. Legislation establishing the surveillance over the *Bundeswehr* was approved by the *Bundestag* on April 11, 1957, against the votes of the socialists, who had proposed that the selection of the Defense Counselor should require a two-thirds majority of the *Bundestag*. According to the bill that was passed, a simple majority will suffice for that purpose, so that the government can control the selection.

In 1956 the Social Democrats claimed that as a result of their efforts to ensure the democratic character of the *Bundeswehr,* the future German military establishment, whether based on conscription or voluntary service, could not possibly lead to a revival of German militarism. The creation of a voluntary professional army, they said, was therefore politically safe for the first time in German history.

Advocacy of a smaller defense force and of voluntary service was not confined to the Social Democrats. There were serious military men, particularly in the younger age groups, who believed that technological developments had rendered conscription obsolete. And there were others who doubted that Germany could create a large military establishment without compromising its quality.

In 1955, before conscription became a serious political issue, a number of military informants had spoken of the need for a professional defense force to meet contingencies arising from the East-West struggle. They advanced the following reasons in its favor. The technical demands which the most advanced weapons made upon the men who used them were such that the necessary skills could not possibly be acquired by conscripts in eighteen to twenty-four months. In addition, the far-flung dangers of the cold war made it necessary to dispose of highly mobile and fully trained forces-in-being composed of men of all three services. To rely upon mobilizing reserves in case of a crisis might invite military disaster. Similarly, the economic war potential of the West, which was mobilized in the course of the last two world wars with decisive effect, might be much less important in the future, since atomic and other forces-in-being might decide the issue before there was time to mobilize. A naval spokesman was especially impressed by the combat value of the U.S. Marines. He said that he had proposed to the German Defense Ministry that an equivalent of at least two of the proposed German divisions should be marines.

Such views were not necessarily associated with the idea that a small force, rather than half a million men, should be put under arms, although it would be patently impossible for Germany to form a professional army of half a million long-term volunteers. The idea of forming only a small force was advanced, however, as early as 1953, before Bonin's proposals became public, and was supported in 1954 by some former German officers in private conversation. The idea was associated at that time with doubts about the *combat value* of a large German army.

The older generation of officers have appreciated from the beginning of the rearmament discussion that it would take many years after the removal of all political obstacles (which itself took more than five years) to build from scratch a military organization of 500,000 men. They appreciated this fact long before the German, or any other, public began to do so, if only because they remembered vividly that it had taken Hitler many years to create his war machine out of the 100,000-man army of the Weimar Republic. They remembered also that, even as late as 1939, after six years of concerted national effort, many of the best German professional officers still judged the *Wehrmacht* deficient.

So free were most of the German military experts of illusions about the speed with which a good German army could be re-created, that several of them not connected with the Blank Office voiced concern in the spring of 1954 that Allied military planners might become discouraged about the new German soldier. He might turn out to be a poor soldier. Just as the French dashed widespread illusions about the quality of their army in 1940, so the new German military contingents might not live up to the reputation which they had inherited from the past. These informants did not suggest that Germany's defeat in World War II had broken the German fighting spirit. Nor did they argue that the Allied disarmament policy during the five years following the end of the war had weakened the German military fiber. Instead, they cited the failure and inability of social institutions other than the army to prepare youth for their tasks as soldiers. The family, the school, the press, the voluntary youth organizations—all of these had to contribute to the making of a good soldier. But postwar German society was incapable of furnishing these necessary underpinnings of a viable army. That was why German youth did not hold much military promise. On this view, then, rearmament was not a task that some social engineer could undertake at will, and to regard it as such involved throwing into relief the fact that Germany had, in 1945, ceased to be a living society with cherished traditions. Easy optimism about the prospects of German rearmament failed to recognize that Germany had been beaten down into an amorphous conglomeration of self-centered individuals, who were either enriching themselves or claiming government support as paupers on the basis of the innumerable laws providing for such support. But, prosperous or poor, they were self-centered always.

A younger former German officer, who now earns his living as a journalist, put the issue in a wider context. The deterioration of the fighting quality of modern soldiers, he said, was not confined to Germany, but was rather characteristic of the whole of Western civilization. He spoke of the "failure" of the GI's in Korea, of the British in Malaya, where "only the Gurkhas" were fighting, and of the poor performance of many French noncommissioned officers in Indochina. This, he said, would be the pattern from now on. Modern technology and modern society required a small professional elite army, a Praetorian Guard, backed up by a larger militia. The Praetorian Guard, equipped and trained "to kill, destroy, and rape," would have to supersede universal military service, which had never been a democratic institution, "since conscription was compulsory." It had merely created a form of bureaucratic organization that brought to the top men whose social qualities facilitated promotion, but whose rank bore no relation to the requirements of modern combat. This observer combined Spengler's malaise about the future of Western culture with the same author's enthusiasm for technology, an attitude that became fashionable among some of the more snobbish intellectuals in Europe before the atomic bomb was invented.

Officials in the Defense Ministry, of course, did not share such pessimistic views. They were committed to planning the new German defense effort in support of the Chancellor's policy, and they no doubt would have scorned pessimism regarding the fighting value of the future German soldier if it had come from the socialist opposition. Since the pessimism came from some German military circles, however, employees of the Ministry took it more seriously, but they denied to the interviewer that it was justified. Instead of addressing themselves to the central issue—the inadequate integration of German society—they expressed confidence in the effects of training, organization, and leadership. Once the cadres were formed, they said, the quality of the soldiers would be determined by professional effort, not by the character of civilian institutions. In 1954 this was the view, of course, of the majority of former officers, even outside the Ministry; the contrary views we have discussed were very definitely a minority opinion.

One former officer attributed the pessimistic predictions to the younger generation and brushed them aside with the remark, "Youth lacks judgment." Another was angered when told that some of his former comrades-in-arms thought that the German soldiers of the future might be inferior to those of the past. He called this notion "idiotic," and, when confronted with the further notion, often expressed by the "pessimists," that German youth had no "ideal" worth fighting for, he replied ill-humoredly that, at the time of the German empire, the ideal of the German army had been monarchist; at the time of Hitler's rule, "at least in the first two or three years," there had been enthusiasm for Nazism; now the ideal was "liberty." Was there any reason to believe, he asked, that liberty was any less useful as an integrative force than the previous ideals? The tone of this answer, perhaps more than its content, implied a view that is prevalent among the former German military, as it is, indeed, in modern society generally: what matters is not ideals, but organization, training, equipment, and leadership. In short, the technical and administrative aspects of military power count; the rest is verbiage.

Most of these arguments and speculations concerning the fighting value of a future German armed force were, as we have suggested, absent from public debate, even though that debate did reflect awareness of the fact that German youth was not eager to bear arms again.

In preparing for the parliamentary debates on the Conscription Law in 1956, the Social Democrats made a tactical mistake. They proposed that a group of distinguished former German generals be asked for their professional judgment of the need for a military establishment of 500,000 men based on conscription. Since the SPD distrusted the military specialists in the Defense Ministry, they asked that experts not connected with the government be invited to testify.

The proposal was accepted by the representatives of the government parties, and four former generals were heard by the Committee on Defense, namely Field Marshal von Manstein, Colonel General Reinhardt, and Generals Busse and Sixt.

As the Social Democrats had failed to foresee, these experts supported the government policy. They declared that they were not interested in reviewing the situation with respect to Germany's international obligations, but would confine themselves to the strictly military aspects of the problem. They unanimously considered a force of half a million men as the minimum required to safeguard German security. They also recommended that this force be constituted on the basis of conscription. Finally, they regarded twenty-four months of service essential.[6] Although the record of the hearings and recommendations was not published, enough of the testimony was either cited or alluded to on the floor of the *Bundestag* to leave no doubt about the experts' views. It appears that Fritz Berendsen, in his well-prepared speech on July 6, summed up many of the arguments presented earlier by the experts.[7]

The July debates in the *Bundestag* on conscription centered around two main points. The socialists now charged that the Western allies themselves had begun to doubt the wisdom of their policy of German rearmament, and speakers for the government took great care to prove that a force smaller than 500,000 would be unable to protect Germany in a *localized* conflict. The opposition repeated that the Soviet threat to Western Europe had lessened since Stalin's death and added that many important American and other Western statesmen had publicly expressed interest in a revision of the policy of German rearmament.

That policy dated from 1950, said Fritz Erler, but "the arguments of the cold war no longer are valid; the crusade does not take place."[8] Erler quoted Defense Secretary Wilson and General Gruenther to the

[6] The professionally most competent justification of a longer service was published by former General Hans Reinhardt, "Die Länge der aktiven Wehrdienstpflicht in der neuen Bundeswehr," *Wehrkunde*, September, 1956. Leo Freiherr Geyr von Schweppenburg, who had advocated a short military service of six months ever since the beginning of the rearmament debate, restated his views at the time of the debate on conscription before the Parliamentary Defense Committee and in the *Münchner Merkur*.

[7] *Bundestag Record*, July 6, 1956, p. 8775.

[8] *Ibid.* The term "crusade," if applied to hot or cold war, has a pejorative meaning in modern German; it is often used as a hostile allusion to the title of Eisenhower's memoirs, *Crusade in Europe*.

effect that no Soviet attack on Europe was to be expected in the foreseeable future, and proceeded to cite a long list of American sources against the policy of German rearmament, including George Kennan, Senators Flanders and Mansfield, Walter Lippmann, the *Christian Science Monitor,* and the *Washington Post.*

As usual, spokesmen for the government vigorously denied that the new Soviet diplomacy offered any reason for complacency and asserted that continued vigilance was required. Adenauer himself pointed to "the [communist] encirclement of Europe" and to the dangerous Soviet activities in the Middle East and the Mediterranean area.[9] Similarly, Kurt-Georg Kiesinger said that the new Soviet policy was "more dangerous" than Stalin's methods had been, and that unpleasant surprises were possible.[10] Herbert Schneider closed his speech with a quotation from Dmitri Manuilsky, "former intimate collaborator of Lenin's, long-time chief of the Comintern, and later Minister-President of the Ukraine Republic," who according to Ambassador André François-Poncet had characterized the problems of Soviet policy in 1931 as follows:

War to the end between communism and capitalism is inevitable. To-day, of course, we are not strong enough to attack. Our time will come in twenty to thirty years. In order to win we need the element of surprise. The bourgeoisie must be put to sleep. We shall therefore begin with the initiation of the most spectacular peace movement which has ever existed. There will be thrilling proposals and unusual concessions. The capitalist countries, simple-minded and decadent, will joyously collaborate in their own destruction. They will seize upon the new opportunity for friendship. When their vigilance abates we shall crush them.[11]

The government was weak and poorly informed in countering the argument of the opposition that Allied spokesmen themselves had been advocating a revision of the policy of rearmament, and that reductions of conventional forces had been effected or were being contemplated in the Soviet Union, the United States, and Great Britain. While the government did not deny the existence of such tendencies, they insisted that one motive underlying them had been

[9] *Ibid.*, p. 8782.
[10] *Ibid.*
[11] Quoted from *Baseler Nachrichten*, May 26, 1956, in *Bundestag Record*, July 6, 1956, p. 8807.

disillusionment with the Federal Republic as an ally. West Germany had to prove her political reliability by proceeding with rearmament according to the obligations she had accepted, they said. The government contended again that the real danger that might result from Western disillusionment about Germany was an American agreement with the Soviet Union in which the division of Germany would be recognized by the United States.[12]

Thus the government spokesmen discounted the possibility that a change in U.S. policy might result from developments in the United States itself, or from changing power relations in the world at large. Instead, they continued to present German compliance with present U.S. policy as the prerequisite of continued American interest in Germany as a European ally, and they falsely regarded all American criticism of U.S. policy toward Germany as nothing but an indication of distrust of the political reliability of the Germans. While the opposition cited American critics of American policy to buttress its own position, the government cited the military authorities of NATO —Generals Gruenther and Schuyler—to prove its case.

The opposition used the debate on conscription to attack the goal of a large army on military as well as political grounds. We have discussed these arguments above; there were four in the main:

1. Major war is unlikely because it would be equivalent to suicide for all the belligerents.
2. The plans according to which Germany was to put up a force of 500,000 men were made in 1950. These plans are obsolete today, not only because of the relaxation of international tensions, but also because nuclear weapons now play so important a role in Western defense plans as to lower the required number of conventional forces.
3. Should there be war involving the major powers in Europe, it would not matter whether Germany had a small military establishment or a large one: even a force of half a million men would afford no protection to Germany.
4. In the event of war, tactical atomic weapons will be used in the defense of Europe regardless of the size of the German defense contribution.

In the July debates, the SPD did not explain in detail what purpose a small army would serve. They failed to make clear whether

[12] Kurt-Georg Kiesinger, *ibid.*, p. 8813, and Herbert Schneider, *ibid.*, p. 8805.

they proposed a small force primarily because they considered it sufficient in the event of atomic war in Europe, or because they thought it only necessary to create a West German capability that would balance East German armament. Some commentators ascribed to the SPD an intention to create a force which could without the help of NATO prevent a military *coup d'état* in the event that East Germany attempted to force unification along communist lines.[13]

The coalition parties argued in reply that any civil war between East and West Germany would involve other communist satellites on the side of East Germany, even if the Soviet Union itself did not intervene directly. For this reason, a 200,000-man army would be too weak to resist limited aggression successfully, they said. The military experts who had testified before the Parliamentary Defense Committee had carefully considered the military risks of a war between East and West Germany, and Fritz Berendsen discussed this aspect of the rearmament issue in unusual detail on July 7.

He first assumed an invasion of West Germany by East German forces after the pattern of the Korean war, in which the Red army would abstain from participation. The East German forces, he said, would number 95,000 men when, as announced by the Pankow government, the military police formations in Communist Germany were reorganized as the National People's Army. In addition, East Germany disposed of 55,000 to 60,000 military forces under the Ministry of State Security. Since the total of 155,000 men corresponded to about 1 per cent of the East German population, Berendsen said, the military peacetime potential of East Germany was in fact already under arms and, "in view of the prevailing economic situation," could not yield additional forces "with or without conscription." He continued that, in the event of a war after the Korean model, the forces of East Germany would be increased by Czech and Polish volunteers corresponding to the support given to North Korea by the Chinese. Thus Berendsen and his political friends reached the seemingly paradoxical conclusion that the West German forces had to exceed 200,000 men, because the East German forces were *too weak* to attack in a local war without the aid of other communist satellites: "it is an established fact," said Richard Jaeger, "that the aggressor has every reason to be stronger than the defense. . . ."[14]

[13] *Deutsche Zeitung,* April 16, 1956.
[14] *Bundestag Record,* July 4, 1956, p. 8588.

In discussing next the possibility of a major war in Europe, with the participation of the Soviet Union, the coalition parties left the ground on which they had stood in 1955. At that time, the opposition had seized upon the NATO exercise CARTE BLANCHE to contend that "conventional mass armies" had been rendered obsolete by atomic weapons, and the coalition had answered that conventional weapons were still important, because both the employment and effectiveness of nuclear weapons were open to doubt. In 1956, the opposition reiterated its argument, but the coalition changed its reply. It contended that a force of 500,000 men did not constitute a mass army, and that any adaptation of ground forces to the conditions of atomic warfare would affect their organization and structure but not their size. Reduction of the size of military *units*, the government now argued, did not mean that the total number of troops required would sink below the 500,000 limit.

The government still was hard pressed by the opposition, however, on the point which has been crucial in German rearmament ever since December, 1954. The socialists insisted that, according to NATO plans, tactical atomic weapons would be used in the defense of Europe. In the event of war, therefore, Germany would become a theater of atomic war regardless of the size of the German defense contribution. The coalition passionately denied the truth of this contention, and based its whole argument on the controversial belief that Germany's conventional armament would render *atomic* war in Europe less likely. The heated exchange that ensued revealed the difficult ground on which the government had chosen to stand:

FRITZ ERLER (SPD): I repeat: The strategy of NATO leaves no room for doubting that an armed conflict in Europe—even with [the participation of] 500,000 German soldiers—will not remain a conventional conflict. The NATO plans are based upon immediate and direct employment of atomic weapons in the event of a conflict in Europe. Colleague Kiesinger, you are shaking your head.

KURT-GEORG KIESINGER (CDU): May I ask a question?

FRITZ ERLER: You must read what has been said on this point—officially, and not only secretly.

VICE-PRESIDENT DR. JAEGER: Deputy Erler, will you yield for a question?

FRITZ ERLER: Yes, sir.

KURT-GEORG KIESINGER: Deputy Erler, since you have addressed me: don't you know the utterances concerning this point that have constantly been made by the responsible politicians and military men of the West? Today, *Die Welt* has published an observation on this point by General Schuyler. How can you say, then, that the Western world is unanimous in its belief that war cannot be restricted to the use of conventional weapons? You seem not to have taken account of these views.

FRITZ ERLER: Colleague Kiesinger, I am not talking about opinions. I am talking about the declarations of those men who are responsible for the [NATO] plans and who have left no room for doubting . . . that the plans of NATO are based upon the immediate employment of atomic weapons in the event of a conflict in Europe. An official resolution to that effect was passed in December, 1954. (*Applause by the SPD. Shouts from the CDU.*) No, these are the plans, even if we were to have 500,000 German soldiers.

FRITZ BERENDSEN (CDU): That is wrong.

FRITZ ERLER: There can be no doubt about it.

FRITZ BERENDSEN: That is wrong.

VICE-PRESIDENT DR. JAEGER: Will you yield for another question?

FRITZ ERLER: Gladly.

KURT-GEORG KIESINGER: Colleague Erler, have you not heard in the conversations with those who are responsible in NATO that the danger of the extension of a possible conflict into an atomic war is reduced by the fact that the conventional ground forces are being augmented on the European continent (*applause by the government parties*) and that, therefore, the more we contribute in this direction, we work all the more for peace and for the avoidance of a terrible atomic conflict? (*Renewed applause by the government parties.*)

FRITZ ERLER: If you wish to hear it explicitly, no one responsible in NATO has ever declared in my presence that the NATO powers will not use their tactical atomic weapons when we will have put up 500,000 German soldiers; on the contrary. (*Hear! Hear! and applause from the SPD. Shouts from the government parties.*) . . . It is important to destroy the illusion that by putting up 500,000 soldiers we may hope in the event of conflict . . . to protect ourselves against the employment of atomic weapons in the Federal Republic. Unfortunately, that is not true. . . .

VICE-PRESIDENT DR. JAEGER: Mr. Deputy, will you permit yet another question?

FRITZ ERLER: Yes, sir.

ROLAND SEFFRIN (CDU): Colleague Erler, as I recall, you were present when General Gruenther expounded his plans to the members of the Committee on Defense here in Bonn. Do you no longer recall that he explained quite clearly and very convincingly that the contribution by the Federal Republic of 500,000 men was necessary in order to meet his plans? (*Shouts and laughter from the SPD.*)

FRITZ ERLER: Yes, I will gladly recall for you what General Gruenther told us. . . . It is correct that General Gruenther said, first, in order to meet his plans (to use your language) 500,000 soldiers are needed. Secondly, he said also that these 500,000 soldiers are needed in order to force the Soviet Union in the event of an imminent attack so to concentrate its forces as to create the possibility for the use of atomic weapons. (*Hear! Hear! from the SPD.*) And now somebody should dare to stand up and tell me that NATO planning with 500,000 German soldiers [at its disposal] will forego the use of atomic weapons! (*Applause from the SPD.*)

VICE-PRESIDENT DR. JAEGER: Will you allow an additional question, Deputy Erler?

ROLAND SEFFRIN: Deputy Erler, aren't you, too, of the opinion that what you just said contradicts your previous statements? (*Shouts and laughter from the SPD.*)

FRITZ ERLER: No, I merely called attention to the fact, about which unfortunately the people have been left all too often in the dark in consequence of our discussions, that in view of regrettable weapons developments in the world even as many as 500,000 German soldiers are not able to protect the German people against the use of atomic weapons in the event of conflict. (*Applause from the SPD.*) [15]

There were more interruptions and more questions, but none succeeded in disconcerting the speaker. In their rebuttal, the deputies supporting Adenauer's policy again avoided discussing the strategy of NATO and confined themselves to general declarations on the relationship between conventional and atomic weapons. Kurt-Georg Kiesinger offered the most conciliatory summary of their views. Addressing Fritz Erler personally, he pointed out that fear of nuclear weapons might conceivably induce the Western powers not to use atomic weapons in defense against a conventional Soviet attack. "What would be the consequence?" he asked:

There would be only two alternatives for the West. One of them is capitulation: one cannot and will not use atomic weapons, but one has no conventional armies strong enough to halt the attack. The other alternative, to be sure, is that one does not want to capitulate and has no other choice but the initiation of general atomic war, which would be fatal for mankind. Is it therefore not true when we say that we serve the cause of peace by supporting the idea of general land armies in

[15] *Bundestag Record*, July 6, 1956, pp. 8777–8778.

Europe and that we contribute at least our share, in the form of the German defense contribution, to the end of avoiding the use of the most horrible of all means of destruction, if the worst comes to the worst? [16]

As is evident from the cited exchange, the speakers for the coalition simply asserted that German rearmament would either lead to a change of NATO's plans for use of atomic weapons or in some way contribute to reducing the risk of atomic war in Europe. Thus by July, 1956, the standard argument of the coalition parties that German rearmament would help to deter Soviet aggression had been replaced, in part, by the contention that the value of German soldiers consisted in helping to deter *atomic* war. This shift in emphasis corresponded to a modification of general apprehension. In the early fifties, at the beginning of the rearmament debate, German politicians had had to deal with the fear of Soviet aggression. In 1955 and 1956, this fear had abated, and had been replaced by the fear of nuclear weapons.

The Conscription Law was passed in the *Bundestag* by a vote of 276 to 174, with 22 abstentions. The Social Democrats were convinced that the *Bundestag* vote did not reflect the views of the Germans. On July 11, four days after the votes had been cast, Ollenhauer submitted to the 72d Congress of the Social Democratic Party in Munich a program for the elections of 1957 which demanded repeal of the law.[17] There is little doubt that the socialist position will find favor with many Germans.

[16] *Ibid.*, p. 8814.
[17] Erich Ollenhauer's speech at the SPD Congress was published as a pamphlet in English under the title *German Politics at a Turning Point*, Bonn, 1956.

TWELVE

Rearmament Revised

After the passage of the law on conscription in July, 1956, German opposition to Adenauer's and Blank's plans of rearmament spread rapidly beyond Social Democratic circles. In the government parties themselves, both Blank's plans for longer military service and his procurement program were criticized. In the spring of 1956, at the Party Conference of the CSU in Stuttgart, Blank's old rival Franz-Josef Strauss had attacked the plans of the Defense Ministry for a large army of conscripts in favor of a "quality army." Later in the same year, during the parliamentary debate on conscription, Richard Jaeger, Strauss's party colleague, had opposed the government plan for eighteen months' service. It had become evident that the technical and organizational preparations for a relatively quick build-up of the German forces were inadequate, and the value of Blank's whole performance was questioned. It appeared to a growing number of observers that the experts in the Defense Ministry had either failed to create some of the essential preconditions for the projected build-up or else had failed to inform their Minister of the difficulties which the realization of his announced plans would encounter. Confidence in Blank, who had been unskillful and unsuccessful in his dealings with the Parliamentary Defense Committee and with the press, waned rapidly in the government parties, in NATO, and, finally, in the Chancellery itself. At a caucus of the Christian Democratic Party leaders on September 26, Blank's timetable for rearmament and his policies for receiving, training, and arming the first conscripts were severely assailed by his own party colleagues. Finally, on October 5, 1956, after a three-day investigation, the *Bun-*

destag Defense and Budget committees reduced Blank's procurement program by one billion marks.

Under these and other pressures, Adenauer changed his armament policies in three important respects. On September 28 the cabinet announced that the period of military service for all conscripts would be reduced to twelve months. In a cabinet shake-up early in October, the Chancellor sacrificed Theodor Blank and appointed as his successor Franz-Josef Strauss, the energetic CSU Minister for Atomic Affairs. Strauss resolved a conflict that had arisen over the matériel-procurement program and changed the force goals for 1957. Finally, Adenauer made some surprising international efforts to obtain atomic arms for Germany.

In shortening the service of conscripts, Adenauer acted against the advice of Theodor Blank, his own Defense Minister, and his top military officials as well as against the best judgment of nearly all German military experts who had expressed their professional views on this subject. Thus the decision represented a defeat for the older German military leaders. Adenauer's chancellery issued a statement which tried to place the responsibility for the development on the so-called "Radford Plan," about which news stories had recently appeared. The official statement said that "when plans about a strong diminution of the U.S. Armed Forces became known from reports in American newspapers," Adenauer became convinced that "thereafter parliamentary approval of eighteen months' service could probably no longer be secured."[1] In effect, the announcement of the Chancellery was tantamount to making a concession to the Soviet Union without getting anything in return. Adenauer acted in response to domestic political pressures and used the Radford Plan as a convenient pretext for the concession he felt it necessary to make.

Abroad, Adenauer's decision was immediately understood to mean that Germany would not meet her treaty obligation to put up a force of half a million men in NATO, since there were not enough volunteers to fill the gap created by the shortening of the service of conscripts. At the NATO Council in Paris on September 28, the previous day's curtailment of the German military service was criticized with special severity by the British, Belgians, Dutch, Danes, and Norwegians, who pointed out that their countrymen would find it difficult to understand why Germany, one of the main

[1] Quoted in *Der Spiegel,* October 3, 1956.

countries in need of protection, had adopted a defense burden less onerous than that carried by the other border states of NATO. The German representatives were requested to ascertain how their government hoped to maintain the quality and quantity of the German defense contribution to NATO on the basis of a twelve months' service. The decision of the German government also found little favor when the Consultative Assembly of the West European Union met in Strasbourg in October, 1956. The Dutch deputy Fens said that the West would face catastrophe if the German example were followed in other countries. He expressed the hope that the deputies of the member states of WEU would have courage enough to reject in their own parliaments any proposals to curtail the length of military service.[2]

Adenauer's decision created not only international difficulties but also domestic dangers. Since efficiency in handling modern weapons requires more than twelve months' training, conscripts will necessarily not be the mainstay of the German armed forces. The emphasis will have to be on volunteers. The ratio of volunteers to conscripts will be about three to two, a reversal of the ratio originally envisaged by Blank.[3] Volunteers will be enlisted for eighteen months or more, and will include virtually all army officers, noncommissioned officers, and air force and navy personnel.[4]

A shortage of suitable volunteers to meet the new requirements could lead to an influx of former SS officers into the *Bundeswehr* that would jeopardize the democratic character of German defense. Even before the twelve months' service was decided upon, the Defense Ministry had accepted some former SS officers as volunteers, and had thereby caused concern among those Germans who feared that rearmament might resurrect military institutions that were indifferent or hostile to the new democratic order in their country.[5] The German public, the *Bundestag* deputies, and the Chancellor

[2] *Wehrkunde,* November, 1956, p. 574.

[3] In an interview in December, 1956, Strauss said that in the army the ratio of volunteers to conscripts would be 55 to 45 (*Der Spiegel,* January 2, 1957, p. 22).

[4] The amount of reserve training for conscripts will be a total of nine months, to be served by the conscripts prior to their thirty-fifth birthday. This constitutes a lengthening, by about 50 per cent, of the reserve training originally planned for enlisted men.

[5] Those who had advocated accepting former members of the *Waffen SS*—and many conservative officers have taken this stand—argue that the SS had not consisted entirely of fanatical Nazis. Many young Germans, they claim, had been unable to escape such service under the Hitler regime.

himself learned of this practice only after it had been adopted. Even dispassionate critics could not help accusing the Defense Ministry at the time of a "capital lack of political instinct." [6] It seemed to them that the Ministry had abandoned its own avowed objective of building up a democratic army. It is possible that the reduction of the term of service will create conditions conducive to even less scrupulous processing of applications for volunteer service. [7] In any event, neither Count Baudissin's efforts in the Defense Ministry nor the uncompromising screening activities of the Personnel Selection Board nor the constitutional amendments made on Social Democratic initiative in the spring of 1955 had convinced the Germans that the basic rights of the individual would be safeguarded in the new armed forces. A German poll, conducted in July, 1956, showed only 20 per cent of the West Germans to be confident that life in the *Bundeswehr* would be different from what it had been in the *Wehrmacht*. [8]

Shortly after the reduction of the term of military service, Blank's matériel-procurement program came under heavy fire in both Germany and Britain. In June, 1956, after much hard bargaining, the federal government had agreed to continue supporting the cost of foreign troops on German territory only on a reduced scale. The British had been particularly displeased by the German attitude, but had been given reason to believe that Germany would place substantial German orders for the British Centurion tank and thus ease Britain's financial burden in participating in the defense of the Continent. Up to October, 1956, there was little evidence, however, that such purchases were in the offing. It was expected that Germany would buy seven British frigates, thirty-six landing craft and

---

[6] *Die Gegenwart,* October 20, 1956.

[7] This danger was pointed out also by *The Times* (London), September 28, 1956.

[8] The *Institut für Demoskopie* included in its poll the following question: "Some people say that one behaves at first as if many things will now be different in the service. Later everything will be exactly as it used to be. In your opinion, is this correct, or is it incorrect?" The replies, as published in *Der Spiegel* (July 18, 1956, p. 31), were divided as follows:

	Will Be As Before	Will Be Different
Men, 30–59 years old	68%	22%
Men supporting the CDU	51	36
Men supporting the SPD	80	12
Total sample	55%	20%

The percentage figures in each line do not add up to 100, because *Der Spiegel* failed to publish the percentages of those who expressed no opinion.

other small vessels, some sixty-eight Sea Hawks, sixteen Fairey Gannets, and some Bristol Sycamore helicopters. But all this was no consolation for the failure to order the Centurion tank, Britain's star product on the international weapons market.

By 1960, Blank planned instead to acquire no less than 4,000 M-47 Patton tanks. He could justify this plan on grounds of economy, since the Patton tank was less expensive than the Centurion, and on grounds of standardization, since large additional numbers of Patton tanks were available from the American military aid program. But both the size of the procurement program and the selection of the Patton tank were harshly criticized by German politicians and tank experts. Thus domestic criticism was added to the British, although on different grounds.

The British were disturbed by Blank's preference for American tanks for strategic as well as commercial reasons.[9] Blank's plan was evidently derived from the traditional notions of mobile tank warfare that were current in the Defense Ministry almost from its inception. In contrast, the British Army of the Rhine, made up of large infantry divisions and a minimum of transport, presupposes use of tactical atomic weapons in war. It is an army with an order of battle for *atomic defense*. To some British observers it appeared that Blank was planning, rather, for an army that could wage conventional *offensive,* mobile warfare.[10]

In Germany, influential members of Blank's own party joined the Social Democrats in charging that by the time the *Bundeswehr* was fully armed with tanks its armament would be obsolescent. Some critics quoted unfavorable opinions about the Patton tank that had been expressed by American generals. In addition, some German military experts, in particular Fritz Berendsen, believed that Germany should build her own tanks and be independent of imported armaments. It became known that German heavy industry was developing a keen interest in the procurement program of the Defense Ministry. The procurement program was complicated further by West Germany's embarrassingly favorable position in the European

[9] *The Times* (London) wrote on October 5, 1956, "The real problem is to find armaments which Britain can supply and which Germany has no compelling reason to buy elsewhere."

[10] They also criticized the NATO co-ordination plan, pointing out that the highest-ranking German officer in the liaison group attached to the Army of the Rhine was only a major.

Payments Union. In 1956, when West Germany was the third greatest trading nation of the world, her credit position against other members of the Union had risen by 500 million dollars to a high of $2,625,000,000.

When the *Bundestag* committees curtailed Blank's procurement program by one billion marks in October, the reduction in tank purchases accounted for four-fifths of this saving.[11] One of the first tasks that Franz-Josef Strauss set himself as Defense Minister was a review of the conflict that had arisen over the policy on armaments. In November, 1956, his position was officially described as follows:

> The members of the *Bundestag* Defense Committee will have an early opportunity to inspect not only the American-made M-47 and the British-made "Centurion" (both of the medium class), but also the British heavy tank "Conqueror," the British counterpart of the "Joseph Stalin III." German tank crews are now testing these three types as to their speed, maneuverability, and penetration power of their guns. In the long run, the Federal Republic hopes to develop a tank of its own design which would be considerably lighter but faster than the tanks now available. This would not be in contradiction to Germany's avowed intention not to manufacture guns of caliber greater than 40-mm. The German-built tanks could mount cannon produced by Germany's NATO partners.[12]

On December 6, 1956, however, Strauss announced that he would not call upon West German industry to manufacture tanks and large-caliber guns. The ordnance needs of the new German forces would be met through 1957 by the United States with equipment of the type used in the Korean war and given to Germany as a gift in 1956. Beginning in 1957, Germany would buy additional equipment required for the further build-up of her forces. Strauss said that $710,000,000 worth of purchases had been scheduled for the years 1957 to 1960. Since these purchases will be made in countries that are members of the European Payments Union, the transaction will reduce Germany's favorable balance of trade in the Union. Strauss explained that he expected the U.S. tank M-47, which now is basic equipment in the West German forces, to prove inferior in the forthcoming tests to the British Centurion medium tank, and he added that West Germany "expected to modify and improve" the basic

---

[11] The reduction applied only to the first procurement period ending on March 31, 1958.

[12] *The Bulletin*, a weekly survey of German affairs issued by the Press and Information Office of the German federal government (English ed.), November 15, 1956, p. 5.

material that it would buy abroad so as to bridge the gap between the Western and the superior Soviet types.[13] Similarly, General Josef Kammhuber explained that the new *Luftwaffe* intended to drop the F-84 jet fighter plane now in use and to acquire a type that would out-perform the Soviet MIG-21. He expected to begin buying this new high-performance fighter toward the end of 1958.[14]

Perhaps the most startling departure from the armament policy that Adenauer had followed since 1950 was his attempt, in September, 1956, to raise the international question of providing West Germany with tactical atomic weapons. In the debate on conscription, two months earlier, neither the opposition nor the government had alluded to this possibility. The opposition might conceivably have proposed that the government ought to press a request for such support in order to lower the need for conventional forces. Similarly, the government parties might have suggested that such arrangements would increase Germany's deterrent power, but that a development in this direction could not be considered unless the Federal Republic made every effort to meet its international obligations concerning conventional armaments. Or the government might have replied to the opposition that the smaller force it advocated would suffice only if Germany were to dispose of tactical atomic weapons. But the subject was never publicly mentioned in any form. Even in private conversations with German military and political leaders in the winter of 1955, it was referred to only once. A *Bundestag* deputy belonging to the Refugee Party (GB/BHE), who took pride in divulging to the interviewer his anti-American feelings, mentioned that Germany "needed" atomic weapons. He said that this was "no nationalistic, but merely a natural demand." Reasons of secrecy could not be adduced in refusing it, he said; "the Russians know everything anyhow." As a politician, he could not meet his constituents and tell them that "everything is O.K. since we have General Gruenther: I would be thrown out if I tried that." Similarly, he suggested that Germany needed atomic weapons more urgently than the United States because his country was in greater danger. "The U.S. farmers buy air-raid shelters, as though Denver—Good Lord!— is in greater danger than Brunswick."

The only other reference to Germany's need for tactical atomic

[13] See the dispatch by Arthur J. Olsen in *The New York Times*, December 5, 1956.
[14] *Ibid.*

weapons was made in a written communication from a former German general. Alarmed by the growing tendencies of anti-NATO feeling in Germany, he suggested in March, 1956, that the basis of such "neutralism" could be destroyed only by equipping the German forces with atomic weapons and integrating the German air forces more closely with those of their NATO allies. In subsequent correspondence, after the July, 1956, debate in the *Bundestag*, he wrote that he had been mistaken on this point. The German government, he said, "clings to conventional weapons mainly because it believes that atomic war of any kind can thus be avoided. As you know, this belief is not shared by the atomic powers. They would react atomically in any case [in the event of war] in Europe."

Soon after the passage of the Conscription Law, Adenauer had publicly reaffirmed his belief in the importance of conventional armaments. Angered by press reports about the Radford Plan, he had taken the unprecedented step of publicly criticizing American military policy. On August 21, he declared that he regarded the shift of emphasis to atomic weapons "as a mistake." [15] In the middle of September, the Council of Ministers of WEU met upon German initiative for a special session in Paris in order to discuss the repercussions of the Radford Plan. Germany was satisfied that other members of WEU shared her objections to plans for "too drastic a diminution of conventional weapons and a decrease of American-British forces on the Continent." More than that, it was considered imperative that the WEU nations close the existing gaps between armament goals and performance.[16] Only a few days later, however, the German government reversed its position. As opposition to the longer term of service mounted in the coalition parties themselves, the government suddenly seemed to discover that there was no irrefutable reason why the principle of the Radford Plan should apply only to the American defense posture. If this principle was sound, why should it be valid only for the atomic powers of NATO and not also for the atomically destitute nations? Could not a plan to share atomic weapons help to reduce the manpower contributions both of West Germany and of all the Allies? The whole NATO defense, after all, was based on the idea that tactical atomic weapons would compensate for Western weakness in ground-force strength.

[15] See Chap. 1, p. 15.
[16] *Wehrkunde*, October, 1956, p. 512.

Thus suddenly toward the end of September, 1956, it was widely reported in the German and foreign press that the German government was entertaining the idea of equipping the *Bundeswehr* with tactical atomic weapons to compensate for its shortage in military manpower.[17] Adenauer broached the subject on the occasion of his visit to Brussels at the end of September, while Blank was still Defense Minister.[18]

Evidently such plans had to take account of the political problems which a policy of atomic armament would raise in the relations of the smaller and medium powers, not only among themselves, but also with the United States. It was not likely that the French and the Belgians, or the Dutch and the Danes, would regard with indifference the acquisition of an independent atomic capability by the German *Bundeswehr*. But perhaps Adenauer hoped that, despite their probable alarm at any independent German effort to acquire atomic weapons, the members of WEU would share his new views on transarmament, since a possible reduction of American military forces in Europe would affect all the European members of NATO.

If this was Adenauer's hope, it was disappointed at first. In October, 1956, the Consultative Assembly of WEU concerned itself with the issue of transarmament and reaffirmed the need for conventional defense contributions to NATO. The WEU, which lacked the supranational features and authority of the defunct EDC, was not a suitable forum for defining the common interests of its members vis-à-vis the United States.[19]

It is likely, moreover, that the German representatives at this meet-

[17] *General-Anzeiger*, Bonn, September 22, 1956, and *The Times* (London), September 28, 1956. *Time* reported on October 29, 1956, that one of the three conditions Strauss had laid down to the German cabinet before he accepted the appointment as Defense Minister was that he be given cabinet backing for a tactical atomic weapons program.

[18] *The Times* (London), September 25, 1956. *Der Spiegel*, October 17, 1956, attributed Adenauer's interest in atomic arms for the German *Bundeswehr* to a conversation with Secretary Quarles in Bonn on September 10. Quarles was reported to have convinced Adenauer that there was an irreversible trend toward "transarmament," and Strauss was quoted as saying, "The conversation with Quarles has made a tremendous impression upon Adenauer." In its issue of January 2, 1957, however, *Der Spiegel* attributed Adenauer's new belief in the value of atomic arms to the influence of Franz-Josef Strauss himself. The idea of giving atomic weapons to Germany was discussed in the German press as early as August, 1956. See Adelbert Weinstein's articles in *Frankfurter Allgemeine Zeitung*, August 20, August 29, and September 4, 1956.

[19] Adenauer, apparently aware of this, had tried in September to arouse interest in the formation of a European confederation that was to function as a "third force" in relation to the United States and the Soviet Union.

ing found that their position was compromised by the reduction of the German military service. The resolution to repeat the emphasis on conventional weapons was in part the result of West European displeasure at this development.[20] The Assembly resolved only that the Council of Ministers of WEU clarify whether or not, and to what extent, an adaptation of the armed contingents of the member states to the new weapons was necessary and practical. The resolution added significantly that no member of WEU should make independent decisions affecting the transarmament of its own forces.

In December, 1956, however, the issue came up for discussion once more, this time at the NATO Council, a forum more appropriate than the Consultative Assembly of WEU for dealing with a matter so vital to the Western alliance. The discussion showed that Germany was not alone in her interest in receiving tactical atomic weapons, and since the British representative took the lead in the debate, Germany could avoid giving the embarrassing impression that her fresh interest in atomic support stemmed from the new plans to reduce the German manpower contribution to NATO. The defense ministers of Germany, France, and the Netherlands, and the Foreign Minister of Turkey supported British Defense Minister Anthony Head's suggestion that American tactical nuclear warheads be made available to European forces. Britain, prompted by her desire to reduce the size of her costly Army of the Rhine, pointed out that arrangements for nuclear sharing would lower the need for manpower contributions from all nations receiving such support. In reply, U.S. Secretary of Defense Charles E. Wilson commented that the United States would continue to supply her European allies with modern weapons, but given American legal prohibitions against transfer of nuclear warheads to alien forces, he could not, of course, promise to meet the specific European request.

Thus the German government used the Radford Plan as a pretext for curtailing conscription, but failed in its efforts to use it as a springboard for obtaining nuclear weapons, or for initiating a WEU request for such weapons. It could be satisfied, however, that in the NATO Council various European nations individually advised the United States of their common interest in nuclear sharing, though without immediate results. It appeared that the only compromise

[20] This resolution was passed unanimously, with seven abstentions. Six German Social Democrats and a liberal deputy from Luxembourg abstained.

which was legally possible consisted in providing one or several members of NATO either with dual-purpose rockets and guns that could fire both high-explosive and atomic weapons or with missiles of intermediate range capable of carrying atomic warheads; the atomic warheads themselves would remain under American control. Such arrangements were indeed made in the spring of 1957. At the Bermuda parley of President Eisenhower and Prime Minister Macmillan, Britain was promised U.S. missiles of intermediate range, and on April 12, 1957, NATO announced that the United States would make advanced weapons available to certain member states. These weapons include the Honest John, the Matador, and the Nike.

By the end of 1956, West Germany claimed to have 96,000 men under arms—about 66,000 in the army (including 9,500 men of the former Border Police), 14,000 in the air force, 9,000 in the navy, and 6,500 in territorial organizations. Some German newspapers said, however, that the actual total was only 70,000 men. Blank's plans for the build-up of the German forces were changed by Strauss so as to speed up the availability of German cadres for NATO, although this measure involved a drastic reduction of the original unrealistic force goals for 1957. In November Strauss announced that by the end of 1957 the *Bundeswehr* will have 120,000 men under arms instead of the 270,000 envisaged by his predecessor.[21] There will be three grenadier divisions, two armored divisions, one mountain brigade, one air-borne brigade, and a number of cadres for purposes of home defense. The planned strength of the grenadier and armored divisions will eventually be 12,000 men each. The grenadier divisions will be fully motorized, and armored units will be attached to them. Each armored division is scheduled to have roughly 220 tanks and additional special-purpose tanks for mine-clearing and bridge-laying.[22]

The grenadier and armored divisions will be so organized and trained that they can be split up, according to a plan approved by NATO, and used as cadres for two divisions each.[23] This organizational change was referred to in the American press as Strauss's crash program to meet the emergency in the cold war highlighted by the Soviet suppression of the revolution in Hungary.

[21] *The Bulletin* (English ed.), November 15, 1956, p. 5.
[22] *Ibid.*
[23] *Tatsachen über Deutschland,* published by the Press and Information Office of the German federal government, Bonn, 1957, p. 54.

Thus more than six years after German rearmament was first discussed among the NATO allies, the new German Minister of Defense could take credit for a "realistic" armament effort. At the NATO meeting in December, 1956, he had made known Germany's new interest in receiving tactical atomic weapons and had persuaded Germany's allies that a smaller German "quality army" that could be counted on was preferable to his predecessor's promises of a larger force, which had so long remained unfulfilled.

Although, in the years to come, the total contribution of German manpower to NATO will probably fall short of the half-million mark that was first mentioned when the European Defense Community was proposed, five to seven German divisions will be available to NATO in 1957. This can be compared with France's division-and-a-half on the Continent at the end of 1956—the remainder of her army was engaged in Africa—and to the four divisions of the British Army of the Rhine, which will be reduced in size as German divisions become available or as U.S. missiles are given to Britain. The German contribution, therefore, though reduced, will compare favorably with that of the other West European powers. Furthermore, at the time of the NATO Council meeting in December, 1956, it transpired that in the spring of 1957 a German general was to take command of all NATO ground forces on the central front which extends from Switzerland to the Baltic. General Hans Speidel was appointed to that post in January, 1957.

German air force goals have not yet been scaled down from the projected strength of 100,000 men in 1959. The main problem of building up the tactical forces that Germany is to contribute to NATO consists in training the requisite pilots. By July, 1955, the German Defense Ministry had received only 12,000 applications for volunteer service in the new *Luftwaffe;* most of them were from air force veterans too old for extended duty or otherwise ineligible for service.[24] The training in the United States of the first German group of instructors was concluded in the summer of 1956. It is expected that beginning in the summer of 1957 German training schools will graduate twenty-five pilots a month.[25]

When Strauss was still competing for office with Blank, he used to

[24] Lewis J. Edinger, "Concept of the West German Air Force," *Air University Quarterly Review*, Vol. VIII, No. 2 (Summer, 1956), p. 52.
[25] *Tatsachen über Deutschland,* p. 54.

stress the need for German home defense forces. As new Defense Minister he has not yet made public his plans for such forces. It is rather certain, however, that the establishment of German home defense in addition to the creation of the NATO contingents according to the new schedule would meet with political difficulties that cannot be overcome in an election year. Nor is it likely that Strauss could solve the financial problems of adequate home defense within the approved German armament budget.

Conclusion

THIRTEEN

Prospects

The major political and military problems of the North Atlantic alliance stem from two salient features of the prevailing balance of power, the virtual nuclear bipolarity of the world with the United States and the Soviet Union as the two giant powers, and the virtual American monopoly of nuclear power in NATO.

If other members of NATO as well as the United States, and to a considerably lesser extent Great Britain, possessed *strategic* deterrent power, the present bipolarity of the world would diminish. The European countries would be able to pursue a more independent policy and some measure of the multipolar balance of power that existed in the pre-atomic age would be restored. In such a world, smaller nations that are now atomically destitute would each be able to reap the benefits of peace under the agonizing conditions of multilateral strategic deterrence. A variant of this development would consist in a redistribution of the strategic deterrent capability of the West so as to endow not individual countries but a group or groups of nations with the independent strategic deterrence which at present only the United States and the Soviet Union (and Great Britain) possess. Such redistribution of strategic nuclear power would not fully restore political multipolarity, however, since strategic deterrence would strengthen merely the defensive posture of smaller countries against atomic blackmail and nuclear attack. While it would enable them to withstand pressure both against and within the Western coalition with more equanimity, they would not necessarily be in a position to exert pressure themselves. For that purpose they would still need supplementary conventional power. In fact, if the acquisition of a strategic deterrent capability were to accelerate the present trend toward curtailment of nonatomic armament, the smaller countries would find their political choice further restricted whenever they faced issues unrelated to atomic blackmail or nuclear war.

Nuclear multipolarity will emerge in the course of time, as other nations follow the Soviet Union and Great Britain in breaking the American monopoly in nuclear weapons. And there is no *technological* reason why the development of multipolarity could not be speeded up by the present nuclear powers themselves if they were willing to share nuclear capabilities with some other nations. Loan or sale of arms is no novelty in military history. But the general reluctance of great powers to lend or sell their most advanced means of destruction to others is multiplied in the case of nuclear weapons: these weapons are of unprecedented destructiveness; the nuclear powers derive an increment of security from secret leads in nuclear science and technology; and they are concerned that sharing such weapons with others might entail their use by allied powers in their minor wars.

The doctrine of "the sword and the shield" obscures the political significance of the unequal distribution of nuclear capabilities among the members of NATO. "The sword" stands, by and large, for the nuclear capabilities of the U.S. Strategic Air Command (and the U.S. Navy), "the shield" for the NATO forces in Europe. But until 1957 both the strategic nuclear capability of the West and the nuclear armament in Europe were largely under American control. None of the atomic weapons in Europe was integrated into the NATO defense system. The American nuclear weapons were either under the authority of the U.S. Air Force (like the B-61 Matadors) or of the Supreme Commander of NATO (like the atomic 280-mm guns, the Honest John rockets, and the Corporal missiles); but he had this authority as commander of the U.S. forces stationed in Europe and not in his role as Supreme Allied Commander, Europe. Furthermore, the atomic firepower of the American ground forces in Europe may be increased in the future while their numbers may be reduced. The American contribution to the common ground defenses in Europe might be confined to atomic support groups.[1] The military posture of

---

[1] The importance of such atomic task forces was recognized in Germany when the neutralization of Austria cut the contiguous contact over land routes through NATO territory between West Germany and northern Italy. For a German discussion of the Southern European Task Force, see Wilhelm Ritter von Schramm, "Atom-Sperrverbände," *Deutsche Soldaten-Zeitung,* October, 1955, p. 3.

NATO might then be stronger than it is today, but the cleavage between the United States and the atomically destitute powers in NATO would be deepened. The United States would be superior to her European allies not merely because she possessed "the sword" in the form of intercontinental striking forces, but also because her ground forces in Europe would be modernly equipped elite units, while those of her allies would be auxiliary forces armed with less advanced weapons.

In order to buttress the defensive strength of the coalition despite its reduced military manpower, the United States decided in April, 1957, to make available to her continental European allies certain advanced weapons that could be used in tactical atomic warfare. This aid will not extend to the atomic warheads themselves. Nor will it affect strategic inequalities within NATO. If anything, the latter have been exacerbated by the new defense policy of the British, who will rely in the future primarily upon a strategic deterrent capability of their own. While the U.S. decision has narrowed somewhat the nuclear weapons gap within NATO, the British decision will create new inequalities and try the political viability of NATO, if not its ability to survive.

Technological differentiation of military capabilities among allies is not new in the history of alliances. A division of military functions and a gradation of military technology among various units of a military establishment has often existed not only in individual nations, but also on an international level, in military alliances. Strictly speaking, there has never been a coalition in which all partners were equally strong and possessed armaments of equally advanced technology. In particular, alliances of the past between sea powers and land powers testify to the fact that viable arrangements for common defense can be made on the basis of functional specialization among the partners. An international division of armament functions among the partners of a coalition, however, is bound to generate certain frictions which in their mildest form may be said to correspond to service rivalries in a national defense establishment and which in their strongest form may sap the strength of the alliance.

German generals have not challenged the nuclear pre-eminence of the United States in NATO. If as a group they have not yet fully accepted the notion that tactical atomic weapons are part of the "conventional" armament of modern forces, it can be predicted that they will do so in the near future, partly because it is impossible to resist progress in the technology of destruction, partly because the need to compensate for insufficient manpower contributions exists in Germany as well as in the United States—it is a phenomenon of modern Western civilization at large—and partly because Germany's political comeback would be arrested if she voluntarily resigned herself to a qualitatively inferior armament status for her ground forces. It is not to be expected that the military will be among those Germans who are prepared for such resignation. Both Franz-Josef Strauss and Adenauer have indicated their interest in tactical atomic arms for the German *Bundeswehr*. In the future, this German interest is bound to increase despite German socialist and French opposition.

German military attitudes toward the acquisition of a strategic capability differ from those toward tactical nuclear weapons. German generals have not ventured to examine the possibility of sharing *strategic* deterrent power more widely in NATO. The possibility that the Federal Republic or Western Europe might acquire a strategic nuclear capability has been mentioned in Germany only by journalists. For example, in September, 1956, Weinstein suggested that, since the real production of West Germany was dependent on "indirect [i.e., strategic] atomic deterrence," and since under conditions of nuclear parity the United States could not be expected to risk using its strategic capability for winning a European war, "France, Germany, possibly also Italy and Turkey" would have to become atomic powers.[2] This, he said, would enable the United States to reduce or withdraw her ground forces without weakening the military strength of NATO in Europe. The requisite atomic arms could be lent or sold. He added that such *strategic* transarmament would involve consequences for the structure of the German air force. It could no longer consist mainly of fighter planes. Instead, the nucleus of West German defense would have to be "a highly qualified, small, long-range bombing force, which as an atom bomb carrier would be capable of strategic deterrence."[3] Furthermore, this bombing force would have to be allowed to use Western air bases "beyond our frontiers."[4]

[2] *Frankfurter Allgemeine Zeitung,* September 4, 1956.
[3] *Ibid.,* August 28, 1956.
[4] *Ibid.,* September 4, 1956.

Such speculations about the military requirements of the defense of Europe were much bolder than the strategic considerations of the German officers who thought along traditional lines. Some former German air force officers did resent the fact that the future German *Luftwaffe* would have no bombing force of its own, and regarded this deficiency as evidence of continued Allied discrimination against Germany as the loser in World War II. However, the informants who reported in 1955 that some people held such views attributed them to others rather than stating them as their own. They claimed moreover to have explained to their grumbling comrades that a division of military functions in the Western alliance was inevitable and necessary. One air force general remarked, "Why should we Germans have bombers? You have them. Besides, Germany is too small a territory for their safe and effective use." The general who made this remark agreed with many other military specialists that there was a need for supranational arrangements concerning certain strictly *defensive* functions of armament, such as warning systems and civil defense, but he accepted the existing distribution of *offensive* capabilities in the Western alliance without regret or resentment.

Many German generals regard strategic nuclear capabilities as a privilege of the strongest partner in the coalition which Germany or other powers on the European continent cannot hope to attain. These views are often reinforced by economic considerations.[5] It is widely, though not generally, held that no country, including the United States, can afford to finance both a strategic deterrent capability and a large ground-force establishment. And what is too burdensome for the United States, it is felt, cannot possibly be borne by Germany. Thus nuclear developments from 1950 to 1956 had generated among German military leaders no desire for strategic weapons and long-range bombers, but merely a keener appreciation of the division of military functions among the members of the coalition.

In some other respects, however, the viability of NATO and the official doctrine of "the sword and the shield" have been occasionally questioned ever since 1954. While these doubts were not widespread in 1956, it is possible that they will gain wider currency in the future.

[5] Economic considerations did not encumber Weinstein's speculations. Weinstein failed to indicate whether he expected the United States to lend or sell not only nuclear warheads, but also the carriers of Germany's "highly qualified small long-range bombing force."

Whether they do or not will depend partly on technological developments, partly on the influence that American and Soviet policies will be able to exert on the global balance of power, and partly on the impact of the new British defense policy on the structure of the coalition.

American policy cannot entirely remove the fear of nuclear war in Europe, and this has a potentially corrosive effect upon the North Atlantic alliance. As has been shown, this fear provides the Soviet Union with possibilities for atomic threats designed to undermine or destroy the solidarity of NATO. Early in November, 1956, the Soviet Union was quick to exploit the deep rift that had developed between the United States on the one hand and Britain and France on the other over the war in Egypt. In January, 1957, the Soviet press issued new warnings of atomic retaliation against those countries which would tolerate U.S. atomic support groups being stationed on their soil. Tass explained to Western Europe, Iran, Japan, and the island of Okinawa, all of which were mentioned explicitly, that by sending atomic forces to these countries the United States intended, in the event of atomic war, to divert the main Soviet blows from her own territory.[6] The latest Soviet threat, on April 27, 1957, took the form of a diplomatic note in which the federal government was warned that nuclear retaliation could turn Germany into "a veritable graveyard." The note, which made reference to "all kinds of modern weapons, including guided missiles," was delivered on the eve of a *Bundestag* debate on atomic armament. Adenauer spoke of an attempt to exploit internal political controversy in Germany, and the Bonn government said sharply that the Soviet note was "a massive threat and an attempt at intimidation with a view to separating the Federal Republic from her allies."[7]

It can readily be seen that any effective ban on large, "unconventional," nuclear bombs could not reduce the fear of atomic war in Europe, where atomic weapons could be used for tactical purposes. A disarmament arrangement that would not cover small "conventional" atomic weapons would not reduce apprehensions among our allies that their territory might become a theater of nuclear warfare; in fact, such an arrangement might have the opposite effect, since it would eliminate the American strategic capability of deterring

[6] For the text of the Tass statement, see *The New York Times,* January 24, 1957.
[7] See *The New York Times,* April 28 and April 30, 1957.

general war and thereby increase the danger of localized war in areas close to the Soviet empire. For this reason, no Western European power can really afford to make or endorse seriously any differential nuclear disarmament proposal aimed at abolishing large atomic and hydrogen bombs. Such a policy would be reasonable only if Soviet superiority in these weapons was manifestly overwhelming; in that case, however, all disarmament proposals would be without any interest whatever to the Soviet Union.

In two press conferences early in 1957, Adenauer favored a ban on nuclear weapons, but neither he nor any of Germany's military experts seem to have recognized that of all policies concerning nuclear armament, the least reasonable from the viewpoint of Western Europe is acceptance of the "conventionality" of tactical nuclear weapons and the outlawing of strategic, "unconventional" ones.

The United States can best forestall Soviet attempts at intimidating the weaker members of the Western coalition by maintaining superiority in strategic nuclear weapons and long-range delivery capabilities. If such deterrence cannot eliminate the fear of nuclear war in Europe, it can reduce it by preventing the crassest forms of its political exploitation through Soviet threats, and by giving assurances that derive from strength. The balance of nuclear power, however, has shifted in an adverse direction.

A second way in which the United States might deter Soviet attempts to intimidate the smaller powers in NATO would be to help them to acquire a strategic nuclear capability of their own, individually or jointly. The effects of such a policy on international affairs would be momentous, but no less shocking than a bare outline of the present balance of nuclear power would have been ten years ago. Only two possible political implications of an arrangement for the sharing of strategic nuclear weapons need be mentioned. First, to protect their bases from destruction by surprise attack, the participating European powers might have to share their bases as well, and presumably locate a large proportion of them in Africa, Canada, and possibly in the United States. If in the course of time the smaller countries were to develop a strategic capability of their own, it is possible that each of them might strive to render a Soviet attack on its territory as costly as possible but withdraw from any responsibility for the fate of its neighbors. If the United States were to play an active part in the creation of such capabilities, however, she might be able to control any politically disruptive tendencies and use nuclear sharing as an additional spur to unity, if not political union, of the European countries involved. It might also permit the United States to repay the present host countries of U.S. bases in Europe in kind. In any event, by diffusing the capability required for strategic nuclear war more widely, frictions in the alliance generated by the present American monopoly on the West's strategic deterrent power would be reduced.

Second, if smaller countries were given a certain retaliatory strategic capability, they might thereby acquire an unexpectedly great *deterrent* power. An aggressor who dared to defy that power would know that he risked damage to himself so great that even the total destruction of the small country would not be worth that price. The *deterrent* power of small countries with a nuclear capability does not necessarily correspond to the destructive power of their weapons. Correspondingly, the political (deterrent) value of the strategic nuclear capability of a coalition appears under certain conditions to be sensitive to the distribution of that capability among the members of the alliance, although the military worth of that capability may not be affected in the same way.[8] The total deterrent power of the coalition may exceed the military worth of its nuclear capability, if the latter is not monopolized by one nation, but distributed among several.

Considerations of this kind, which are in need of much analytical refinement, have not received much attention in Europe. In Germany, by 1956, if not earlier, the development which had led politically myopic observers to speak of a state of "mutual deterrence" (as though the United States were aggressive enough to be in need of deterrence) had merely created doubts in the minds of some observers as to whether the United States could be counted upon to come to the help of its European allies in the event of a communist attack on Western Europe. As long as the United States was safe from Soviet nuclear attack, her help was confidently expected. Recently, however, even some conservative German generals have publicly intimated the possibility that conflicts might arise in Europe which the United States (and the Soviet Union) might not be able or *willing* to arrest; instead, they might try to avoid strategic involvement.

For example, Field Marshal von Manstein developed this idea in

[8] It may indeed be affected adversely.

the following way.[9] In the past, he said, a certain degree of inferiority in weapons could always be compensated for by other means—by allies, better leadership, or by favorable geographical position. Under the threat of total destruction, the possibility of such compensation had disappeared. In order to survive, the United States was therefore compelled to try to stay ahead in the nuclear armament race. At the same time, Manstein continued, Germany, a nonatomic power, could not afford to forego building up forces for "classical" war, if only because all military conflicts since the end of World War II—in Indochina, Indonesia, Morocco, Algeria, Korea, and the war between Israel and the Arab states—had been waged by nonatomic forces, and it was not certain that another war in Europe would necessarily involve the use of atomic weapons. Thus far the argument is familiar from earlier conservative justifications of German rearmament, but Manstein added a point that had not been made in the early fifties. He considered the possibility that the United States might not use her strategic thermonuclear power for the defense of Europe. Neutralized by the Soviet threat of nuclear attack on the United States, she might confine her strategic power to the purpose of deterring such an attack while the war in Europe would be running its course. Thus Manstein suggested that the United States could not be definitely relied upon to fight a global war for the sake of freedom in Europe; he implied that the NATO strategy of "the sword and the shield" was no dependable guarantee of German and European security in all circumstances.

Some journalists put the same idea more bluntly.

In the event of an aggression by the satellite powers the Atlantic solidarity of the Americans and the British would always [sic] disintegrate in consequence of the balance of terror which they as atomic powers have themselves created. For the sake of Düsseldorf and Frankfurt nobody will provoke an attack upon London or New York, which would lead to retaliation upon Leningrad and Moscow. The world cannot allow itself to be exploded for West Germany.[10]

Other military analysts pointed out in addition that a European country hard pressed by local aggression might ask the United States

[9] See the articles by Manstein in *Die Welt,* September 4 and September 20, 1956.

[10] Adelbert Weinstein, "Über den Terror des Schreckens," *Frankfurter Allgemeine Zeitung,* August 29, 1956. Note that Weinstein, in one of the emotional *non sequiturs* with which his writings abound, ascribed the existence of nuclear parity itself to British and American efforts.

for thermonuclear support and the enlargement of the conflict into global war, but most of the *European* countries not directly involved in such local aggression would unquestionably oppose their ally's demand for American support of this kind in order not to expose themselves to the danger of nuclear annihilation.[11] In other words, in these considerations the strategic nuclear capabilities of the United States were seen not primarily as *unusable* in local war, but rather as a possible *political liability* to a common defense effort of the NATO powers in the event of such a war.

German military doubts as to the reliability of the United States as an ally should not be taken as doubts of American morality in international relations. From the point of view of German military observers, the question as to whether or not the United States will continue her European policy is not an ethical problem, but a matter of American national interest. The members of the former German military class know that the basis of defense through coalition is compatibility of national interests.

In general, the interest of the weaker partners in protection by the stronger is more readily appreciated than the interest of the strongest partner in maintaining an association with the weaker. Fundamentally, however, the interest in the coalition which the strongest nation has resides in the simple fact that in certain respects it is not strong but weak. It finds it useful to protect the weaker partners either because it wants to prevent their defection and their exploitation by the enemy, or because it derives benefits from their support in fighting him. But in peacetime the utility of this calculation is measured by the price to be paid for the expectation of gain, and not by that gain itself. Unfortunately, in a military coalition price and gain have to be estimated in peacetime and can be computed only after a war. It is evident, however, that under four general conditions any coalition may appear to be unprofitable or useless to the strongest partner:

1. When the threat by the enemy disappears or is believed to disappear—a condition which one German general dubbed "the coexistence narcosis"—the peacetime cost of the coalition may appear too high.

2. When the weaker partners fail to pay their share, the principle of equity in the distribution of peacetime costs may be violated.

---

[11] Joachim Ruoff, "Umrüstung und angemessene Verteidigung," *Wehrkunde,* October, 1956, p. 483.

Accordingly, Adenauer has feared, and has often warned those who opposed his foreign policy, that the United States might lose interest in the Federal Republic as a partner in the coalition, if West Germany failed to rearm. With reference to the same principle, the socialist opposition maintained conversely, at least until Stalin's death, that her own national interest would impel the United States to defend Germany against communist aggression regardless of the size or timing of West Germany's contribution to Western defense.

3. When it appears to the strongest partner that supporting weaker members of the coalition in the defense of their security against limited armed aggression entails the risk of having to defend its own security against unlimited aggression, the probable wartime cost of the coalition may be deemed to have risen excessively. In this case, the strongest partner may elect to circumvent or violate the terms of mutual assistance. It is this third possibility to which Manstein and some other German military observers called attention in view of Soviet nuclear capabilities and of the danger to American security attending them. These observers may be said to be concerned that the United States may turn isolationist in a local European war.

Some German military observers have been more radical than Manstein and voiced apprehension that the United States might return to an isolationist policy *in peacetime*. The reasons they adduced are related to a fourth general condition under which any coalition may become unprofitable from the viewpoint of the strongest partner. This condition may be stated as follows:

4. If changes in the technology of weapons reduce the relative military value of the weaker partners in the eyes of the strongest, the latter loses interest in contributing to the protection of the former's security. Despite such changes, the strongest partner may of course remain a member of the alliance, either because he is interested in preventing a *rapprochement* between the weaker partners and the enemy, or because of economic calculations, cultural tradition, or other nonmilitary interests, but since the military worth of the coalition has diminished, in the strategic judgment of the strongest power, the coalition is that much less viable.

German military observers first spoke of an American "endeavor to reach the 'Fortress America'"[12] when they observed that the over-

[12] Hans Kissel, "Gedanken zur Verteidigung der Bundesrepublik Deutschland," *Wehrkunde*, December, 1956, p. 597.

seas base system of the United States had been *politically* weakened in recent years, particularly in Africa and the Middle East. Some observers, however, soon shifted the emphasis and looked at this political development in the light of current and expected advances in weapons technology, thus arguing in fact with reference to the fourth, technological set of conditions under which the solidarity of a coalition is jeopardized. If it were technologically possible, some German military experts asked as early as 1954, to defend the American continent without the use of advance bases near the perimeter of the Soviet Union, would the United States not welcome her military independence from the Western allies? Surely the U.S. Strategic Air Command "must press" for concentrating its great offensive potential in the United States in order to be able to attack the Soviet Union with full power on the shortest route "via the Arctic." This concept was often referred to as "the peripheral strategy, which is so much feared by us." Other observers remarked that the United States might adopt a form of defense which was "less than 100 per cent peripheral in character": overseas bases might be used in the first phase of the war, as long as they could be held against Soviet attacks; but they might fall quickly and the United States would then be forced to resort to a peripheral strategy in the second phase of such a war.

Concern that the United States might adopt a policy of atomic isolationism emerged in consequence of the nuclear bipolarity of the world, but received new impetus by speculations about the strategic effect which the availability of long-range missiles would have upon the NATO alliance in the future. Inevitably, these speculations have been tentative and vague.

German military observers seem inclined to believe that under the assumption of a bipolar distribution of intercontinental missiles capable of carrying nuclear warheads, the probability of a major war will be smaller than it is today. This belief is based on the opinion that the risk of "mutual national suicide" through unrestricted war would be even greater than it is today, since the probability of destroying the strategic capability of the enemy before it can be employed in retaliation would be lower, unless it is assumed that the technology of identifying, intercepting, and destroying enemy missiles moving far beyond the speed of sound will advance beyond all expectations. Strauss himself once declared in an interview, it may happen that, from a purely military point of view, Europe will become less interesting to the Americans. The main routes for long-range weapons in war between the United States and the Soviet Union need no longer pass over Europe.[13]

The third and fourth conditions under which the strongest partner in a coalition may lose interest in the alliance—that is, fear of the common enemy and advances in weapons technology—are also the general conditions under which the political issue of the reunification of Germany may assume a different political complexion. It has been stated previously that the Western policy of strength cannot in itself bring about reunification, since neither American military policy nor NATO are designed to enlarge the territory held by the Western powers. The German Democratic Republic, which Germans refer to as "Middle Germany," is ruled by a communist government, and large Soviet forces are stationed on its territory. The Soviet rulers cannot be expected to cede control over Middle Germany, unless they misunderstand the policy of strength to imply the danger of a war that they want to avoid. The strategic deterrent capability of the United States and the military capabilities of NATO were conceived and are being maintained in a *defensive* spirit. They are meant to *hold* territory now under the control of the West. Conversely, since the Soviet Union has a nuclear capability of its own, neither the United States nor NATO can *force* a revision of Soviet control over any satellite nation, be it Poland, Hungary, or Middle Germany, unless the West is ready to risk war in order to attain these objectives.

When the East Germans rose against their communist rulers in June, 1953, the West watched the fight for freedom with sympathy and the resolution not to interfere. Similarly later, when Soviet military forces suppressed the popular revolution in Hungary in 1956, both the United States and NATO stood by without giving help to the Hungarian fighters for freedom. Moreover, at the time of the uprising in Hungary it was reported that some Western governments were *alarmed* by the possibility of an anticommunist uprising in Middle Germany, since they feared that such an event might lead to war.

Projecting this attitude further, fear of nuclear war may intensify Western desires for coexistence. In particular, it is conceivable that

[13] Interview with Franz-Josef Strauss in *Der Spiegel*, January 2, 1957.

some time in the future the United States may hold it to be in her interest to remove potentially explosive issues by making concessions to the Soviet Union that she has been unwilling to make in the past. Such a policy would be an indication of weakness, but the European powers would realize that even when weak the United States is considerably stronger than they are. None of the European members of NATO is in a position to pursue its individual national interest by military or other means, by pressure or concession, unless either the Soviet Union or the United States tolerates such ventures. Britain and France were reminded of that fact when their efforts at an independent policy in Egypt were thwarted by both the Soviet Union and the United States.

If the United States were interested in bringing about the reunification of Germany without war, to reduce fear of an armed conflict over this issue or to attain any other objective, she would have to accept all or most of the conditions which the Soviet Union has stipulated. In the military sphere the decisive conditions are (1) withdrawal of all non-German forces from Germany, (2) termination of West German membership in NATO, and (3) limitation of the all-German armed forces to 125,000 men. In view of American security interests, meeting these conditions would entail shifting the advanced defensive positions of the West to Great Britain, Africa, and the Middle East, since it is doubtful that NATO would survive the neutralization of Germany or that the attempt to hold a Western European bridgehead in France and the Iberian Peninsula would be strategically sound. In the event of war under such arrangements, a neutralized Germany would probably not be spared Soviet occupation and destruction. In present German explorations of the roads that might lead to reunification, this contingency is less urgent, however, than realization of the fact that no German policy of reunification can succeed which is not supported or tolerated, by design or default, by the United States.

Thus far the United States has given no indication that she is ready to permit the Soviet Union to score a momentous victory in her anti-NATO policy. There have been unofficial intimations, however, that novel approaches to the question of reunification ought to be considered. In the summer of 1956, John J. McCloy suggested that the West German government might renounce its claims to part of the former German territory which Poland received at the end of

World War II in compensation for Polish territory given to the Soviet Union with British-American consent.[14] According to the Potsdam Agreement of 1945, the Oder-Neisse line separating the four occupation zones from the German territory under Polish administration is only a provisional frontier. Furthermore, it has been U.S. policy that the permanent location of that border remains to be settled. In 1950, the communist East German government concluded an agreement with Poland in which this line was recognized as "the eternal frontier of peace" between Poland and Germany. Without mentioning the Oder-Neisse line or the East German agreement of 1950, McCloy argued that a West German renunciation of territorial claims might be a forward step toward achieving the unification of West and Middle Germany. At the same time, he suggested that such a West German step might satisfy more general Western interests vis-à-vis the Soviet Union. It would make it "more difficult for the Soviet rulers to dominate" their satellites, because if fears of German expansionism were reduced in Poland and Czechoslovakia, "the communist rulers of those countries would no longer be in a position to pose as defenders of the national-territorial interest."[15] Their fears assuaged, the Poles and Czechs would be less reliable allies of the Soviet Union, and Soviet control over its satellites would thus be weakened.

This argument overlooks the fact, demonstrated most recently in Hungary, that the Soviet leaders are capable of violating the national interests of a satellite if they hold such violation to be in their interest and can proceed with impunity. No West German renunciation of territorial claims to territories under communist control will impress the Soviet Union merely because it might please the Poles and the Americans. In order to be effective, it must please the Russians. The argument also overlooks the importance of Middle Germany to the Soviet Union as a staging base for military operations not only against the West, but also against unreliable satellites. Finally, it is utopian to expect the conflict between the United States and the Soviet Union, the two super-powers, to be reduced by agreements between minor powers, such as West Germany and Poland.[16]

[14] John J. McCloy in the Foreword to Henry L. Roberts, *Russia and America,* New York, 1956.

[15] *Ibid.,* p. xviii.

[16] About McCloy's proposal, a German observer said it appeared to him "so truly American that it could have been made by Franklin D. Roosevelt. It admonishes both Germans

Some observers, especially German and British socialists, however, have followed McCloy and disregarded the fact that on the communist side it is the Soviet Union, rather than Poland or Czechoslovakia, which controls the future of German reunification. Early in October, 1956, Carlo Schmid initiated a German debate on the Oder-Neisse line by suggesting that an agreement be reached first on the future of the territories east of the Oder-Neisse line. He spoke of the political taboos that would need to be violated in West Germany in order to make progress toward reunification, by which he evidently meant that McCloy's ideas should be viewed with favor.[17]

German military observers are not subject to the delusion that war will be abolished when both the United States and the Soviet Union have the capability of using intercontinental missiles with nuclear warheads against each other. Instead, they believe that if the likelihood of unrestricted war is lowered under such circumstances, the political and military importance of restricted war and other forms of conflict will be heightened. Therefore they conclude that, given the possibility of a technologically yet more highly advanced form of nuclear warfare, the need for conventional ground forces will not vanish. Instead, the need for *graduated defense* in the many-faceted and continual struggle against communist aggression will become even more pressing. For, besides unrestricted war, there are other forms of aggression that must be met. They range from the diplomatic struggle for the solidarity of the coalition and the fight for economic influence to virulent border incidents, civil war, partisan warfare, aggression by proxy with nonatomic weapons, and direct communist aggression in Europe leading to localized war involving or not involving the use of "conventional" atomic weapons.

If fear of a world holocaust prevents the use of long-range nuclear weapons, and if political and humanitarian considerations inhibit atomic defense against certain restricted forms of local communist aggression in Europe, the absence of forces capable of fighting a "classical" war might be an invitation to disaster. Germany is not only in need of contingents that are prepared to participate in a "conventional" atomic war, but must also have forces for "classical"

and Poles: Be reasonable, each of you yielding a little, and come to an agreement; perhaps this will create the atmosphere in which the deeper conflicts between the world powers will disappear" (Kurt Borries, "Das Dilemma der Oder-Neisse-Linie," *Aussenpolitik*, October, 1956, p. 652).

[17] Carlo Schmid, "Das böse Tabu," *Der Spiegel*, October 17, 1956, p. 17.

warfare. According to present plans, this double requirement will be met by (1) the contingents contributed to NATO, which ultimately will be dual-purpose forces trained to fight both kinds of war; (2) the home defense forces, not within NATO, which will perform a supporting function in either atomic or classical war; and (3) ground forces for air defense.

In December, 1956, Defense Minister Strauss was asked in an interview how many men West Germany would eventually have under arms when her projected NATO forces, home defense forces, and the anti-air ground defenses had reached their full strength. He replied:

This question cannot be answered within the next six months. The organization of the home defense forces still depends on an agreement within WEU. But we have a free hand up to a total strength of 500,000 men.

When he was then asked whether it is planned to exceed this limit, he replied, "Not in peacetime." [18] All these figures pertain to the future. At present, Germany's military strength still is way below the maximum of 125,000 men which the Soviet Union suggested for Germany in her international disarmament proposals; but Strauss clearly expressed his view of the desirable total relative strength of Germany when he declared, "In principle, we must aim at parity with England and France." [19]

The German military experts, who do not expect nuclear weapons to be used in the future, are inclined to press for *large* home defense forces. Some writers have pointed to the need for a militia that could repulse "weaker enemy attacks" in the frontier regions without allied help. According to some estimates, such a militia would have to number three million men.[20] Its mission would not be confined to "the active air defense of important centers" and "the defense against possible attacks by paratroopers," which General Heusinger once mentioned as the tasks of the German home defense forces.[21] Instead, it would be a large defensive nucleus of the old mass armies that fought in the last two world wars, with the specific mission to prevent the occupation of West Germany by Red forces.

[18] Strauss, *loc. cit.*
[19] *Ibid.*
[20] See the article by Kissel, *op. cit.*, and the literature cited there.
[21] See *Frankfurter Allgemeine Zeitung*, March 3, 1956.

The argument about the required size of the military forces is familiar from the American armament discussions. No general of the U.S. Army, however, has expressed his opinions so bluntly and aggressively as the former German general who, in a review of the impact of nuclear power upon warfare, called the atomic weapon "the Maginot Line of the unwilling taxpayer and *bon vivant* in which he seeks to take shelter in order to avoid sacrifices." This general pointed out:

Despite its larger population, the West is incapable or at least believes itself incapable of mobilizing armed forces equaling in strength those of the East. The West fails to do so because its peoples lack the necessary will and its governments the necessary power. One prefers to live well and not to sacrifice too much time and money for his freedom. One is afraid that Bolshevism may enter through the back door if the standard of living is lowered in order to improve the defenses. . . . If we prepare voluntarily for a situation in which we can counter a nonatomic attack only with atomic weapons, because we lack adequate classical forces and have failed to prepare for civil war, we are already marked in the future annals of history as "atomic war criminals born of degeneracy." If the West shrinks in the last minute, however, from resorting to the suicidal atomic weapons, the only alternative that remains is capitulation.[22]

Generally speaking, a coalition is of value to its weaker members if they have confidence in the power of their strong partner to protect them against the common enemy and in the strong partner's reliability, should the need for assistance arise. In NATO today, fear of atomic war is fear of that protection. This is the hidden paradox of NATO. Removing it is anything but easy, since more is involved than the acceptance by military and political leaders of tactical atomic arms as "conventional" weapons. It is necessary for the people themselves to have a realistic understanding of the nature of war, of the stakes for which it would be necessary to fight it, and of the measures that must be taken to increase the likelihood of moral and physical survival.

[22] Lieutenant General (Ret.) Helmut Staedke before a membership meeting of the *Arbeitskreis für Wehrforschung,* Frankfurt, printed as manuscript, without date (1956).

Appendix

German Popular Opinion on Air War and Nuclear Weapons

Opinions of military leaders about war and weapons are not representative of the views held by the man in the street. The average layman has less information on the military worth of weapons than the former professional soldier may be assumed to possess. Moreover, the soldier considers armaments with the interest of a consumer, whereas the civilian views them with the apprehension of a potential victim; that, at least, is the case in Germany. When asked about modern weapons, the average German finds it difficult to remain as cool as the professional soldier. Instead, he is likely to betray his fear of war, destruction, and death. It is nevertheless worth while to review what is known about German popular attitudes toward air war and nuclear weapons, because these attitudes cast some new light on the characteristics of German military opinion, and afford insights into German politics that the press does not offer.

The following pages are compiled from surveys of popular opinion conducted in West Germany and West Berlin by German research organizations during the last few years.[1] A few general remarks on the meaningfulness of the results of such surveys may be made in order to put the summary of their findings into proper perspective.

Opinion surveys are a useful tool for ascertaining what people know about foreign and military affairs, or about decisions that have been made by various governments, and for discovering how many people "like" or "dislike" the issues and decisions they do know about. It is considerably harder to ascertain accurately by means of surveys *why* people feel the way they do.

Surveys can also be useful for predicting, with varying degrees of

[1] Some of these results have not yet been published, but were kindly made available to the author on an informal basis by the organizations concerned.

inaccuracy, how many people will "like" or "dislike" certain decisions that may be made in the future. Findings of this third kind are not without value; but for a number of reasons, popular response to the actual event when it occurs in the future may differ from the predicted response before the event. Present attitudes about assumed future events may be influenced by likes or dislikes of the men whom the respondents erroneously believe will be responsible for events. Similarly, the answers to questions of this sort may be colored by wrong notions about who will benefit or suffer from the anticipated event. Finally, personal fears, hopes, or indifference may influence the way in which the respondents understand and react to the assumed event.

Popular expectations as expressed in surveys must not be confused with the predictions of experts. For example, public-opinion surveys in Germany found many people expecting that atomic weapons would not be used in another world war, and that, if they were used, Germany would be a more likely target than either the Soviet Union or the United States. Such expectations are not accurate forecasts of what may in fact happen, although they deserve close attention as expressions of popular fears.

When government leaders face a choice among various courses of action, opinion surveys are valuable instruments for determining the preferences of the people. But the expression of such preferences as a rule provides no guidance to autocrats, and it may also be irrelevant to democratic leaders. In a democracy, popular attitudes influence political decisions only to the extent that they are known and shared or respected by the men who make the decisions. On military issues, for example, democratic leaders are more likely to be guided by professional advice than by popular preferences, and it is impossible to predict how a leader will resolve conflicts between expert and lay opinion. Even in a democracy, popular preferences for a certain course of action—or for inaction —may be construed as no more than an indication that the people should be given more information about the issues and the implications of relevant facts, and more education about the importance of concern with the common welfare in addition to personal interest. Such information and education, of course, represent efforts to change, rather than to heed, popular wishes. When laymen are asked questions that only experts can answer, the opinion-survey technique merely reveals the distance between the laymen and the experts; it cannot yield any other valid result.

Opinions on War in the Air: 1952

According to a survey made in the summer of 1952, 74 per cent of the West German respondents had lived through air attacks in World

War II, and 30 per cent had been bombed out. In Berlin these proportions were higher: 98 per cent and 50 per cent, respectively.

When the respondents were asked about air raids in the event of another war involving Europe and Germany, 75 per cent (81 per cent)[2] expected that air raids would take place. Forty-six per cent (40 per cent) either expected, specifically, that air raids would be carried out by both East and West, or foresaw, generally, heavy raids and widespread destruction. Twenty-eight per cent (34 per cent) mentioned only air attacks by the Russians, while 4 per cent (7 per cent) mentioned only attacks by the Western powers. It is possible that the latter difference reflected not so much differential expectations of air attacks from East and West, as differential estimates of the aggressiveness of the two powers.

More important perhaps than these figures were the words used by the respondents to characterize the consequences of a future war. Many of the comments recorded by interviewers appear to have been born of a deep sense of anxiety: "Germany would become a desert"; "Then we could say our last prayers, because our country is right in the middle"; "It would mean the downfall of Europe and Germany"; "All of them will raid this country; none will spare us"; "Compared to what happened in the years 1939 to 1945, the things that would happen then would be much more terrible"; "Everything would be lost"; "Any future war will be even more cruel"; "Things will be much worse, as we won't even have air raid shelters." These were typical comments.

A high percentage of respondents condemned the bombing of cities. While three out of every four persons expected air attacks in the event of war, only one out of every four considered that the bombing of cities was justified "under certain circumstances," such as the presence in cities of armament factories or enemy troop concentrations.

Sixty-one per cent (51 per cent) expressed the opinion that city bombing was not justified under *any* circumstances. This opinion was held by 77 per cent of the women and 58 per cent of the men. When the sample was broken down according to other criteria, the highest degree of unqualified condemnation of city bombing was found among persons who had had only elementary schooling, among skilled and semiskilled laborers, and among farmers and veterans with families. Differences in religious denomination or party preference did not seem to affect the findings. Among age groups, the highest percentages of unqualified condemnation were found among those who were 35 to 44 years of age, and those who were 55 and over.

An attempt was made in the survey to determine whether the opinion that air attacks are unjustifiable would be altered if city bombing were

[2] The figures given in parentheses are those for West Berlin.

envisaged as a step toward liberation from enemy occupation. Because of its delicacy, this question was asked in a historical context. Opinions were elicited on the justice of the American bombing of French cities during the period of German occupation of France in World War II. Perhaps because the idea of subsequent liberation was only implicit, the inquiry failed to produce any appreciable change in the strong condemnation of bombing.

As regards present German attitudes toward the conduct of air warfare by the Americans during World War II, exactly half of the respondents said that the U.S. Air Force had not been a chivalrous opponent; 30 per cent expressed "no opinion." The reasons for the negative attitudes were distributed as follows, with some of the respondents giving more than one reason:

Americans destroyed cities and houses	15%
Americans directed their attacks at the civilian population	13
Americans killed defenseless people by ground strafing	7
Americans bombed civilian targets, instead of only military targets	5
Americans killed women, children, and old men (the three groups were specified)	7
Americans bombed hospitals, refugee camps, churches, etc.	4
Americans destroyed Dresden and other (specifically identified) cities	3
Americans dropped phosphorus bombs	2
Other reasons	1
	57%

It is interesting to note that the bombing of Dresden, which has been discussed as a particularly cruel and shameful action in various West German books that have often quoted British military opinions to the same effect,[3] was spontaneously mentioned by only very few respondents.

When those who did *not* say that the U.S. Air Force had been an unchivalrous opponent were asked specifically whether they had any complaints about the conduct of the air war by the Americans, another 29 per cent (of the total sample) registered complaints.

The widespread condemnation of city bombing, and of the way in which the U.S. Air Force had conducted its bombing operations, was

[3] See Rodenberger, *Der Tod von Dresden,* Land Verlag, Dortmund; Hans Rumpf, *Der hochrote Hahn,* Darmstadt, 1952, pp. 134ff.; Jürgen Thorwald, *Es begann an der Weichsel,* Stuttgart, 1950, pp. 126ff.; Kurt von Tippelskirch, *Geschichte des Zweiten Weltkriegs,* Bonn, 1951, pp. 586–587.

not associated with antagonistic feelings toward American air force personnel. Fifty-four per cent of the respondents from West Germany, and 85 per cent of those from Berlin, said that American personnel should not, as men, be condemned for their wartime actions.[4] This response can probably be attributed in part to the fact that the war ended more than seven years before the survey was made, although only 4 per cent of the respondents gave reasons such as "time heals all wounds" for their present lack of hostility. Two out of five explained their opinion by pointing out that the American airmen had merely performed their duty and had carried out the orders of their superiors. The frequency of this explanation is interesting, not only because of its sobriety, but also in view of the fact that German officers who were accused of war crimes in World War II usually claimed that they had only been carrying out orders.

Opinions on Atomic Weapons and Atomic Policy: 1954–1955

In the spring of 1954 and the summer of 1955 a number of surveys inquired into West German public opinion on some of the new weapons of war. Highlights from these surveys may be summarized as follows:

1. *In West Germany the opinion is preponderant that atomic and thermonuclear weapons will not be used in another world war.* This result was obtained in 1954, but no comparable inquiry was made in 1955. "Preponderance" does not mean "majority." In all opinion surveys, a fraction of the sample expresses "no opinion." "Majority" refers to an opinion which is expressed by more than 50 per cent of the sample. "Preponderance" is here used arbitrarily to refer to the majority of those who state their opinions.

The following question was asked:

> If a new world war were to break out—which, of course, nobody desires—do you consider it more likely that atomic and hydrogen bombs would be used or do you consider it more likely that both sides would avoid using atomic and hydrogen bombs?

The answers were as follows:

More likely that A- and H-bombs would be used	33%
More likely that A- and H-bombs would not be used	49
No opinion	18
	100%

[4] It may well be that the big difference in the figures for West Germany and Berlin in this instance reflect favorable attitudes toward the U.S. Air Force on the part of Berliners as a result of the experience of the Berlin blockade and airlift in 1948–1949.

About half the people who said that such weapons would not be used gave no specific reasons for their views; typical comments were, "No, they won't dare to use them"; "I, too, don't believe it"; and the like. Another quarter of the respondents who answered in the negative seemed to do so in view of the disastrous effects of such weapons. Answers were of this sort: "Atomic bombs mean complete destruction"; "No country wants to risk that"; and so forth.

2. In 1954, West Germans believed *either that the United States should not use atomic weapons under any circumstances, or that the United States would be justified in using atomic weapons only if others did so first. West Germans who held either opinion together represented a preponderant group.*

The question read:

What circumstances, in your opinion, would justify the use of atomic weapons by the United States?

The answers were distributed as follows:

	West Germany	
No use of atomic weapons under any circumstances	14%	40%
Use justified only if others use them first	26	
Use justified under other (specifically identified) circumstances		32
No opinion		28
		100%

The question was so phrased as to discourage the negative response given by 14 per cent of the sample. If the question had been differently phrased, it is likely that this percentage would have been higher. Even so, it appears that only 32 per cent of the West Germans would "approve" of American use of atomic weapons in circumstances not involving retaliation. The question was not repeated in 1955. A more specific implication of the German predisposition is indicated in the next table.

3. *The majority of West Germans opposed American use of atomic weapons in defense against any nonatomic Soviet attack on West Germany. From the spring of 1954 to the summer of 1955, this opposition increased.*

The question:

Supposing Russia were to attack West Germany *without using atomic weapons:* would you personally then agree to America's using atomic and hydrogen bombs on Russia in order to defend West Germany, or wouldn't you?

The answers:

	West Germany	
	April, 1954	September, 1955
Would agree to using A- and H-weapons	22%	15%
Would not agree to it	60	65
No opinion	18	20
	100%	100%

In 1954 those who "would not agree" gave various reasons for their negative opinion, as follows:

Because Russians would retaliate in kind	16%
Because consequences would be especially hard for Germany	12
Because the effects would be too disastrous	11
Because the use would violate humanitarian principles	8
"If the Russians don't use them, the Americans shouldn't either"	7
Other reasons	11
	65% *

* Five per cent gave more than one answer.

In 1955 those who gave a negative reply to the previous question were asked further:

And supposing Russia were to attack West Germany *with atomic weapons:* would you *then* agree to American use of atomic and hydrogen bombs on Russia in order to defend West Germany, or wouldn't you?

The result showed that, even assuming these more extreme circumstances, only 48 out of each 65 who had originally disapproved of American nuclear bombing switched over to the group of 15 per cent who had originally approved of such bombing. After the second question was asked in 1955, the total of those who said they would approve American use of nuclear weapons was 63 per cent. If the "no-opinion" group as well had been asked the second question, the corrected total might have been higher still.

4. Knowledge that atomic weapons are stored in Germany increased

among West Germans from 23 per cent to 36 per cent during the year and a half between the two surveys. This increase in knowledge was not accompanied by increased approval. *The number of West Germans who disapproved of the United States having stored atomic weapons on the territory of the Federal Republic rose between April, 1954, and September, 1955.*

In reply to the question:

> Do you approve of America's having stored atomic weapons here in West Germany, or don't you approve?

the following answers were given:

	West Germany	
	April, 1954	September, 1955
Approve	35%	30%
Disapprove	39	45
No opinion	26	25
	100%	100%

The replies to this question, as to all other questions, showed that Germans in the Western sectors of Berlin held more "favorable" attitudes toward United States policy than did the West Germans. For example, in 1955, 56 per cent of the West Berliners approved of the storing of atomic weapons in West Germany, and only 39 per cent disapproved. Also, the proportion of those who had "no opinion" on political and military issues in West Berlin was consistently *lower* than in West Germany: with regard to the location of atomic weapons, only 5 per cent of the people in West Berlin had "no opinion" in 1955, whereas in West Germany the percentage was 25. But, for the eighteen months under review, the trend of decreasing approval and increasing disapproval of atomic weapons being located in Germany could be observed in Berlin as well as in West Germany.

What were the reasons given for disapproval? In September, 1955, only a small percentage of those expressing such disapproval stated that they feared that the storing of atomic weapons in West Germany would provoke the Soviet Union, or would lead Russia to locate her own atomic weapons in East Germany. A large majority of these respondents said instead that the storing of nuclear weapons in West Germany endangered German lives; that they did not want to have anything to do with it all; or that it increased the danger of war. Interestingly enough, those who feared that German lives would be endangered were not apparently thinking primarily of the danger of war, but of explosions in peacetime (as a result of thunderstorms and accidents!) or of radiation in consequence of atomic tests that might be conducted in Germany! These fears indicate that public information on nuclear weapons in West Germany is inadequate.

5. In April, 1954, a question was asked which tried to ascertain West German opinion on Secretary Dulles' first statement on "massive retaliation," which was made in his speech of January 12, 1954. It was determined first that *only 10 per cent of the West Germans had heard or read that in the past few months authoritative statements had been made about a change in American defense plans.* Then Mr. Dulles' position was restated, in a greatly simplified form, with the result that *there was preponderant approval of the policy of massive retaliation;* but the replies to a follow-up question showed that *a substantial minority of the respondents did not interpret the statement about massive retaliation to mean the possible use of atomic weapons.*

The question read:

America stated that, in the future, an attack on a country in the Western camp will not be countered only on a local basis, but that America is resolved to employ massive retaliation where and with what means it deems appropriate. Do you personally approve of this American statement, or do you disapprove of it?

The answers were as follows:

	West Germany	West Berlin
Approve	46%	72%
Disapprove	22	16
No opinion	32	12
	100%	100%

Of those who approved, approximately 75 per cent gave one of the following reasons for their opinion: "This statement increases our security"; "The only way to deal with the Russians is to employ a policy of strength"; "This statement acts as a deterrent to Russia." Many of those who disapproved the statement on massive retaliation did so "because such a statement increases the danger of another world war."

In response to the follow-up question,

In your opinion, does this statement mean that America would also employ atomic and hydrogen weapons in its retaliatory measures, or don't you interpret it this way?

these replies were given:

	West Germany
Statement means that atomic weapons will be used	42%
Do not interpret it that way	33
Don't know	25
	100%

The large number of those who gave the second answer is another indication that many Germans still think of a possible future war in the image of World War II, and do not take account of the technological developments in the means of warfare that have occurred since 1945.

6. A question on "atomic blackmail" was also asked in the spring of 1954. Although this question differed from that raised in the interviews with former members of the German military class in the spring of 1954,[5] the response to it affords insights into German opinion that are not available from any other source. Unfortunately, the question was not repeated in later surveys.

The question was:

> Supposing Russia would make the following offer to the West European countries: If the West European countries make America give up its bases in West Europe, Russia pledges herself not to drop atomic or hydrogen weapons on West Europe. Would you like to see the West European nations accept such an offer, or reject it?

It was found that, in the event of such Soviet overtures, *the majority of West Germans do not wish European nations to prevail upon the United States to relinquish its bases in Europe.*

The distribution of the replies was as follows:

	West Germany	West Berlin
Favoring acceptance of Soviet offer	24%	14%
Favoring rejection	52	78
No opinion	24	8
	100%	100%

The percentage of those who favored rejection of the offer was higher among men than among women, and among persons who had had more than elementary schooling than among those who had gone only through elementary school. The percentage of rejections also rose with increasing income. This pattern of response is, incidentally, characteristic

[5] See Chap. 5, p. 108.

of all issues mentioned in this Appendix. A somewhat oversimplified way of describing it would be to say that U.S. policy is most popular in West Germany among fairly educated men who are relatively well off. Since in the case under review the pattern shows up very clearly, it is presented here for illustrative purposes:

	Accept Offer	Reject Offer	No Opinion	Total	Number of Cases
Sex:					
Men.....................19%	65%	16%	100%	271
Women..................27	42	31	100	347
Education:					
Elementary school........26	48	26	100	506
Beyond elementary school..14	68	18	100	112
Income:					
Up to 149 DM.............21	42	37	100	99
150–299 DM..............26	45	29	100	173
300–399 DM..............25	60	15	100	143
400–499 DM..............32	52	16	100	86
500 DM and more.........16%	68%	16%	100%	93

7. In the summer of 1955, the NATO exercise CARTE BLANCHE, in which tactical air forces were tested, aroused a storm in the German press and in the *Bundestag,* because the exercise involved the dropping of several hundred mock atomic bombs. A question pertaining to the exercise was included in the survey of West German opinion the following September. It was found that only 46 per cent of the respondents had heard or read "about the recent air maneuvers of NATO, which have recently taken place in Western Europe and in the Federal Republic." Those who had heard of the exercise were asked:

By and large, have you been favorably or unfavorably impressed by these maneuvers of NATO in West Germany?

The unfavorable impressions outweighed the favorable by approximately two to one:

	West Germany	West Berlin
Favorable impressions	7%	17%
Unfavorable impressions	15	15
Neither	20	8
No opinion	4	5
	46%	45%

8. In September, 1955, seven out of every ten West Germans had heard "something about tests which have been carried out recently with atomic and hydrogen bombs." An attempt was made to determine German public opinion on the continuation of the American test program. *Opposition to the continuation of atomic and thermonuclear tests by the United States had increased since April, 1954.* In September, 1955, almost half the adult population was opposed to such tests.

The question read:

> As you (may) know, America has carried out new tests with atomic weapons in the last year: Are you for or against America continuing these tests for the development of atomic and hydrogen bombs?

The answer broke down as follows:

	West Germany		West Berlin	
	April, 1954	September, 1955	April, 1954	September, 1955
For	37%	29%	56%	42%
Against	35	46	35	53
No opinion	28	25	9	5
	100%	100%	100%	100%

Those who opposed the continuation of the tests were asked a second (somewhat loaded) question:

> Supposing Russia were to continue its atomic tests for the development of atomic and hydrogen bombs, would you even [*sic*] then be against American continuation of its tests, or would you be for it in that case?

The opposition crumbled. A majority now favored continuation of the American test program. In April, 1954, the answers to the first question were as follows:

For continuation of American tests	37%
Against continuation of American tests	35
No opinion	28
	100%

When the second question was asked of the 35 per cent who opposed continuation of the tests, the following new distribution was revealed:

For continuation of American tests	62%
Against continuation of American tests	6
No opinion	32
	100%

In September, 1955, the first question yielded the following distribution:

For continuation of American tests	29%
Against continuation of American tests	46
No opinion	25
	100%

After the second question to the 46 per cent who were against continuation of the tests, the distribution changed:

For continuation of American tests	58%
Against continuation of American tests	12
No opinion	30
	100%

Index

Index

Blank, Theodor, 30, 38–40, 43, 78, 147–49, 185–89, 191–92, 195–97, 211–13, 215–16

Blank Office, 30, 32, 35, 35n, 39–40, 57, 75–76, 80, 141, 145, 196, 200; *see also* Defense Ministry, West German

Blomberg, Werner von, 20

Blumentritt, Günther, 69n, 82n, 113n, 134n, 137n, 147–48

Bolshevism; *see* Soviet Union

Bonin, Bogislav von, 75–83, 85, 89, 124, 144, 182, 192

Bonin Plan, 75–83

Bor, Peter, 19n, 139n

Border Police, West German, 196–97

Borries, Kurt, 241n, 242n

Boveri, Margret, 22n, 28n, 67n, 179n

Bradley, Omar, 6, 9

Brandt, Willy, 156n

Brentano, Heinrich von, 15, 162–63, 166, 180–81

Brüning, Heinrich, 73

Bulganin, Nikolai A., 87, 91, 106

Bullit, William C., 92n

Bundesrat, 195

Bundestag, military representation in, 37–41

Bundestag debates
  in 1952, 156–61, 173, 175
  in 1954, 38, 162–68
  in 1955, 37, 38, 169, 173, 180–87, 189–92, 194
  in 1956, 149, 195, 203–10

Bundeswehr, 77–78, 194–95, 199–203, 205–7, 212, 221–22, 243; *see also* Air Force, German; Conscription; Defense Ministry, West German; Home defense forces, German; Military leaders, German; Naval officers, West German; Opinion polls, German; Rearmament, West German; SS officers; Volunteers, German; Weapons, conventional

Bundeswehr—continued
  equipment of, with strategic nuclear weapons, 230–32
  equipment of, with tactical atomic weapons, 17, 40, 44, 147, 217–19, 221–22, 230, 243
  military leaders in, 40, 42, 43–44

Busse, Theodor, 79, 203

Buzzard, Sir Anthony W., 98–99

Byrnes, James F., 5

Canaris, Wilhelm, 22n

Carney, Robert B., 114, 114n

Carte Blanche, 40, 96, 124, 142, 144, 146, 147n, 182–93, 207; *see also* Opinion polls, German

CDU; *see* Christian Democratic Union

Chamberlain, Neville, 24

Cherwell, Sir Frederick, 63

China, 51, 53, 64

Christian Democratic Union, 38–39, 164, 175–77, 195; *see also* Adenauer, Konrad

Christian Social Union, 39–40, 45, 175–77, 195, 211

Churchill, Winston, 4, 7, 12, 62–64, 86, 92, 97, 118, 140, 186

Civil defense, 142, 145, 184, 231

Clay, Lucius D., 5, 5n, 175

Coalition, nature of, 236–39

Coexistence, 11, 12, 19, 62, 86, 87, 91, 106, 121, 125, 162, 165–66, 236, 239, 244

Command of the sea, 112

Communism, 7, 56; *see also* Satellites, Soviet; Soviet Union

Conscription, 14, 16, 39, 194, 197–98, 210
  and length of service, 195, 197, 211–12; 214; *see also* Bundeswehr; Volunteers

Conscription Law, 13, 149, 210

Containment, 4, 11; *see also* Deterrence; Retaliation

Corporal missiles; *see* Missiles

Council of Europe, 5, 7
Cowles, John, 114n
Craig, Gordon A., 20n, 26n
Crüwell, Ludwig, 79, 82n
CSU; *see* Christian Social Union
Cyprus, 90
Czechoslovakia, 4n, 206, 241–42

Davison, W. Phillips, xi
Defense, graduated, 242
Defense Committee, Parliamentary, 39–41, 80, 82, 198, 206, 208, 211, 216
Defense Ministry, West German, 30–31, 35, 39, 43, 75, 79, 82, 82n, 145, 183, 185, 187, 191–93, 197–98, 200–201, 211, 214–15; *see also* Blank Office
Defense Production Act of 1950, U.S., 6
Dehler, Thomas, 74, 75, 91, 163, 166n
Demilitarization; *see* Disarmament of Germany
Deterrence, 17, 105, 111–13, 116, 125, 185, 210, 227, 230, 233–34
  economic cost of, 231
  graduated, 96–99; *see also* Containment; Retaliation; U.S. atomic monopoly
  mutual; *see* Parity, nuclear
Dethleffsen, Erich, 32n, 69n, 124n, 134n, 186
Deutsch-Englische Gesellschaft, 78n, 175
Deutsche Partei; see German Party
Deutscher Club 1954, 81
Deutscher Soldatenbund, 31, 41
DeWeerd, Harvey A., 109n
Disarmament of Germany, 5, 7–8, 14, 41, 50, 156
Dollfuss, Engelbert, 24
Douhet, Giulio, 33
DP; *see* German Party
Dulles, Allen, 44n
Dulles, John Foster, 15, 61n, 93, 97–98, 108, 119, 141n, 178, 178n

East Germany
  armament of, 6, 79, 206
  June 17, 1953, uprising of, 164, 239
Eberbach, Heinrich, 79
EDC; *see* European Defense Community
Eden, Anthony, 15, 63, 74, 106, 118
Eden Plan, 74
Edinger, Lewis J., 222n
Egypt, 51, 106
Eisenhower, Dwight D., 9, 14, 61n, 91–93, 101, 101n, 140, 141, 165, 170n, 186, 203n
Erler, Fritz, 39, 159–61, 173, 182n, 183–84, 207–9
Europe, defense of; *see* NATO, strategy of
Europe, unification of, 93, 154, 157–58, 163; *see also* European Defense Community, West European Union
European Coal and Steel Community; *see* Schuman Pool
European Consultative Assembly, 8
European Defense Community, 9, 30, 50, 55–60, 69, 73, 112, 153–56, 158, 163
  failure of, 30, 57, 75n, 153; *see also* NATO, membership of West Germany in; West European Union
European Payments Union, 216
European Recovery Program, 5

Faber du Faur, Moriz von, 25, 25n, 26
Falkenhayn, Erich von, 23
FDP; *see* Free Democratic Party
Federal Republic of Germany; *see* West Germany
Fett, Kurt, 77
Flanders, Ralph, 204
Fleig, Hans, 179n
Foerster, Wolfgang, 20n
Folttmann, J., 20n
"Fortress America"; *see* Isolationism

Horne, Alistair, 7, 157n
Hossbach, Friedrich, 79
Hungary, 1956 uprising in, 16, 239, 241
Hunt, Victor, xi

Iberian Peninsula, 240
ICBM; see Missiles
Iceland, 90
Indochina, 53, 58, 61–63, 86, 118, 120, 201
Iran, 105n, 232
IRBM; see Missiles
Isolationism, 11, 15, 106, 121, 237–39
Italy, 105n, 108, 110, 135, 195

Jaeger, Richard, 37, 39, 44, 195, 206–9, 211
Japan, 51, 105n, 232
Jodl, Alfred, 20, 25, 26n
John, Otto, 71n, 83, 198n
Juin, Alphonse Pierre, 160
July 20, 1944, 19, 24n, 28, 29, 31 32n, 76
Just, Arthur W., 123

Kammhuber, Josef, 44, 217
Keitel, Wilhelm, 20, 25n, 26n
Kennan, George, 12, 92, 165, 204
Kenya, 55
Kern, Erich, 21n
Kesselring, Albert, 20, 20n, 27n, 41, 44n, 72
Kiesinger, Kurt-Georg, 166, 204–5, 207–10
Kintner, W. R., viii
Kirkpatrick, Sir Ivone, 7
Kirst, Hans Hellmuth, 41
Kissel, Hans, 237n, 243n
Knauss, Robert, 25
Knowland, William F., 61n
Korean war, 6, 52, 103, 114, 165, 201, 206
Krushchev, Nikita S., 87, 88n, 91
Kühn, Fritz, 175n
Kuntzen, Adolf, 79, 82n

Laegeler, Hellmuth, 77
Landesverrat, 20, 28
Leites, Nathan, xi
Lemmer, Ernest, 175
Liddell Hart, B. H., viii, 34
Lippmann, Walter, 204
Lisbon force goals; see NATO
Lloyd, Selwin, 15
Locarno, 73, 157
London Conference
of 1947, 6
of 1954, 162
Lüttwitz, Smilo Freiherr von, 79
Luftwaffe; see Air Force, German; Air Force officers, German

MacArthur, Douglas, 51
McCloy, John J., 7, 8, 12, 92, 240–42
Malenkov, Georgi, 141
Mansfield, Michael J., 204
Manstein, Erich von, 34n, 79, 82n, 203, 234–35
Manteuffel, Hasso von, 38, 40, 56, 168n, 190, 191n
Manuilsky, Dmitri, 204
Marshall, George C., 6, 9
Marshall Plan, 4
Matador missiles; see Missiles
Matériel-procurement program, German, 212, 214–17
Mediterranean, 135
Mellies, Wilhelm, 183
Mende, Erich, 74, 80, 112, 186n, 191, 198n
Merkatz, Hans-Joachim von, 164, 166n
Middle East, 53–55, 101n, 135–36, 204, 238
Middle Germany, 239–41; see also East Germany
Miksche, F. O., viii
Militarism, German, 18, 33, 38, 41, 59, 71, 199; see also Opinion polls, German
Military leaders, German, 18–45
economic status of, 34

Uhlig, A. W., 147n
Ultimatums, 104, 106, 109–10
  atomic, 100–101; *see also* Threats,
    atomic
Union of South Africa, 55
U.S. atomic monopoly, 51, 96–97; *see
    also* Deterrence; Parity, nuclear;
    Weapons, nuclear and atomic
U.S. foreign policy, 3–17, 50–54, 61–
    62, 64–65, 73, 91–94, 97–98, 101,
    103, 107–8, 114–21, 125–26, 141,
    149, 178, 189, 196, 203, 219n,
    220–21, 232, 234–41; *see also* Con-
    tainment; Deterrence; Isolation-
    ism; NATO; Neutralism; Rad-
    ford Plan; Rearmament, West
    German; Retaliation; Reunifica-
    tion, German

Vasilevsky, Alexander M., 105
Veterans' organizations, 41
Vishinsky, Andrei, 141n
Vistula, defense at, 154–55
Volunteer Law, 39, 196
Volunteers, 70, 77, 195, 196–97, 199–
    200, 212, 222
  ratio of, to conscripts, 213, 213n

War, 50, 53, 73, 100, 112–13, 119–49,
    168
  fear of, 104, 184, 232; *see also*
    Opinion polls, German
  limited, 98–99, 103, 119–31, 208,
    235–36, 242–43
  preventive, 100, 109, 114–19, 121–
    22
  probability of, 112, 126, 164–66,
    184
  unlimited, 12, 97–98, 104, 106, 121,
    123, 126, 130, 184, 190–93,
    206–9, 232–33, 239, 242, 244;
    see also Surprise, in war
War criminals, 5, 41, 68
Warfare, mobile, 81, 133–34, 215
Warne, J. D., 140n

Warsaw Pact, 84, 180
Weapons, conventional, 13–14, 129,
    132–49, 186–91, 207–9, 218, 227;
    see also Bundeswehr; NATO;
    Rearmament, West German
Weapons, dual-purpose, 221, 243
Weapons, nuclear and atomic, 34, 51,
    95–108, 124–26, 138–39, 141n,
    143, 187, 190–91, 220, 228, 233–
    34, 244, 254–55
  sharing of, 219–20, 228, 233–34
  strategic, 98, 148, 230–32
  tactical, 13–14, 17, 81, 98, 101–5,
    107, 124, 126, 144, 146–47, 167,
    183–86, 191, 205, 219–20, 233,
    244; *see also* Missiles; Opinion
    polls, German; Parity, nuclear;
    support groups, atomic;
    Threats, atomic
Weapons tests, 86, 96, 142, 181n; *see
    also* Opinion polls, German
Wehner, Herbert, 159, 165–66
Wehrbeauftragter, 198
Wehrmacht, 21–24, 26–27, 200; *see
    also* Reichswehr
Weimar Republic, 23, 25, 26n, 73,
    174–75
Weinstein, Adelbert, 32n, 78, 78n, 79,
    82, 89–90, 134, 144–45, 183,
    184n, 192–93, 230, 231n, 235
Welles, Sumner, 4n
Wenck, Walther, 44
West European Union, 10, 162–64,
    170–72, 180
  and atomic weapons, 219–20
West Germany
  class structure in, 18, 36
  democracy in, 36–37, 71
  economic position of, 5, 7, 17, 36
  importance of age differences in, 37
  sovereignty of, 10, 162
  strategic position of, 7, 192, 209
  territorial claims of, 241
  as theater of war, 61, 132–34, 161,
    184, 186

OTHER VOLUMES OF RAND RESEARCH

COLUMBIA UNIVERSITY PRESS, NEW YORK:

Soviet National Income and Product, 1940–1948, by Abram Bergson and Hans Heymann, Jr., 1954

Soviet National Income and Product in 1928, by Oleg Hoeffding, 1954

Labor Productivity in Soviet and American Industry, by Walter Galenson, 1954

McGRAW-HILL BOOK COMPANY, INC., NEW YORK:

The Operational Code of the Politburo, by Nathan Leites, 1950

Air War and Emotional Stress, by Irving L. Janis, 1950

Soviet Attitudes toward Authority, by Margaret Mead, 1951 (out of print)

Introduction to the Theory of Games, by J. C. C. McKinsey, 1952

The Organizational Weapon: A Study of Bolshevik Strategy and Tactics, by Philip Selznick, 1952 (out of print)

Weight-Strength Analysis of Aircraft Structures, by F. R. Shanley, 1952

The Compleat Strategyst: A Primer on the Theory of Games of Strategy, by J. D. Williams, 1954

THE FREE PRESS, GLENCOE, ILLINOIS:

Psychosis and Civilization, by Herbert Goldhamer and Andrew W. Marshall, 1953

Soviet Military Doctrine, by Raymond L. Garthoff, 1953

A Study of Bolshevism, by Nathan Leites, 1953

Ritual of Liquidation, Communists on Trial, by Nathan Leites and Elsa Bernaut, 1954

Two Studies in Soviet Controls: The Party and the Peasant—Moscow in Crisis, by Herbert S. Dinerstein and Leon Gouré, 1955

A Million Random Digits with 100,000 Normal Deviates, by The RAND Corporation, 1955

PRINCETON UNIVERSITY PRESS, NEW YORK:

Approximations for Digital Computers, by Cecil Hastings, Jr., 1955

International Communication and Political Opinion: A Guide to the Literature, by Bruce Lannes Smith and Chitra M. Smith, 1956